ENTANGLED EMANCIPATION

Women's Rights in Cold War Germ

In 1900, German legislators passed the Civil Code, a controversial law that designated women as second-class citizens with regard to marriage, parental rights, and marital property. Despite the upheavals in early twentieth-century Germany – the fall of the German Empire after the First World War, the tumultuous Weimar Republic, and the destructive Third Reich – the Civil Code remained the law of the land. After Nazi Germany's defeat in 1945 and the founding of East and West Germany, legislators in both states finally replaced the old law with new versions that expanded women's rights in marriage and the family.

Entangled Emancipation reveals how the complex relationship between the divided Germanys in the early Cold War catalysed but sometimes blocked efforts to reshape legal understandings of gender and the family after decades of inequality. Using methods drawn from gender history and discourse analysis, the book restores the history of the women's movements in East and West Germany. *Entangled Emancipation* ultimately explores the parallel processes through which East and West Germany reimagined, negotiated, and created new civil laws governing women's rights after the Second World War.

(German and European Studies)

ALEXANDRIA N. RUBLE is an assistant professor of history at the University of Idaho.

GERMAN AND EUROPEAN STUDIES

General Editor: James Retallack

Entangled Emancipation

Women's Rights in Cold War Germany

ALEXANDRIA N. RUBLE

UNIVERSITY OF TORONTO PRESS
Toronto Buffalo London

© University of Toronto Press 2023
Toronto Buffalo London
utorontopress.com

ISBN 978-1-4875-5026-4 (cloth)   ISBN 978-1-4875-5031-8 (EPUB)
ISBN 978-1-4875-5027-1 (paper)   ISBN 978-1-4875-5029-5 (PDF)

Library and Archives Canada Cataloguing in Publication

Title: Entangled emancipation : women's rights in Cold War Germany /
    Alexandria N. Ruble.
Names: Ruble, Alexandria N., author.
Series: German and European studies ; 52.
Description: Series statement: German and European studies ; 52 | Includes
    bibliographical references and index.
Identifiers: Canadiana (print) 20230497004 | Canadiana (ebook) 2023049708X |
    ISBN 9781487550271 (paper) | ISBN 9781487550264 (cloth) |
    ISBN 9781487550318 (EPUB) | ISBN 9781487550295 (PDF)
Subjects: LCSH: Women's rights – Germany – History – 20th century. |
    LCSH: Domestic relations – Germany – History – 20th century. | LCSH: Equality –
    Germany – History – 20th century.
Classification: LCC HQ1236.5.G3 R83 2024 | DDC 305.42094309/045 – dc23

Cover design: Val Cooke
Cover image: Poster for the International Women's Day from the Democratic Women's League of
Germany advertising opposition to nuclear rearmament (1955).

We wish to acknowledge the land on which the University of Toronto Press operates. This land is
the traditional territory of the Wendat, the Anishnaabeg, the Haudenosaunee, the Métis, and the
Mississaugas of the Credit First Nation.

The German and European Studies series is funded by the DAAD with funds from the German
Federal Foreign Office

Deutscher Akademischer Austauschdienst
German Academic Exchange Service

University of Toronto Press acknowledges the financial support of the Government of Canada,
the Canada Council for the Arts, and the Ontario Arts Council, an agency of the Government of
Ontario, for its publishing activities.

Canada Council   Conseil des Arts
for the Arts   du Canada

ONTARIO ARTS COUNCIL
CONSEIL DES ARTS DE L'ONTARIO
an Ontario government agency
un organisme du gouvernement de l'Ontario

Funded by the   Financé par le
Government   gouvernement
of Canada   du Canada

To my grandmothers, Barbara and Lila

Contents

Illustrations

Acknowledgments

This book would not exist without the support of many archivists, librarians, organizations, faculty members, colleagues, friends, and family. I am forever grateful for their input, help, and support.

This project has its roots in my undergraduate years at Christopher Newport University, where I first learned about post-war German history and gender history during a fateful semester abroad. I developed a strong interest in understanding how Europe recovered from the destruction wreaked by the Nazis, the role women played in rebuilding Germany after the war, and what happened to women's rights in East and West Germany. Three of my professors, Brian Puaca, Laura Micheletti Puaca, and Laura Deiulio, were exemplary mentors and encouraged me to pursue my interests in graduate school.

I was fortunate to attend the University of North Carolina at Chapel Hill, where the History Department provided a collegial and stimulating intellectual environment. My adviser, Karen Hagemann, constantly supported and challenged me. Several other faculty members – Christopher Browning, Chad Bryant, Konrad H. Jarausch, Susan Dabney Pennybacker, Donald M. Reid, and Katherine Turk – left their mark on this book as well. I was surrounded by many wonderful friends: Julie Ault, Friederike Bruehoefener, Adam Domby, Lexi Domby-Kosmin, Trevor Erlacher, Peter Gengler, Jenna Polles Gengler, Lorn Hillaker, Jen Kosmin, Scott Krause, Max Lazar, Emily Lipira, Bee Lehman, Sarah McNamara, Andal Narayanan, Caroline Nilsen, Stephen Riegg, John Robertson, Michal Skalski, Philipp Stelzel, Lars Stiglich, and Pearl Young. Their camaraderie made the early stages of this project enjoyable.

I completed this book at the University of Idaho with the support of several colleagues in the Department of History, especially Rebecca Scofield, Ellen Kittell, and Alyson Roy. I also want to thank my friends at Spring Hill College for their support through early stages of writing: Sarah Duncan, Nicholas Wood, Vlad Kravtsov, Kathleen Orange, Cinthya Torres, Paige Vaughn, Harold Dorton, Lisa Hager, Bret Heim, Tom Ward, and Shane Dillingham. In Mobile, colleagues from the University of South Alabama – Claire Cage, Timothy Lombardo, Beca Venter-Lombardo, David Meola, Kelly Urban, and Brian Whitener – have rounded out my cohort of vibrant scholars. I have also benefited from many professional connections outside of my institutions that have evolved into deep friendships. Alissa Bellotti, Adam Blackler, Jane Freeland, Lea Greenberg, Scott Harrison, Kathryn Julian, Andrew Kloiber, Jennifer Rodgers, Lauren Stokes, Robert Terrell, Daniela Weiner, and Laura Yacovone have been great friends and collaborators. From afar, Jessica Keene shared the ups and downs of graduate school and early career travails. To Lauren Corrigan, who has shared many coffees, memes, and new experiences with me: I am lucky to have you, my dear.

The research featured in this book has been sponsored by numerous institutions and fellowships, including a Foreign Language and Area Studies (FLAS) grant through the UNC Center for European Studies, a Social Science Research Council Dissertation Proposal Development Fellowship, the Fulbright US Student Program, the UNC History Department's Clein and Mowry funds, the Central European History Society, the German Academic Exchange Service (DAAD), a UNC Graduate School Dissertation Completion Fellowship, a Dr. Richard M. Hunt Fellowship for the Study of German Politics, Society, and Culture from the American Council on Germany, and a Mitchell Grant from Spring Hill College. Most recently, an American Association of University Women American Postdoctoral Leave Fellowship in 2021–22 provided critical support for revising my manuscript before its final submission.

This funding supported research at several institutions. The archivists at the Bundesarchiv in Koblenz and Berlin, the Friedrich-Ebert-Stiftung in Bonn, the Konrad-Adenauer-Stiftung in Sankt Augustin, the Friedrich-Naumann-Stiftung in Gummersbach, the Kempowski archive in Berlin, the Parlamentsarchiv in Berlin, the Archiv der deutschen Frauenbewegung in Kassel, the Katholischer Deutscher Frauenbund in Cologne, and the Bundesbeauftragte für die Unterlagen des Staatssicherheitsdienstes der ehemaligen Deutschen Demokratischen Republik in Berlin deserve many thanks for their assistance at critical junctures in this project. I have also had the good fortune of working in many libraries over the years, including the Staatsbibliothek Berlin, the Davis Library at UNC, and the Burke Library at Spring Hill College.

Parts of this book have been presented at the Social Science Research Council, the Council for European Studies annual conference, the German Studies Association annual conference, the Berkshire Conference of Women Historians, the German Historical Institute's Transatlantic Doctoral Seminar, and the Southeast German Studies Workshop. I am grateful for the in-depth commentary provided by Dorothy Hodgson, Pamela Scully, Carola Sachse, Dagmar Herzog, and others at different stages of development. Also, parts of this research have been published in *Central European History* as well as in *Gendering Postwar Germany:*

Entanglements, edited by Karen Hagemann, Donna Harsch, and Friederike Bruehoefener, and *The Family in Modern Germany*, edited by Lisa Pine.

I am also grateful to my editor at the University of Toronto Press, Stephen Shapiro. From the very beginning, he endorsed the project and critically engaged with its core concepts. At every step along the way, he has offered important insights and asked the provocative questions necessary to shape its early drafts into a final manuscript. To the anonymous reviewers who generously took the time to comment on the manuscript and engage its ideas: thank you.

One has to find a life outside of academia. I have always found mine in Shotokan karate clubs, everywhere from Newport News to UNC to Berlin to Mobile. To my friends at all those clubs, thank you for making me always feel at home.

One does not need to search archives or study post-war European society to know that families are a source of comfort and support. My parents, Joyce and Daniel Ruble, encouraged me as a child to become a doctor, so I did. They also encouraged me to learn German and study abroad, which set me on this path. My grandmother, Lila Waite, too, has always offered her love and support. My brother, Charlie, is the epitome of fraternity. When book writing got tough, I could always rely on the antics of Shelby, Kendall, Cora, and Twig to keep my spirits up. Finally: all errors within are my own, and I hope I have done justice to the stories told here, especially of women who struggled for equal rights then and continue to fight for them now.

Abbreviations

ACC	Allied Control Council
AFA	Antifascist Women's Committees
BGB	Bürgerliches Gesetzbuch
CDU/CSU	Christian Democratic Union/Christian Social Union
DFD	Democratic Women's League of Germany
EKD	Protestant Church in Germany
FDGB	Free German Confederation of Trade Unions
FDP	Free Democratic Party
FGB	Familiengesetzbuch
FRG	Federal Republic of Germany
GDR	German Democratic Republic
KPD	Communist Party of Germany
LDPD	Liberal Democratic Party of Germany
NSDAP	National Socialist German Workers' Party
OMGUS	Office of Military Government, United States
SED	Socialist Unity Party
SMAD	Soviet Military Administration in Germany
SPD	Social Democratic Party of Germany
USSR	Union of Soviet Socialist Republics
ZFA	Central Women's Committee

ENTANGLED EMANCIPATION

Introduction

Cold War Battles over the Family

In 1949, the provisional constitutions of the two newly founded German states, the Federal Republic of Germany (FRG) in the West and the German Democratic Republic (GDR) in the East, made the same bold and unprecedented promise to their citizens: "Men and women have equal rights." Furthermore, both constitutions declared that all laws that undercut this principle of equality were to be invalidated. In East Germany, the one-party communist dictatorship immediately overturned all laws opposing gender equality. In West Germany, legislators had until 31 March 1953 to alter existing laws.[1] With the constitutional mandates set in stone, politicians in East and West Germany had little choice but to begin overhauling any legislation that undermined women's equality with men.

It was not coincidental that the two states adopted similar equality clauses and mandates. Indeed, that was the direct outcome of an early Cold War battle over women's rights that played out in the parallel constitutional conventions in the Western and Soviet occupation zones in 1948 and 1949. As the Cold War developed in the late 1940s, it became increasingly evident that the Soviet Union and the Western Allies would be unable to agree on Germany's future. In 1948, as tensions mounted, German politicians in the Soviet and Western occupation zones began drafting separate constitutions for the new German states. Prominent women in both occupation zones insisted that the new constitutions include broad equality clauses as basic rights – rights that had been a point of unresolved contention in Germany in the decades preceding the Second World War. These women's rights activists perceived the devastation of post-war Germany as offering a tabula rasa for women's rights. After much struggle with their male peers, they prevailed, largely because the escalating Cold War had spawned a competition between the two occupation zones. East German communists were the first to include an equality clause in their draft constitution. West German politicians then followed up with their own version of the same clause. Then, in a shocking twist, West German political leaders were the first to approve the constitution of the new FRG in May 1949 – complete with an equality clause. In response, East German politicians vowed to change their laws first. To ensure that these promises would not go unfulfilled, female activists on both sides insisted on including strict deadlines for implementation. Clearly, gender and women's rights were from the beginning at the centre of the Cold War competition between what were now two separate Germanys.

The marriage and family law section of the Civil Code (Bürgerliches Gesetzbuch, BGB) was the most prominent existing German law that required reform. The BGB – introduced in the 1870s, approved in 1896, and in effect since 1900 – designated women as second-class citizens with regard to marriage, parental rights, and marital property. Among other discriminatory measures, men could make all decisions for their wives and families, prevent their wives from working, and claim full control over their wives' property as well as custody of the children. Throughout all the upheavals that beset twentieth-century Germany – the disintegration of the German Empire after the First World War, the tumultuous years of the Weimar Republic, and the destructive Third Reich – the Civil Code remained the official law of the land. At the time, some people viewed the old law as a powerful point of reference and as a means to stabilize German society in the wake of the chaos and destruction caused by the Second World War. Others, though, viewed the law as outdated and as no longer meeting the needs of a post-war society dominated by a "surplus" of 7 million women.[2]

As the Cold War intensified, the Civil Code's prescriptions for women's roles became a point of contention between the two Germanys. From the earliest stages of the constitutional conventions, female activists in both occupation zones cited the Civil Code as a discriminatory law that needed to be overhauled. Notwithstanding all disparities between their competing systems, the two German states made the same promise: to deliver equal rights to men and women. From this point on, women in both Germanys would stake a claim to legal equality that had been denied to them for decades. In doing so, they encountered resistance from conservative factions in both states. Although it was supposed to happen quickly, change took time. Finally, legislators in both German states passed two new, competing laws: the 1957 Equal Rights Act in the FRG and the 1965 Family Code in the GDR. These laws overturned more than half a century of measures that discriminated against German women.

Entangled Emancipation analyses the parallel processes whereby East and West Germans reimagined, negotiated, created, and followed these new laws as both states sought to end sex discrimination in marriage and the family. This book argues that the complicated relationship between the divided Germanys in the early Cold War alternately catalysed and halted efforts to reshape legal understandings of gender and the family. The results were mixed. The new laws expanded women's rights in critical ways that were unprecedented in German history. Yet those same laws were often limited in their implementation by the context of the Cold War. In each of the Germanys, discourses and decisions regarding gender roles were created largely with an eye on developments in the "other" Germany. In the end, each state constructed its own separate model of an ideal family – the male-breadwinner/female-homemaker family in the West, the dual-earner family in the East – with each model a reflection of its own, seemingly antithetical economic, political, and social system. This book also describes the complexities of putting law into practice. It shows that among East and West Germans, adherence to the old Civil Code was inconsistent: some followed its prescriptions closely, others did not. For East and West Germans alike, however, the ultimate obstacle was often the courts – that is, the approach they took when adjudicating the law. Without more expansive laws, and the fair enforcement of those laws, men and women could not expect full legal equality, regardless of what the constitutions promised.

Post-war Europe was saddled with the Herculean task of rebuilding after the destruction of the Nazi era. As noted earlier, Germans had long tended to view family law as a stabilizing force in uncertain times, especially during and after global conflicts such as the First World War. The aftermath of the Second World War was no different. Much as they had after the First World War, Europeans, and Germans in particular, viewed gender imbalances, rising divorce rates, increasing illegitimacy rates, marital strife, and the proliferation of "non-traditional" family structures with alarm. As before, Europeans across the continent interpreted these trends as part of a post-war crisis of the family. That particular crisis was continent-wide, but it had special resonance in post-war Germany.[3] For one thing, the gender imbalance was more striking in Germany than anywhere else in Central Europe.[4] For another, the German case was special because Germans also had to grapple with their Nazi past. Nazi racial policies had strongly shaped many families in Germany, not least Jewish and racially "other" families, through a regime of positive and negative eugenics. High casualty rates during the war and the ensuing social changes had further altered the structure of many German families.

Dealing with these factors alone would have created enough obstacles for Germans after the Second World War. But add to this a factor that was even more significant: the escalating Cold War, which had divided Germany into the liberal democratic, capitalist FRG, locked into a transatlantic alliance dominated by the United States, and the communist GDR, a satellite state of the Soviet Union in the Eastern Bloc. Germany was unique, in that it was the only European state to have been cleaved in two in the war's aftermath. For the next forty-five years, until reunification in 1990, the two post-war German states would face a special relationship of "entanglement and demarcation."[5] At the same time, the two German states came to represent different sides in a broader debate within each sphere of influence over women's rights, gender, and the family. Gender, women's rights, and the family came to serve as battlegrounds in the Cold War struggle between East and West Germany and, by extension, between the Soviet Union and the US-dominated West. Competition between the two Germanys both drove and complicated efforts to achieve equality between men and women.

This book also examines the complex implications these legal revisions held for ordinary Germans in the context of the Cold War. The Civil Code of 1896 had established a patriarchal family and marital structure that would indelibly shape Germans' lives for more than half the twentieth century. For some Germans, the law's prescriptions mattered immensely in how they structured their home lives. For a variety of religious and social reasons, they elected to follow the law's patriarchal regulations. For others, the law had little bearing on how they chose to arrange their families. Some Germans opted to follow more egalitarian models, to the degree the law would allow. Whatever the case, it mattered greatly how the courts applied the law. In conflicts between partners over marriages, children, and households, judges would uphold the law, regardless of how egalitarian the partnerships and families had previously been. For opponents of the Civil Code, an unchanged law had powerful potential to continue limiting women's rights with regard to marriage, parental custody, and marital property. On top of this reality, the Cold War posed an additional obstacle, especially for partners and families divided by the political cleavage, who needed clearer answers when it came to how the new laws applied to their lives.

The new laws passed in 1957 and 1965 thus represented fundamental change for both Germanys, albeit to different extents. The 1957 Equal Rights Act was not as far-reaching as its proponents would have liked but nevertheless signified a major shift for West Germans. For example, it removed the right of men to make all decisions for their wives (*Stichentscheid*), which meant that women now had equal input into matters such as where to domicile and how to raise their children. Also, married women were now allowed to work outside the home without their spouse's consent. But their rights were still limited in certain ways: they were permitted to do paid work outside the home only if it was reconcilable with their "obligations" to the household and family.[6] Some of these provisions would not change until the passage of the First Bill for the Reform of the Marriage and Family Law, passed in 1976.[7]

The 1965 Family Code of the GDR was much more progressive than its West German counterpart. According to it, spouses had equal rights and duties in marriage and family, including in childrearing. They also shared all property and were equally responsible for contributing income to the household. In

West Germany, married women and mothers were supposed to work at most part-time; in East Germany, by contrast, state policies encouraged women to work full-time, even as mothers,[8] and the state enabled them to do so by providing necessary all-day facilities for children.[9] In East Germany, however, a gap persisted between the legal standard and how life was actually lived. An unequal division of labour in the workplace and at home continued even after full equality was promised by a legal reform in 1965 and a new constitution in 1968.[10]

Even so, the legal reforms had a lasting impact: for younger generations, the new laws created new expectations. Most Germans in the FRG and the GDR in the first two post-war decades believed that men and women were naturally different and thus should not hold the same roles in society. For the older cohorts, the gendered division of labour did not change radically even after the new laws were fully in place. Younger generations, however, began to respond differently.[11] In the GDR, for instance, younger men were more willing to embrace a more equitable division of labour at home. In contrast, while the 1957 and 1976 laws offered important reforms, West German women still faced several hurdles, such as a shortage of affordable childcare, and they were still not entitled to keep their own surnames upon marriage. These differences remained in place until German reunification in 1990, at which point the GDR was absorbed into the FRG, compelling East Germans to adapt to the West German model.

Gendered Entanglements in Cold War Germany

Given their common history, language, and culture, it was inevitable for the two post-war Germanys to be closely intertwined. Yet for a variety of logistical and ideological reasons, the division of Germany immediately after the Second World War led historians to privilege isolated narratives of East and West Germany.[12] Only recently have scholars begun to write "integrated" German histories (this book is one of them).[13] These are not just parallel histories that started in 1945 and came together in 1990. Rather, they are entangled histories in the sense that the two Germanys constantly influenced each other during the Cold War. Addressing the entangled nature of the two states' developments is a complicated endeavour. Not every topic in either Germany can be compared; not every topic was as "entangled" as gender relations; and the relationship between the two Germanys was not always symmetrical.[14] All of that said, this book's examination of family law offers an intriguing and organic entry point into recent German history. Diverging social, political, and economic systems in the context of an intensifying Cold War pushed the two states apart; yet a shared legal history and similar cultural norms regarding gender and the family continued to link them intimately in ways that other scholars have previously discounted.[15] Cold War competition further enmeshed the two states as each sought to portray the other as backward.

The division of historical narratives into East German and West German history has trickled down to the field of gender history.[16] Indeed, the differences in legal treatment faced by East and West German women that were still evident after German unification in 1990 have long marked both the public discourse and the scholarship surrounding women's rights in the post-war Germanys. Most commentary on the subject has assumed that women's rights in the two Germanys were always separate and distinct due to the states' divergent ideologies. But it was far from a given that women's rights would end up looking different in the two states. Some recent publications have compared the two; fewer have examined the construction of gender relations from an integrated or "entangled and demarcated" German–German perspective.[17] This book maintains that the complicated Cold War relationship did much to determine how East and West Germans redefined gender roles, women's rights, and the family. It goes beyond simple comparisons to show how changing gender roles through reforms to family law linked and complicated the bonds between the two states – and, by extension, between Eastern and Western Europe, and the Soviet Union and the United States – in ways that were especially critical in the early Cold War.[18] Only by examining the dialogue between East and West from 1945 to the 1970s can one fully understand the changing contours of these debates over "gendered entanglements."

Conversations about the family and gender roles between East and West were also conducted beyond the borders of the two Germanys in Cold War Europe. This book thus also situates the German–German dialogue over gender and the family in a broader pan-European context.[19] Across the continent, Europeans faced crises of the family sparked by the Second World War. In the immediate post-war years, female activists went to work across Europe rectifying decades of political, social, economic, and legal inequality. They also looked to their allies in Eastern and Western Europe and the United States and the Soviet Union for guidance. Moreover, their decisions were often shaped by wider developments in both blocs.[20] The debates within the two Germanys ultimately served as microcosms of larger conversations about women's rights in each sphere of influence, but those same debates also had their own unique twists and turns. The problems posed by family law reforms presented unique challenges for both Germanys that other European states did not face. When East and West Germans rethought gender roles in marriage and the family, they had an opposing model right over the border to observe and counter.

The complicated, entangled relationship between the two Germanys during the Cold War was not the only driver of changes in family law. Domestic developments, such as protests by women's movements and the Protestant and Catholic churches, also did much to colour discussions of new family laws in each state. Female activists in both Germanys were important actors in this discourse, although scholars of the new women's movement in West Germany that emerged in the late 1960s tend to downplay their predecessors' activism and accomplishments.[21] Other scholars have dismissed the women's associations of the 1940s and 1950s because the earlier generations' conceptions of women's rights often had very different goals and strategies than the women's movements that emerged post-1968. This book paints a different picture. After 1945, female leaders of independent women's associations and political parties began to rebuild their organizations, many of which had existed prior to 1933, when they were outlawed by the Nazis. Using methods employed by previous German women's movements – circulating petitions, drafting legislative proposals, promoting media coverage, and writing letters – these women applied enough pressure on the West German Bundestag to achieve some significant reforms, even if the law was not ultimately as far-reaching as many of them had hoped. This book highlights their achievements and situates them within a longer movement for equality in a way that past scholarship has not.[22]

In the same vein, this book shows how female leaders in East Germany significantly influenced reforms of family law initiated by the SED-controlled government. To be sure, East German women, especially in the SED and the state-sponsored communist mass organization, the Democratic Women's League of Germany (DFD), did not enjoy the same level of manoeuvrability as their West German counterparts; this is because civil society in the GDR was so limited.[23] Nevertheless, women were instrumental in pressuring the SED to change its employment and family policies to better accommodate working women's needs as mothers and breadwinners.[24] This book does not change the established narrative but does build on it, besides recontextualizing it within a broader Cold War framework by exploring the links between the East and West German women's movements. Many of these women had known one another before 1933; some had cooperated in women's groups right after the Second World War and during the early stages of the Cold War. By dividing Germany, the Cold War restricted the mobility and collaboration of women's associations on both sides of the border, with particular impact on female communists and social democrats in West Germany. Any resemblance to the SED in the GDR opened these women's groups to allegations of communist subterfuge and influence, which made some of their positions precarious to hold and undercut their ability to fight for more aggressive reforms. This book thus illuminates the important role that various women's associations on both sides of the German–German border played in resisting and advancing their respective governments' proposed family laws in the 1950s and 1960s.[25] It ultimately demonstrates that female activism was alive and well in both Germanys long before the late 1960s.

This study also highlights the special and paradoxical role played by churches in these discussions in both East and West Germany. The standard narrative has been that in West Germany, the Catholic Church (and, to a degree, the Protestant churches) held quite a bit of sway with the Catholic chancellor, Konrad Adenauer, and the reigning Christian Democratic Union, influencing their policies related to gender and the family.[26] This book argues that while leaders within the Catholic Church exerted influence over Western political leaders, their strategies did not ultimately have the intended effect. Meanwhile, in East Germany, Protestant churches (and, to a lesser extent, the much smaller Catholic Church) had an antagonistic relationship with the ruling SED government. Despite these testy relations, the Protestant churches played an unexpectedly significant role in delaying the SED's reforms in the mid-1950s. The Protestant and Catholic churches in the GDR exposed that "the dictatorship's rule was more limited than assumed by theories of totalitarianism."[27] In other words, internal forces affected the dictatorship in East Germany more than scholars have previously recognized, and they did so at an earlier stage.[28]

Finally, this book traces gradual shifts in behaviour against the major legal revisions in both Germanys. By the 1950s, the bourgeois notion of marriage and the family as patriarchal institutions was deeply ingrained in most European societies.[29] Moreover, these patriarchal institutions were still crystallized in law. As the rest of society liberalized, civil laws were left behind, and many citizens continued to follow them, a phenomenon referred to as the "cultural lag."[30] At the same time, it must be recognized that laws are not simply products of social, political, and cultural change; they are also "the driving force behind it."[31] As such, this book explores and compares the complex and paradoxical relationships between the law and everyday life in both Germanys. In the GDR, the Civil Code was technically overturned in 1949, yet many families and judges clung to old practices, at least in the early years. In the FRG, where the Civil Code technically remained in force until 1953, Germans interpreted the law in different ways. As sociological surveys and autobiographical texts show, many families had already begun to practise more egalitarian marital and familial structures; many others, however, had not. This book demonstrates that despite all differences, the gendered division of labour remained remarkably similar in the two Germanys. At the same time, it acknowledges that the two German states were on different trajectories. In the GDR, the next generation seemed to move faster than in the FRG in terms of creating more egalitarian partnerships and family structures.

As alluded to earlier, the related concepts of comparison, entanglement, and demarcation are at the core of this book. On one level, this book is a comparative study, in that it compares and contrasts similar laws, policies, institutions, and groups in the two post-war German states. At the same time, this study pays special attention to the different and unique properties of the major actors, institutions, and driving ideologies involved in the debates over civil law reforms in each state. Moreover, it places these debates in the larger pan-European context. Here, comparison serves to pinpoint what was unique about the German–German context. This study also acknowledges that these debates ran on at times synchronous and at other times slightly asynchronous timelines.

On another level, while parts of this analysis are indubitably comparative, the overall framing of the book transcends comparison and ventures into the territory of *histoire croisée*, or "entangled history." For one thing, the two Germanys were not isolated, diachronic entities, as many comparative studies aver; rather, they remained closely linked and were able to "modify one another reciprocally as a result of their relationship."[32] For another, *histoire croisée* places "exploration of particular objects or as a group of societal processes" at the centre of examinations of various levels of connections.[33] Both approaches are useful for a study that interrogates particular objects – in this case, legal reforms – that ran on slightly different timelines. The complicated chronologies of the reforms in the divided Germanys resulted from processes that often overlapped with and responded to key changes in the other state.

Even as far as "entangled" histories go, the case of the two Germanys stands out, since "continuity, entanglement, demarcation, and division" always marked the relationship between the FRG and the GDR in ways that other European states did not endure.[34] Continuity is key here, because the "postwar gender order and gender relations within each state were entangled with the shared past of the German Empire, the Weimar Republic, and Nazi Germany."[35] This factor set Germany apart from many other European states that did not have fascist pasts (with Italy as one exception). In terms of entanglement, the two Germanys were linked on numerous levels ranging from the discursive to the tangible. Discourse at the time, for instance, constantly employed the other Germany as a bogeyman, especially when it came to discussions about women and gender. These discursive constructions shaped the decisions made on both sides. Although discursive analysis certainly plays an important role throughout this book, the outcomes laid out in this study cannot be reduced purely to discourse.[36] After all, the law had real consequences for its adherents, many of whom remained mired in past legal practices, which had become cultural norms.

At the same time, there were moments when the two Germanys went down separate paths for different reasons specific to their states and societies. As much as they shared a history, there were still new institutions, ideologies, and social norms that were products of the post-war era. Thus, this study opines that various economic, political, social, and cultural factors combined to shape and determine the separate paths on which the two Germanys embarked regarding women's rights, gender roles, and family law.[37] For ordinary East and West Germans, changes in family law had enormous implications for their employment status, alimony payments, and child support payments, among other things, and these were outcomes of the new post-war economic and political systems put in place. These problems were compounded by the German–German border, which divided partners and families, and by policies defining, among other things, labour conditions. Germans in the FRG and the GDR always viewed family law reforms through the lens of the special "entangled and demarcated" German–German relationship.

To get at these complicated, entangled debates and negotiations, this book examines a wide variety of primary sources. First, memoranda, petitions, letters, legislative drafts, meeting minutes, and opinion pieces highlight the discussions and negotiations among members of governing political institutions in both Germanys, namely the SED-controlled communist government in the GDR and the Christian Democratic Union/Christian Social Union (CDU/CSU)-led government in the FRG, and their respective ministries and parliaments. Here, the opposition parties, such as the leftist Social Democrats (SPD) and the liberal Free Democrats (FDP) in the FRG, are especially critical. Second, memoranda, party newsletters, faction protocols, and depositories of party leaders draw out the debate in society. Third, regional- and national-level newspapers and women's magazines summarize the debate in the media. Finally, petitions, correspondence, sociological surveys, and autobiographical texts shed light on the impact of family law on daily life in both German states.

Each of this book's five chapters explores the links among these four levels of analysis, compares parallel and entangled processes and discourses in East and West Germany, and explains points of "entanglement and demarcation" in the two states. Chapter 1 analyses debates over the family among the Western Allies, the Soviets, and the Germans in the immediate post-war reconstruction years. Germans at the time determined that society was in the midst of a post-war "crisis of the family," citing increasing numbers of divorces, illegitimate births, and "non-traditional" family structures. Meanwhile, the Soviet Union and the Western Allies overturned all Nazi-era legislation and enacted a law in 1946 that largely reiterated the old provisions of the Civil Code. In response, first women's committees and then, soon after, newly founded women's organizations in the East and West began to reimagine partnerships and the family in the post-war era, eventually drafting their own versions of a new civil law that became the template for later versions.

Chapter 2 looks at constitutional reforms in the Soviet and Allied occupation zones in 1948–49. In discussions over basic rights, the idea of equal rights for men and women – a subject dating back to the Weimar era – became highly contested in both occupation zones' constitutional conventions. Throughout their debates, delegates relied on allusions to the other German occupation zone's policies on women and gender to defend and disparage competing notions of equal rights for men and women. Furthermore, changes to the Civil Code were already on the table in both occupation zones from an early stage as constitutional convention representatives debated how to create equality in their respective new states. This chapter argues that even at this early stage, gender and the family were already central to the Cold War competition between the two sides.

Chapter 3 explores the first stages of debates over the new marriage and family laws in each German state from 1949 to 1953, which failed to produce new legislation by mandated deadlines. Spurred by Cold War competition, the SED-led government of the GDR quickly put together a new Civil Code by early 1950, but internal conflicts of interest prevented its approval. Meanwhile, the Christian conservative-led government of the FRG attempted to keep a more patriarchal version of family law, but faced staunch opposition from independent women's associations, trade unionists, the FDP and SPD, and the Communist Party of Germany (KPD). The West German Bundestag thus remained unable to pass the legislation by its self-imposed deadline of 31 March 1953.

Earlier chapters emphasized the close links between the two Germanys; chapters 4 and 5 reflect the increasing divergence of the two states. Chapter 4 covers the years 1953 to 1957. In West Germany, a period of "legal chaos" in 1953 gave way to a second round of debates over the legislation, ultimately leading to the approval of the 1957 Equal Rights Act, a set of compromises between Christian conservatives and progressives that expanded women's rights in marriage in some aspects even while continuing to limit them in others. Meanwhile, in East Germany, the uprisings of 17 June 1953 brought to power a new justice minister – the well-known women's rights activist Hilde Benjamin, who revitalized interest in family law and introduced the draft legislation to the public in June 1954. The East German government quickly abandoned the reforms, however, after a storm of protest from citizens, especially Protestants and Catholics.

Chapter 5 examines the final stages of family law reforms in both states between 1957 and the 1970s. In East Germany, the SED laid low after the 1954 protests and did not return to the reforms for another decade, well after the construction of the Berlin Wall. It finally passed the new, socialist Family Code in 1965, followed by further reforms in the 1970s. The 1965 Family Code signified a radical departure from the patriarchal civil law of the past. In West Germany, the Bundestag no sooner passed the 1957 law before problems arose with its implementation and the Federal Constitutional Court had to intervene. An SPD/FDP coalition finally replaced this law in 1976 with a modern, liberal family and marriage law that truly granted women equal civil rights. This was a result of the pressure by the new women's movement that emerged in the West in the late 1960s; it was also a response to the 1965 GDR Family Code.

The conclusion compares and contrasts the two German states with other post-war European societies in an attempt to explain the dual uniqueness and representativeness of the German states after 1945 in the context of the Cold War. As it shows, the two Germanys were the front lines of the conflict between the United States and the Soviet Union. As such, gender, marriage, and the family became crucial points of contention between the two broader spheres of influence. Furthermore, the concluding chapter draws critical connections to the present day, a time when Europeans are confronting the rise of far-right parties that wish to destroy gender parity and reinstate the "traditional" family.

1 Reimagining Post-War German Families, 1945–1947

Upon Nazi Germany's capitulation on 8 May 1945, the four Allies – the Soviets, British, Americans, and French – began their formal occupation and rehabilitation of Germany. The task was daunting. Because of the war, much of Europe lay in ashes. In Germany alone, the casualties sustained during the war had left behind an estimated 7 million more women than men. Many of those 7 million had taken on the dual responsibilities of childrearing and full-time work during and immediately after the war. In addition, out-of-wedlock births had increased significantly in Europe, and "non-traditional" family structures had become more and more common. The demobilization of surviving soldiers also had an important impact. Veterans were returning as changed men to destroyed homes and often had a difficult time adjusting to their wives', daughters', and fiancées' newfound independence. Many of them hardly knew their families any longer. The massive conflict had upended the gender order across Europe and triggered a crisis of the family.

Germans and the Allies now had to confront this "crisis of the family" precipitated by the war. Wartime losses had compelled some families to exist in non-traditional structures. For other German families, reunification marked the beginning of a gradual and often bumpy readjustment period. Some couples and families never fully recovered. Many Germans, as reflected in the media and their correspondence with the Allies at the time, wanted to know what their rights and responsibilities were. As a short-term response, the Allies enacted legal stopgap measures to assert their authority over the occupation zones and ease citizens' concerns. As part of this process, the Allies denazified existing laws, passed a new marriage and family law, and reinstated the old Civil Code's (Bürgerliches Gesetzbuch, BGB) regulations on marital property schemes, spousal relations, and parental authority. This meant that after 1945, married women were still legally required to obey their husbands' decisions, turn over management of their property to their spouses, and relinquish full authority over their children. The new Allied law alleviated some Germans' problems, but it also exacerbated those of others. The Allies believed they had chosen the most expedient solution by denazifying the law and re-establishing long-standing regulations on marriage and divorce. In this way, they provided necessary legal parameters for an increasingly chaotic and confusing environment. However, their law was not designed to be permanent or to resolve long-standing issues in German society.

During the first half of the occupation period (1945–47), Germans across the occupation zones began to reflect on the long-term implications of the "crisis of the family" as well the legal situation their country faced. The collision between post-war reconstruction programs and the burgeoning Cold War provided Germans with opportunities to rethink the long-term future of the law. In the early post-war years, in the context of reconstruction and the re-emergence of political parties and social organizations, a variety of party-based and independent non-party women's associations in the West began discussing reforms to the Civil Code. Whether they favoured reform or not, there was a broad consensus among women's organizations that the Civil Code deserved special attention in the post-war era. Their willingness to pursue reforms at this early juncture was a sign that they viewed the post-war years as a "moment of promise."[1] At the same time, women's associations' discussions were subject to the politics of the burgeoning Cold War, which dictated the political space they could inhabit and limited their ability to press for reforms until the Allies resolved the "German problem." Their proposals laid the groundwork for later debates about a new Civil Code; however, these discourses would be shaped by the new problem of Cold War division.

German Law before 1945

The Civil Code had a long and contentious history prior to 1945 that would shape its path in the post-war period, especially as it intersected with the crisis of the family. As the Allies and average Germans began critically re-examining the Civil Code, they reignited decades of heated debates over the legal status of the family that stretched back to the 1870s. In 1871, German chancellor Otto von Bismarck had unified much of German-speaking Europe "from above" after a series of military campaigns.[2] A few years later, in 1874, Bismarck assigned Gottlieb Planck, a prominent National Liberal politician, the task of creating of a Civil Code for the new German Empire, which until that point had consisted on more than twenty-five regions, each with its own separate legal code.[3] Under Planck's careful eye, National Liberal and conservative legislators drafted a new, patriarchal civil law in which husbands exerted authority over their spouses in all areas of marital decision-making, marital property, and parental authority. Among other discriminatory measures, men could make all decisions for their wives and families, prevent their wives from working, and claim full control over their wives' property and custody of the children.[4]

Despite Planck's efforts, by 1896 the German imperial government still had no new civil law on the books. Over the preceding twenty-two years, an uneasy alliance of bourgeois and socialist women, the Social Democratic Party (SPD), and Catholics had put up staunch opposition to the conservatives in the Reichstag, delaying the passage of the law. Women's organizations employed several strategies to protest the proposed legislation, such as petitioning the Reichstag and publishing brochures and articles explaining the pitfalls of the draft legislation. Similarly, the SPD contingent in the Reichstag opposed the law. While the Center Party held mostly conservative views, it initially opposed the Civil Code's provisions out of concern that the law was another attempt to undermine the Catholic Church; the *Kulturkampf* of the 1870s had left a powerful impression.[5]

By 1896, however, opponents of the law had started to lose traction when it came to blocking the law's approval, in no small part because the Catholic Center Party had changed sides. Swayed by the new law's paternalistic tone, the Catholic Center chose to ally with the National Liberals in the debates about it, despite the two parties' long history of mutual hostility. Planck and his peers seized the opportunity to form a new alliance. Now, on the brink of successfully passing the Civil Code, Planck assured the Reichstag in February 1896 that "community order, property, inheritance, marriage, [and] family stand as the wide and firm basis of a common German law."[6] The new Civil Code defined "family" as a paternalistic structure in which men, as fathers, breadwinners, and husbands, held authority over their dependents, that is, their wives and children. According to Planck, this conception of the family, which was derived from German tradition, would set Germany's future course as a culture and society.

The Reichstag approved Planck's version of the Civil Code on 18 August 1896; it went into effect on 1 January 1900. Almost immediately, bourgeois and socialist women and the Social Democrats called for it to be expunged, arguing that it suppressed women's rights. In 1902, the bourgeois women's movement mounted one last unsuccessful campaign against the Civil Code. Meanwhile, proponents of the law argued that it would help unite and stabilize German society. Without political representation – women were barred from joining political parties until 1908 and from voting until 1919 – female activists had few opportunities to overturn the legislation. In the meantime, bourgeois women focused their attention on other facets of women's equality, such as equal access to higher education, better job opportunities, and women's suffrage. After 1908, many bourgeois women also joined political parties, leading them to take up different issues.[7] Then in 1914, the First World War began, and women put their activism on hold because of the demands of the total war effort.

The disintegration of the German Empire at the end of the First World War and the November Revolution of 1918 opened the door for new discussions about women's rights. For one thing, the founding of the democratic Weimar Republic in 1919 with a new constitution signalled significant changes to men's and women's civil rights. Article 109 of the new Weimar constitution promised

Image 1.1. German National Assembly in Weimar 1919, the female members of the
Independent Social Democratic Party of Germany (1919). This photograph, taken
by an unidentified photographer, features Luise Zietz and two other female members
of the National Assembly who were instrumental in adding Article 109 to the new
constitution. Image courtesy of the Bundesarchiv Berlin-Lichterfelde.

"the same" civic "rights and duties" for men and women "in principle."[8] Article 119 declared that marriage "as the cornerstone of family life and the nurturing and growth of the nation" stood under the special protection of the state; it also guaranteed mothers and families state assistance.[9] Out-of-wedlock children now had status equal to that of legitimate children; their mothers were not. The 1919 constitution offered new opportunities and equal rights for men and women in principle; in practice, though, equality was constrained in most areas of society, the economy, and domestic life.[10]

Political discussions of women's equal rights often went hand in hand with society-wide anxiety about the "crisis of the family." In the eyes of many politicians and government officials, the First World War had precipitated a crisis of the family, exemplified by the "surplus" of 2 million women, rising rates of divorce and out-of-wedlock births, and single motherhood.[11] The divorce rate had increased significantly during the war, from 14.66 per 10,000 marriages in 1914 to a peak of 32.57 per 10,000 in 1920, before declining slightly in the early Weimar years.[12] Similarly, the illegitimacy rate hovered around 11 per cent until 1933.[13]

Liberals and socialists responded with proposals to change the family law sections of the Civil Code, but these faced opposition from conservative forces in the Weimar-era Reichstag. For instance, female Reichstag representatives belonging to the SPD and the newly established Communist Party of Germany (KPD) wanted to ease restrictions on divorce. Although out-of-wedlock birth rates were not especially high, Weimar policy-makers still perceived illegitimacy to be a symptom of the "crisis of the family" and as well as a threat to the health of the "body of the population," especially because of the high infant mortality rate of out-of-wedlock children.[14] As the Weimar Republic grew increasingly unstable and chaotic, politicians constantly pointed to the Civil Code, with its prescribed gender roles, as a source of stability. As a result, while female activists periodically raised their objections to the old law, the Civil Code remained unchanged throughout Weimar's existence, despite the constitutional promise of equality.[15]

In 1933, Adolf Hitler and the Nazi Party (NSDAP) came to power and female activists' hopes of expanding women's legal rights in marriage and the family evaporated. This was in part because the Nazi Party had set out to transform Germany into a totalitarian dictatorship. In 1933, the Nazis eliminated most dissent in society through its policy of *Gleichschaltung*, or "bringing into line." The first targets of this policy were the opposition parties on the left, the SPD and KPD, followed by independent organizations such as the Federation of German Women's Associations (BDF).[16] These developments eliminated anyone who might have opposed changes to the Civil Code and related laws.

Having stifled political dissent, the Nazi regime was free to pursue its more radical goals, which included social transformation through eugenics. Under the Third Reich, a totalitarian regime with racist and expansionist aims, marriage and the family took on new meanings. During the Weimar years, the state had protected marriage and the family. The NSDAP was about to transform marriage and reproduction into services to the German nation. Various family policies and laws passed between 1933 and 1938 allowed "racially desirable Aryan Germans" to marry and produce children while prohibiting certain groups of Germans – namely Jewish, non-Aryan, and "feeble" men and women – from doing so.[17] The Nazi Party cemented its racial agenda through legislation such as the antisemitic Nuremberg Laws of September 1935. The Nazis then introduced a separate Marriage Law in July 1938 that allowed the easy dissolution of a "racial intermarriage" or a "childless marriage."[18] The same laws would apply to annexed territories such as Austria after 1938.

In addition to all this, the Nazi Party's desire to keep old German legal traditions alive led its leaders to embrace reform rather than elimination of the old Civil Code.[19] In 1939, a Nazi legal commission, the Academy of German Law, began drafting the Volksgesetzbuch ("People's Code"). This amounted to a full-scale overhaul of the old Civil Code's marriage, family, and marital property law sections.[20] The draft People's Code would also gather the disparate policies and pieces of legislation governing marriage and the family under one umbrella. The academy's work would have been impossible had the Nazis not silenced their potential opponents early on. With little opposition, and only occasional admonishment, the academy kept working well into the Second World War, but it never completed its task. The academy set it aside in 1941, planning to return to it after the Nazis won the war. They did not: the Third Reich collapsed on 8 May 1945, ensuring that the People's Code would never materialize. Indeed, the Allies would soon undo many existing Nazi-era laws.

The Post-War Crisis of the Family

The Nazis' efforts to control families, gender roles, and reproduction came to a crashing halt with the war's end. By the last months of the war, German families were already experiencing crisis and chaos. Nazi Germany's defeat left the German population at the mercy of the victorious Soviet Union and Western Allies, who now occupied the territories of the former Reich. Before the end of the war, at the Yalta Conference in February 1945, the Allies had made plans for the post-war occupation. However, they had to shift gears abruptly upon Germany's capitulation when the wartime destruction turned out to be worse than they had expected.[21] As the Allies asserted control over Germany, 6.5 million eastern Germans – a large portion of them women and children – fled westward to escape the approaching Red Army and vengeful neighbours.[22] Allied bombings had reduced many large German cities to rubble, destroying around 3.4 million of 17 million homes.[23] In addition to that, the Allies had attacked major industrial areas of Germany, thus crippling the post-war economy. In accounts of the months immediately after the war, Germans often recalled how this period of chaos and devastation exacerbated their suffering and harmed their families.

A contributing factor to the emerging crisis of the family was the demographic imbalance resulting from the high male casualties in the war, especially in its final months. Germany had faced a gender gap since before the First World War,[24] and, as mentioned earlier, male casualties during that war had exacerbated this difference. The high male casualties in the Second World War further worsened the demographic discrepancies that had existed since 1918. Five million of the approximately 18 million men who had volunteered or been called up to the front never returned home.[25] By the war's end, around 7 million more women than men were living in occupied Germany.[26] To be sure, the numbers varied slightly between the four zones. The 1946 census counted 7 million more women than men, a number that decreased gradually over time.[27] By 1950, in West Germany, there were 3 million more women than men; in the East, it was 2 million.[28] The smaller total population in the East (18 million in 1950) compared to the West (51 million) meant that proportionally the "surplus" was larger in the Soviet zone.[29] Sociologists, the census, and women's magazines all noted this demographic imbalance.[30] The demographic gap would become a source of anxiety for many Germans, for it signalled potential losses, either through the death of a male breadwinner or a shortage of marriageable men in the future.

Many men never returned home; many more did, only to face a slow and complex process of economic and social reintegration. The Allies devoted a significant amount of attention to the demobilization of the military, although their procedures were often haphazard. Unlike after the First World War, there was no revolution or post-war German government: the Allies took over all aspects of governance and did not quickly transfer power to the Germans.[31] Although the Wehrmacht had surrendered unconditionally, its officers never disbanded the military, and the Allied Control Council did not formally dissolve the armed forces until 25 September 1945.[32] The Allies placed nearly 10 million troops in prison camps to await processing, which for some meant a trial. The Allies agreed to release all prisoners of war by December 1948: the West kept that promise; the Soviet Union waited until 1950. Over the next five years, roughly 2 million former Wehrmacht soldiers, as well as civilians and women employed by the military, returned to Germany from prisoner-of-war camps (many on the Eastern Front).[33] The absence of a government, lack of official demobilization policies, and differing procedures created a long, drawn-out process that was not carried out uniformly across the occupation zones. On top of the logistical problems, there was the prevailing sense of a masculinity in crisis. According to discourse at the time, men no longer had a firm grasp

Image 1.2. The arrival of the first German prisoners of war from the Soviet Union (25 July 1946). This photograph, taken by a Soviet photographer named Malischew, depicts former German prisoners of war or repatriates in the Gronenfelde camp, located near Frankfurt (Oder) in the Soviet zone. Image courtesy of the Bundesarchiv Berlin-Lichterfelde.

on who they were.[34] Masculinity in Germany had traditionally been rooted in martial prowess, and Nazi Germany had taken this idea to the extreme. In both occupation zones after the war, medical professionals and politicians emphasized the need to "remasculinize" the starving returnees, but in a distinct contrast from the "hypermasculine, militarized ideal of the National Socialist front-line soldier."[35]

For many in the Eastern and the Western occupation zones, employment was essential to remasculinization. In this regard, German officials across all four zones called for the release of POWs for the sake of the economy.[36] Not that the economy was recovering quickly. The Allies had bombed several key industrial regions such as the Ruhr in Germany, which impeded post-war growth.[37] Moreover, as a punitive measure, the Allies enforced heavy reparations, often paid in the "coin" of factory equipment, which was dismantled and taken out of Germany. In particular, the Soviets stripped eastern Germany of the infrastructure it needed to operate its key industries.

According to the Allies and many German men, re-employing men would require pushing women out of their jobs. To some degree, being pushed out of the workforce was nothing new for the older generation of German women, many of whom had been fired from their jobs in order to open them up for men after the First World War.[38] For younger women, however, this process was a new experience, one that varied across borders. In the Western zones, occupation labour policies, designed to promote capitalism, placed a heavy premium on male labour. After 1948, Western employers began dismissing married women from their jobs in order to grant men their old positions (if available), based on their presumed role as breadwinners.[39] In the Soviet zone, the greater demographic imbalance and ideological factors pushed the Soviets to employ women in much higher numbers than in the Western zones. Women who remained in the workforce tended to be single, widowed, or divorced.[40]

Compensation was another issue where gendered differences were evident. The Western Allies ostensibly allowed equal pay for men and women but ultimately left enforcement up to the employers,[41] with the result that employers typically paid men more than women. The Soviets shied away from that approach, largely out of necessity. In August 1946, for example, the Soviet authorities issued an "equal pay for equal work" order and supposedly barred sexual discrimination (though actual practice in both areas did not live up to these policies).[42] For pragmatic and ideological reasons, they sought out women for employment in their planned economy.[43] Still, even these seemingly egalitarian policies failed to resolve the "double burden" facing many women, especially single mothers, as they attempted to balance family life and employment.

The effects of the demographic imbalance, demobilization policies, and labour policies disproportionately affected the 7 million surplus women, who came to be known as the "generation of German women standing alone."[44] During and after the war, these women had done paid work, raised their families, and endured other tribulations. Pre-war Nazi rhetoric had emphasized domestic roles for women. The realities of war meant that the Nazis had to temporarily draw women into the workforce, which could mean anything from factory work to auxiliary military service.[45] Nazi Germany's surrender brought women's work in wartime industries to an abrupt end. Wartime work conditions had not been ideal, and now, employed women faced new challenges related to survival, demobilization, and voluntary and mandatory labour under the Soviet and Western occupations. After the war, women's focus shifted to their families' survival, which required long hours of unpaid and involuntary labour. Some women, especially in the East, had to toil as "women of the rubble" (*Trümmerfrauen*), clearing the debris from the streets of major cities.[46] Women often bore the burdens of negotiating the black-market economy, housing shortages, ration scarcities, and migrations. For women who had fled from the East (part of a larger wave of ethnic Germans entering the Western zones from modern-day Poland), survival was especially complicated.[47]

Image 1.3. Cleaning up Berlin, Women of the Rubble replace excavators (22 January 1948). This photograph shows several women cleaning up the corner of Friedrichstrasse and Unter den Linden. Courtesy of Bundesarchiv Berlin-Lichterfelde.

For some Germans, issues related to survival, labour, and demobilization fuelled personal crises. Indicative of the difficulties of post-war reunions, the divorce rate soared. In 1948, for example, 87,013 divorces were granted – the highest number after the war and ten times the pre–First World War rate.[48] Many couples credited the difficult wartime separation and reunification as reasons to pursue divorce.[49] Also, illegitimacy rates rose significantly during and after the war. In the West, non-marital births reached their peak in 1946 at 16.4 per cent, declining thereafter to 10 per cent in 1950.[50] In the East, nearly 200 per 1,000 births in 1946 were non-marital, though this rate too declined quickly, to a low point by 1949 of around 120 per 1,000.[51] The "surplus of women," high divorce rates, and rising numbers of out-of-wedlock births meant that non-traditional family structures became more typical: single women often headed households, lived with ex-partners because of housing shortages, or found "uncles" with whom they cohabited.[52]

Autobiographical texts buttress the stories behind the statistics.[53] After years apart, husbands, wives, and children had to reacquaint themselves with one another and with post-war life. Some were elated at the prospect of family reunification. In her diary, Frau S. (b. 1929) wrote that the entire family was extremely happy when her father returned.[54] Others attempted half-heartedly to drum up excitement. Frau R. (b. 1910) admitted that even though she was unhappy about her husband's adultery before and during the war, she hoped for a better marital life after the war for the sake of the children. Despite her hopes, he left her, filing for divorce in 1947. When asked by the judge why he did not bother to support his wife or children, he stated, "I just want to create a new existence for myself."[55] R.'s case indicated gendered differences in men's and women's reactions to family reunification and divorce. Frau R. prioritized the children and likely knew that divorce would be detrimental to her financial and social status, given that divorce at the time rested on the "guilt principle," meaning that under the law, one spouse had to be identified as the "guilty" party; the notion of no-fault divorce did not exist in the law. If she pressed a divorce case and was found guilty, she risked losing everything. Herr R., as an employable man, could more easily shoulder the burden of alimony and child support, as well as the labour market, with less fear of permanent consequences. It was therefore less of a problem for him to accept the guilty label.

For others, the return of the father was traumatic. In the case of Frau A. (b. 1944), the reunion was short-lived. When her mother died in 1947, she was left in the hands of her father, who went through several short-lived marriages in the late 1940s and early 1950s.[56] According to Frau A., he usually sided with his new wife over the children, which eroded their parent–child relationship. At times, he institutionalized her and her three siblings because he was unable to care for them. When she was at home, he sexually abused her. Frau A. got engaged at seventeen (in 1961) to a childhood friend because she saw it as a "safe haven."[57] It turned out to be an unhappy marriage, "almost the same life as earlier in [her] parental home."[58] Her husband was unemployed and demanded that she fulfil her "marital duties" multiple times a day. When she refused, he threatened to withhold her allowance. As a married woman, she was prohibited from working full-time without her husband's permission (this remained the case until the reform of family law in 1976) and thus could not earn her own money. According to a local lawyer, verbal abuse and threats did not constitute grounds for divorce – only physical abuse did that. Frau A. thus provoked her husband into hitting her so she could leave.[59]

Popular attitudes reportedly became more accepting of non-traditional family structures, albeit out of accommodation to circumstances, not ideological transformation.[60] In fact, many Germans in the West began to associate marriage and the nuclear family with stability and order in the wake of wartime destruction. Some Christian commentators expressed disappointment on behalf of the "surplus" women who would never marry.[61] In the East, many Soviet and German Communist leaders labelled marriage a "hopelessly outdated" institution because of its association with women's economic dependence and capitalism.[62] On the ground, however, citizens of the Soviet zone – especially those who were religious – often embraced traditional views of marriage and familial structures.

In all four occupation zones, contemporaries perceived the immediate post-war years as a crisis of the family. Media pundits and politicians emphasized the problems that had arisen because of the "surplus" of 7 million women. Meanwhile, medical professionals and politicians stressed the emasculated state of male prisoners of war and sought to improve their condition through labour policies. At home, Germans confronted the difficulties of reunion. Some couples never recovered from the wartime changes, choosing instead to divorce. In the immediate post-war years, altered family structures became more normal. These families became accepted in both German societies; however, their existence caused the opposite reaction in some circles: a growing yearning for "traditional" family and marital structures.

Allied Legal Intervention in Post-War Family Law

The "post-war crisis of the family" was more than a social crisis. It was a legal nightmare. The absence of a centralized post-war government meant that the legal system had no enforcement arm. Moreover, racist Nazi laws technically stayed on the books a few months into the Allied occupation, until the Potsdam Conference in July and August 1945. From this point on, the Allies had to collaborate to pass new laws to adjudicate the four occupation zones. The Allies' efforts to address the twin social and legal crises had profound implications for the future of family law. In creating a new marriage and family law, the Allies set an important precedent for later legal reforms in East and West Germany.

At Potsdam, Allied leaders met to re-evaluate their earlier discussion at Yalta and plan the next phase of Germany's future.[63] To carry out these plans, they formed the Allied Control Council (ACC), the highest governing body in the occupied sectors; it would function until March 1948, when the Soviets withdrew. The council established the appearance of stability and unity because, unlike other policies, which had been left to the discretion of each military governor, these laws applied uniformly across the four zones. On 20 September 1945, for instance, the ACC declared all Nazi laws null and void in all four zones.[64] The ACC periodically issued orders, laws, and proclamations that asserted its authority over the four sectors. One of these laws was the Allied Control Council Law Number 16 (ACC Law No. 16), issued on 20 February 1946, which established regulations for marriages and families in the absence of other laws.[65] This law went into effect on 1 March 1946.[66]

The Allies settled on partial reforms rather than a radical overhaul. The 1946 ACC law repealed the 1938 law but did not revamp all Nazi-era legislation related to marriage and the family.[67] Besides hanging on to some Nazi-era provisions, the Allies chose to reuse the language from the 1900 Civil Code regarding marital age of consent, incest, bigamy, adultery, engagement, and divorce.[68] The 1946 law provided stipulations on marriage and divorce but did not overturn other existing measures of the old Civil Code. Marital property schemes, for example, still dictated that married women's property and their assets were controlled by the husband.[69] Furthermore, old provisions such as the *Stichentscheid*, or the right of the husband to make all decisions in the family, were still valid.[70] Full parental authority and decision-making were still the domain of the father.[71] Women still had to take their husbands' surnames.[72] If married, their husbands still had the right to bar their wives from working.[73] Women were still considered the head of the household and could only work if their husbands were unable to support the family.[74] The 1946 law expanded rights to divorce and dismissed outdated marriage regulations, but it did not overhaul provisions that had long constrained women's rights in marriage and over their children.

The Allies chose this path of limited reform for several reasons. First, they were primarily interested in denazification. Although the Allies retained parts of Nazi-era laws, they made sure to remove the portions of the 1938 law that most reflected racist Nazi beliefs. Also, the Allies' decision to pursue partial reforms may have been a matter of diplomacy. By February 1946, the four occupying powers already had a history of poor cooperation. The Soviets, for instance, had been obstinate at the Potsdam Conference and had delayed approving the formation of the ACC and voting on other joint decisions.[75] Fully rewriting the law would have required compromise among the Soviets, Americans, British, and French. Any serious discussion would likely have ended in stalemate, especially because the four powers had different conceptions of gender roles in marriage and the family. Additionally, the 1946 law was the expedient choice in a constantly evolving and chaotic post-war environment, especially one in which the Allies prioritized other initiatives, such as currency reform.[76] They wanted to get a new law on the books, and recycling the old BGB's measures was a fast and easy solution. Finally, reusing German text may have made the legislation more familiar to the Germans under occupation since, in theory, they would have known the provisions of the old BGB. This combination of reasons likely pushed the Allies to adopt regulations that were reminiscent of the older Civil Code.

Women and legal experts soon identified issues with the application of the ACC Law. The British Zone Central Justice Administration, for example, received several letters from jurists and other legal officials scattered across the Western zones between 1946 and 1948.[77] One woman wanted to know if there were rules about attaining a divorce from her husband who was in an internment camp.[78] Others wrote with questions about specifics, such as how the age of majority for marriage worked under the new law.[79] On one level, the letters reflected genuine inquisitiveness about the new law; when faced with a quandary, jurists turned to the lawmakers on behalf of their clients. On another level, however, the letters indicated a reckoning with the new legislation. Far from being comfortable with merely reinstating the old law's provisions, Germans wanted to know whether the new circumstances benefited them or whether loopholes existed to help them skirt certain issues (such as obtaining a spouse's signature for a divorce).

Another place to which Germans turned for help was the pages of the women's press. The editors of women's journals often published readers' letters in order to highlight problems and frustrations with the law. In September 1946, for example, *Die Frau von heute* printed a letter from Annedore Z., an orphaned nineteen-year-old, who asked if she could marry without her guardian's permission. Her fiancé had recently returned from a prisoner-of-war camp, and now her legal guardian was forbidding the marriage. Annedore wanted to know if she had to wait to marry.[80] Another writer asked whether her husband, also recently returned from the front, had the right to divorce her without her consent.[81] In each case, the writer expressed some confusion or frustration with the law and was turning to the paper for help. The editors carefully selected letters to print that would resonate with their readers.

The Allies performed a vital service when they laid down a new marriage law for Germans struggling with crises in their families and marriages. But the Allied law did not account for every possible obstacle that the immediate post-war period threw at German families. The law itself was a product of expediency and was meant to be a stopgap. It was not designed to change the entire trajectory of women's rights in occupied Germany. As a result, the limits of the law created even more uncertain situations, which female activists were quick to criticize in the early post-war years. The extent to which female activists could respond, however, depended on the circumstances, which differed between the Soviet and Western zones.

Women's Committees Fight for a New Civil Code

The post-war crisis of the family, the introduction of the 1946 marriage law, and the opportunity to organize spurred women's associations in all four occupied zones to begin crafting their own proposals for a new civil law. While the Western powers encouraged pluralism and decentralization, the Soviets consolidated and centralized Communist rule in the East under the SED. Social and political organizations in the occupation zones played important roles as arbiters in the later debates over family law and women's rights. The most important voices in these discussions belonged to women, who began drafting new versions of the law before the fate of Germany was settled. Their work was significant because it demonstrated that women were deeply involved in grassroots organization at an early stage. Furthermore, their versions would serve as templates for later discussions in the 1950s.

As the Allies promulgated new laws in response to the crisis of the family, they also began rehabilitating Germany's pre-1933 political and social structures. This would have important implications for family law reforms down the line. Within months of the Allied occupation, old parties, such as the Social Democratic Party of Germany (SPD) and the Communist Party of Germany (KPD), as well as new parties, such as the Christian Democratic Union and the Christian Social Union (CDU and CSU), were permitted to form across the four occupation zones. The Socialist Unity Party (SED) was founded in 1946 as a merger of the SPD and KPD in the Soviet zone. In addition, women's organizations, the Protestant and Catholic churches, trade unions, and the press were all permitted to re-form.

As the ones who stood to gain the most from the overhaul of the old Civil Code, women were instrumental in the reform process. At the same time, the extent to which women readily attached themselves to the cause differed in the two zones and was contingent on several factors. In the Soviet zone, attracting women to communism initially proved difficult. Before 1933, German women had traditionally voted for the SPD or the Center Party, not the KPD.[82] The Soviets' support of women's emancipation stemmed from a combination of their own history of revolution as well as contemporary circumstances induced by the occupation.[83] Furthermore, the Soviet Red Army's aggressive campaign of raping German women at the end of the war had provoked a backlash against communism.[84] The long history of "emancipating" women in Russia, a spotty history of female support for the KPD, and a recognition of women's plight under the occupation meant that that the Soviets and their German partners had to struggle hard to draw women into their party.

Almost as soon as the occupation began, female activists across the four zones organized on the grassroots level to help women and their children navigate and survive the crisis years. The Soviets and German Communists then tried to bring women into their fold by taking direct control of women's grassroots activities. For example, the Soviets turned "women's centres," which sprang up immediately after the war, into "antifascist women's committees" (AFAs) in June 1945.[85] On a pragmatic level, the AFAs were responsible for helping women collect food and clothing, operate soup kitchens, and learn their legal rights.[86] On an ideological level, the Soviets and leaders of the re-emergent KPD hoped that the AFAs would unify the fragmented women's movement under the banner of antifascism, antimilitarism, and the promotion of (albeit Soviet-style) democracy. To some extent, the AFAs succeeded, bringing together around 300,000 women from all political persuasions and economic backgrounds (housewives, farm labourers, and white-collar workers).[87]

Within a few months, the Soviets had taken further steps towards bringing the AFAs under Communist control. On 30 October 1945, SMAD issued Order No. 80, which decreed that the antifascist women's organizations were both officially sanctioned and under the jurisdiction of the city administrations.[88] After Order No. 80 came out, the German Administration for Education designated a department to cover all issues related to women. In July 1946, the Berlin Central Women's Committee and the Education Department gathered all women's committees in the Soviet zone to form the Central Women's Commission (ZFA), which soon after, in March 1947, was supplanted by the Democratic Women's League of Germany (DFD).[89] By September 1947, 242,000 women – most of them housewives without party affiliation – had joined the DFD.[90] The DFD became the dominant representative of women's matters in discussions of family law in the GDR.

An early goal of the ZFA (and then the DFD) in the Soviet occupied zone was to reform the Civil Code. To that end, in August 1946, the ZFA established a legal commission, led by Hilde Benjamin.[91] Benjamin had joined the KPD in 1927 and became a lawyer for the party. After the Second World War, she entered the newly founded SED and worked her way up to Chief Prosecutor and Director of the German Justice Administration for the Soviet zone. She had long been an advocate for women's rights.[92] Within the ZFA, she led a commission comprised of women's working groups that aimed both to attract women to the legal profession and to clarify complicated legal matters for women in the Soviet zone.[93] Benjamin specifically identified the "place of women in family law" and "the rights of unmarried mothers and illegitimate children" as laws that "hung in the air" and desperately needed revision. The ZFA planned to collect proposals from regional and local women's committees, discuss them in the commission meetings, and then send on all suggestions to the German Justice Administration. This plan, Benjamin hoped, would bring together "bottom-up" and "top-down" approaches to changing the laws.[94]

Beyond sending proposals to the German Justice Administration, the ZFA and the DFD found other ways to express their opinions about civil law, namely through publishing in the women's press. Between 1946 and 1948, the editors of East German women's magazines such as *Die Frau von heute* and *Für Dich* published series of articles and readers' letters that simultaneously praised the SED for its progressive stances on equal rights and criticized the enduring status of the old Civil Code. An article by SED member Käthe Kern, a former Social Democrat and rising star in the DFD, applauded the ruling party, because "the full equality of women is realized for the first time as a human right."[95]

At the same time, the women's press sought to inform readers about existing obstacles to equality. The press subtly criticized the continued existence of the Civil Code and the SED's lacklustre attempts to change it. The editors and authors conveyed their disapproval through two strategies. The first was to present the limits of the law. In May 1947, for example, *Für Dich* published an unsigned article that began with this rhetorical question: "How would it be if women still wore fashion from 1897? ... We would all find that a bit strange, right?"[96] The article then featured the insights of a male jurist on the sections of the old BGB that had not been changed under the 1946 law. The author made several suggestions, such as changing the *Stichentscheid* to give spouses equal say in all decisions concerning the marriage and family. He also argued that women's rights to work outside the home and represent their husbands legally could no longer be limited. Men should no longer have control over their wives' property. Finally, unmarried mothers should have full authority over their children. Similarly, a series titled "Equality Yes – But Also Equal Rights," published in 1948 by *Für Dich*, outlined each aspect of the old Civil Code that was still valid under the 1946 marriage law.[97] These types of articles told readers about their legal rights and also exposed them to their legal limitations.

Approaching the topic from another angle, authors and editors in the Soviet zone sometimes employed a second strategy of conflicting discourses to sway their readers. In an October 1946 article in *Die Frau von heute*, Elli Schmidt called the work of the Soviet occupiers a "great gift" to women.[98] Schmidt's positive assessment was not surprising, given that she enjoyed close relations with the Soviets and the SED. Trained as a seamstress, Schmidt had joined the KPD in 1927 and spent the war in exile in Moscow. She returned to Germany in June 1945 and became a leader of the women's division of the Central Committee of the SED.[99] Notwithstanding these accolades, leaders of the Soviet zone women's committees also used the Soviets' progress to criticize the SED's work. In an article from September 1948, for example, the author pointed out that in the Soviet Union, a woman was free to keep her maiden name or take on her new husband's name.[100] The article did not explicitly condemn the SED, but the comparison implied that other, better models of family law existed than what remained in effect in Germany.

Finally, the editors of women's newspapers often printed readers' letters that pointed out problems with the legal situation in the Soviet zone. Some of these letters were about the cultural and social barriers women faced at home. In one letter, for instance, Frau F. stated that she was excited to join the DFD until her husband intervened on the grounds that married women should stay home and refrain from political activity.[101] Other letters emphasized the writer's legal confusion. Frau L. wrote in June 1947 to complain that she had been adhering to the BGB and working in her husband's business, but that the Soviet authorities had ordered her to enter the workforce.[102] Another woman wrote to ask if it was really possible that her husband could demand a divorce without her consent.[103] Like the other articles, these letters informed female readers about their rights and offered solidarity, while pointing out legal and cultural barriers that still existed in the Soviet zone.

The SED had asserted its control over the ZFA and the DFD, but there were still some opportunities in the early post-war years for non-Communists (mainly liberals and Christian Democrats) to discuss a new civil law. In October 1947, for instance, the East-CDU's Women's Committee addressed the

ZFA's recent proposals for a new BGB. According to the East-CDU, the ZFA's suggestions focused too much on equality of women, not the family, and this would only leave women "isolated and more vulnerable."[104] They were highly critical of the ZFA's assertion that the law would reflect the "people's opinion," observing that the Nazis had relied on populist sentiments.[105] In the end, the East-CDU put together a list of its own positions, which reflected its Christian views and addressed the limits of the BGB and the 1946 law. These discussions highlight that women's associations of all political persuasions in the East engaged with the problem of the Civil Code at an early stage, which in turn points to a certain degree of pluralism in the Soviet zone. This fluid situation changed when the Cold War began and the Allies found a temporary solution to the German question. As political space tightened in the context of the Cold War, the Christian conservative women's suggestions were sidelined in favour of the ZFA/DFD's in the Soviet zone. As a result, for the rest of the Soviet zone's (and later the GDR's) lifespan, Communist women dominated all discourse on gender roles, labour, and the family.

Meanwhile, women's groups were beginning to organize in the Western occupation zones. Much as they did in the Soviet zone, women's "self-help" groups organized on the local and regional levels within the first few weeks of the end of the war, primarily to help women restore their daily existence, which essentially meant acquiring food rations.[106] Over the next two years, political parties and independent women's associations took over their work.[107] Women's organizing in the Western zones was marked by divisions and logistical obstacles, which had direct and indirect impacts on their ability to lobby for reforms to family law at different stages down the line. One issue facing women's associations was an initial lack of bureaucratic and monetary support from the occupiers.[108] Without guaranteeing much formal or financial help, the British and American occupation governments vowed to assist women by providing citizenship and re-education programs for them. The Allies assumed incorrectly that women lacked political development, were apathetic, or were repressed.[109] The Western Allies therefore designed various programs to reacquaint women with democracy and social welfare while fulfilling their "womanly" desires.[110] The occupation officials had the help of American and British women, such as Ruth Woodsmall, a former teacher and later a representative on the UN Commission on the Status of Women. These "outsider" women set out to empower German women, "albeit in the private sphere"; thus, they made little effort to politicize them or offer other paths to equality (such as equal wages).[111]

Despite Allied perceptions, German women hardly needed an introduction to democracy. Many leaders of the new women's committees and organizations had been politically active during the Weimar Republic, in the Reichstag or the Landtags (the equivalent of state representative assemblies), or at the local level. They had not been politically active after 1933 only because the Third Reich had dissolved all women's associations and forbade women from joining political parties.[112] Many of these women rejoined major political parties after the war, and some of them led the parties' women's committees. The Social Democrats were the only major party with an office devoted to women, having established one in 1946.[113] The Christian Democrats and Free Democrats had regional and local women's groups but did not introduce their own national-level women's committees until the early 1950s.[114] The Communist DFD established a West German branch in 1950.[115] By the early 1950s, every major political party in West Germany had an official, national-level women's committee. These party-level committees would play an important role in family law reform.

Political parties offered one path for women to press their concerns; independent, non-party women's associations provided another.[116] These non-party women's organizations represented a variety of political, professional, and confessional interests. Alongside non-confessional associations were religious (i.e., Christian) women's organizations. These had been founded in the early twentieth century and forced to disband in 1933.[117] They worked closely with both their church leaders and the CDU/CSU in the post-war years. All these women's organizations – non-party, professional, confessional – re-emerged in the immediate post-war years with the tacit support of the Western Allies. They would represent women's voices in later debates over reforms to family law.

To be sure, these categorizations of women's associations in the West are somewhat superficial. Many female leaders represented several organizations or parties at once, which sometimes complicated their allegiances in discussions over family law. Elisabeth Schwarzhaupt, for example, was a powerful voice in the debates conducted in the 1950s. In addition to being a CDU member, she led the Protestant Women's Work and a female lawyers' group, besides working for a Protestant church. Whatever their affiliation, the women who led these organizations brought years of experience and political activism with them. But the variety of associations and multiple affiliations at times caused discord. For example, SPD Frauenbüro leader Herta Gotthelf condemned the work of female SPD leaders like Theanolte Bähnisch who had established independent women's associations. Gotthelf was highly critical of Bähnisch's efforts, forbade her to continue, and asserted that the SPD was the only women's movement that Germany needed.[118] Despite Gotthelf's proclamations, many women, either because of their pre-war experiences or because they had watched the DFD get "brought into line" with the SED in the East, preferred the independent organizations to the SPD. The siphoning off of women to independent groups did not help the SPD gain support for the family law reforms it proposed. Meanwhile, the CDU faced its own problems. Among Christian conservative women, tensions developed between national and local leaders over which women's issues to prioritize (e.g., "practical" versus broader legal and political matters).[119]

These groups, for the most part, escaped the overt politicization faced by their counterparts in the Soviet zone, at least initially.[120] Once the Cold War began in earnest in 1947–48, Western military officials observed mounting divisions among women's groups and feared that disunity among women would create space for communist infiltration. The Americans, in particular, mobilized women's groups to foster anticommunism.[121] By early 1947, the Soviets had eliminated the possibility of political competition in the East and consolidated the women's committees into the DFD, which had a marginal but growing presence in the West.[122] British occupation officials responded to the DFD by supporting the formation of a single women's association (the Deutscher Frauenring) in 1947 to unite all of the regionally based independent women's associations in their zone.[123] The American occupiers would later fund the establishment of the Informationsdienstes für Frauenfragen in 1951, which then became the Deutscher Frauenrat – effectively the successor to the pre-war bourgeois women's movement.[124] The Allies' efforts to unify German women around the twin goals of antifascism and anticommunism, however, were ultimately hindered by old divisions and divergent interests.

Women's groups in the Western zones faced very different circumstances than their Eastern zone equivalents in other ways besides. Logistics were one problem. These groups had little opportunity to work together because so much infrastructure had been destroyed and passes were necessary for travel between zones (unlike in the Soviet zone, which was smaller and under one central authority).[125] Organizing on a national level became easier after January 1946, when the occupation powers licensed women's associations.[126] Still, women's organizations did not hold their first interzonal meeting until May 1947, in Bad Boll.[127]

In the Western zones, the paradigm was reversed. Communist women were in the minority, and the SPD and independent women's associations dominated the critical discourse, which aimed for reforms of women's rights as they related to marriage and the family. For all the divisiveness, many Western women's associations shared the same goal as their Eastern counterparts: to rebuild Germany "as a new democratic state" out of the ashes of the Nazi dictatorship.[128] These leaders maintained that granting women equal rights, especially in marriage and the family, was fundamental to reconstruction. In January 1946, for instance, the Founding Program of the Frankfurt Women's Committee vowed that the organization would fight for the "complete equality of women in all areas" (especially in public offices and in workplaces) and would work to guarantee women equal rights in marriage and marital property.[129] The Dortmund Women's Committee similarly declared its commitment to the struggle "for the equality of women," legal aid for women, and "support and help for employed and breadwinners of their families."[130]

Groups like the Frankfurt Women's Committee were clearly committed to equality in marriage, yet few archival records on Western women's committees' early work on the Civil Code exist, likely because social organizations in the West were so decentralized.[131] The limited evidence available from the SPD and the CDU, however, indicates that discussions about the Civil Code were conducted in the West, even if complete documentation of those debates is unavailable in major archives. The SPD left the most complete paper trail, likely because the party had an official "Women's Office" after 1946 that kept records of local- and regional-level discussions.[132] The SPD brought up the Civil Code again at its September 1948 women's conference and during the Parliamentary Council.[133] Records from Christian conservative women point to discussions about equal rights and civil law in their circles as well. In 1948, for instance, a CDU women's leader prodded her party to introduce an equality clause that would guarantee men and women equality in professional life and promote equal treatment of domestic duties.[134]

The Western women's press was heavily involved as well. The West Berlin magazine *Sie* and the Hamburg-based women's magazine *Constanze*, for instance, published articles that clearly supported equal rights for unwed mothers and urged women to pursue divorce.[135] And the SPD newsletter for female party members, *Genossin*, printed articles that criticized the state of the BGB, homing in on issues that the 1946 ACC law had not addressed, such as the right of men to make all decisions for their families and men's right to control and profit from their wives' property holdings.[136] In this way, the editors of these magazines exposed their subscribers to critical issues surrounding women's rights and status in marriage and the family.

As another way of reaching readers, women's newspapers often published explanations of the law's ins and outs. For instance, *Sie* began publishing a regular series called "Sie und das Recht" [You and the Law]," written by a district court attorney. In a matter-of-fact tone, the column's author explained sticky issues plaguing readers in the chaotic post-war years. For instance, what did the law say about accidental bigamy, in cases where men were presumed dead and later returned home?[137] What about adoption by single mothers, especially with so many orphaned children in need of parents?[138] Did the guilt principle still apply in divorce, or were there ways to work around it?[139] What about the legal obligation to support family members, formerly only applied to immediate family? How did that provision work in the new post-war era in which new family structures were the norm?[140] This column helped shine a light on the fraught nature of the Allied law.

Editors of women's magazines could also use their letters sections to suggest to women how they should understand social perceptions. Of course, social expectations remained difficult to break, as indicated by surveys. In one poll, residents of the American zone and Berlin were asked why women should be barred from participation in public life. Fifty-four per cent in the American zone stated that a woman's place was in the home as the caretaker of the children, while another 26 per cent claimed that women were either uninterested, uninformed, or incapable.[141] The editors sought to undermine these prevailing notions about gender roles by printing critical letters from readers. For instance, one woman complained in her letter about the "legally anchored bulwark of male domination," in particular the stipulation that women had to take their husbands' surnames.[142] Yet another claimed that many women were no longer worried about their marriage prospects and were in fact happy to be single.[143] Publishing such commentary was a subtle way of getting female readers to rethink the old patriarchal restrictions placed on them by the law.

From the beginning, the women's committees in the Western zones faced certain obstacles that their Eastern zone counterparts did not. For one thing, they encountered physical and logistical barriers. Restrictions on travel and much larger territories prevented a national-level movement from forming until later. Furthermore, the decentralized nature of politics and society in the West meant that debates over issues like the future Civil Code often occurred on the local or regional level (and thus are more difficult to trace today in the archival record). Women's committees also faced long-established ideological, class, and confessional differences of the kind that had burdened the German women's movement since the late nineteenth century. Additionally, they encountered the problem of aligning their own goals with those of the Western occupiers, who assumed incorrectly that German women needed democratization. The endeavours that the Western Allies were willing to invest time and money in, such as initiatives to teach women citizenship, were not what women's committee leaders sought for themselves. Unlike the Soviets, the Western Allies did not intervene early on in the women's committees, though they would shower them with more attention later, once they realized what an invaluable tool women were for the project of rebuilding Germany.[144] Finally, as the Cold War began in earnest in late 1947 and early 1948 and the Allies developed a solution to the German question, women's associations found themselves caught up in the tug of war between East and West, with limited political space in which to manoeuvre.

In 1945, a crisis of the family erupted across Europe. For many Germans, the war and its immediate aftermath had thrown their families into disarray. Addressing this perceived crisis became paramount for numerous parties. The Allies recognized the need to provide parameters for imperilled German marriages and families. Thus, their 1946 law largely reinforced earlier provisions lifted from the Civil Code. Meanwhile, female activists in the Western and Soviet zones viewed the post-war crisis year as a tabula rasa for women's rights and were less keen on retaining the old law. The leaders of women's organizations in both the East and the West resisted the old BGB, the 1946 law, and the reinforcement of traditional family roles, but not all Germans did. Soldiers returning from the front were unwilling to stop being patriarchs. Many of the women who had worked and raised families while their men were absent were unwilling to relinquish their new authority, yet they also found the "double burden" tiresome. For some Germans, then, a return to the traditional family was desirable during the post-war crisis.

In many ways, the experiences of other Europeans resembled those faced by the Germans. In recently collapsed Fascist Italy, Italian women had been responsible throughout the war for caring for their families in the absence of their husbands, who were away fighting in France, the Eastern Front, North and East Africa, and the Balkans.[145] These women were expected to return to their traditional roles after the war. In liberated France, many men did not return home, having been killed or sent to concentration camps or having "disappeared into the Resistance."[146] Those who did return home in one piece were quick to engage in domestic violence and expected their wives, who had spent the war shouldering the double burden, to return to subservience and domesticity.[147] British women faced similar sentiments,[148] as did Eastern European women. In Poland, a brief post-war period of women's emancipation gave way to the re-establishment of more traditional gender roles.[149] Even in the Soviet Union, past notions about patriarchy never completely disappeared.[150]

The German post-war family crisis ended up differing from that in the rest of Europe in many ways. For one thing, except for the Soviet Union, Germany faced the most critical demographic imbalance after the war. France, Italy, Britain, and Hungary did not face quite the same differences in their male-to-female ratios.[151] For another, while most European states saw women's organizations re-emerge in 1945, only German women's organizations became subject to the influence of the Western Allies and the Soviets. Finally, the division of Germany and the burgeoning rivalries among the occupying powers did much to shape the nascent discussions of marriage and the family. In other states, such as France and Italy, rule had passed almost immediately into the hands of monarchs or former resistance fighters. In Eastern Europe, the Soviet Union quickly propped up satellite states, with sympathetic local communists at the helm. Only Germany remained divided and occupied. As a result, only Germany had Allied input into its laws, such as the 1946 Allied Control Council law. The Allies recognized the need to provide parameters for imperilled marriages and families. In an attempt to stabilize Germany, the 1946 law largely reinforced old provisions lifted from the Civil Code. However, the 1946 law created more confusion for Germans in the immediate post-war years.

The immediate post-war period in occupied Germany would leave three lingering legacies. First, the post-war context allowed women's organizations to regroup. They did not always see eye to eye, but collectively they would remain instrumental in pushing reforms of the Civil Code. Second, the 1946 law prepared the ground for future debates. It was, after all, merely a stopgap solution, one that did not reflect the comprehensive reforms that women's organizations envisioned. Third and finally, it was clear from the earliest moments that the presence of separate occupation zones would have lasting effects on discussions of gender, women, and the family in the late 1940s and early 1950s.

2 Gender Equality and the Family in the Two German Constitutions, 1948–1949

In January 1949, SED functionary Käthe Kern published an article in the Soviet zone women's magazine *Die Frau von heute* titled "Bonn Opposes Women's Rights." Kern had been active in the SPD women's movement in Berlin before 1933. After 1946, she joined the Socialist Unity Party (SED), rose in the ranks of the Democratic Women's League of Germany (DFD), and became a representative on the People's Council, the Soviet zone's constitutional convention.[1] In her article, Kern relayed to readers that the Parliamentary Council, the Western zones' constitutional congress in Bonn, had recently rejected a proposal to grant women equality with men in their provisional constitution, the Basic Law.[2] In contrast, the SED and the People's Council had already adopted complete equality for men and women as a basic right in its own draft constitution in 1946, although it had not yet officially ratified that document. Kern lauded the People's Council's actions on equality as "a step forward for women and a peaceful future." Meanwhile, she labelled the Western Parliamentary Council's draft as "backward," contending that the council would never embrace women's equality.[3]

Much to Kern's dismay, the Western Parliamentary Council passed the Basic Law first, complete with an equality clause, before the People's Council could adopt its constitution. Shortly after Kern's article came out in the Soviet zone press, the Western Parliamentary Council had decided to reverse course and include an equality clause. On 23 May 1949, the West German Basic Law came into effect, establishing the Federal Republic of Germany (FRG). The Basic Law promised that "men and women have equal rights." Members of the Eastern People's Council were outraged. In the context of the rising Cold War competition, women's equality was one of the issues on which the council had staked its reputation as the superior Germany. It could no longer claim that mantle. Not to be outdone, People's Council representatives declared that they would put women's equality into practice before the West did. A few months later, on 7 October 1949, the East German People's Council finally passed its

own constitution, thus founding the communist German Democratic Republic (GDR). That document, too, included an equal rights clause, which read:
"Men and women have equal rights." Additionally, both provisional constitutions guaranteed the overhaul of all legislation prohibiting "equal rights." In the
GDR, this clause went into effect immediately; the West German government
had until 31 March 1953 to change its legislation.

From this point on, the two states followed forking paths in terms of their
political, economic, and social systems. Yet despite their differences, the two
states shared the same commitment to women's equality, at least on paper. It
was no accident that both sides' constitutions included similarly worded equality clauses. Two entangled impulses drove the adoption of the equality clauses
in each state. First, members of the Western Parliamentary Council and the
Eastern People's Council had made the same deliberate decision to incorporate
these nearly identical clauses in their constitutions because of the developing
Cold War competition between the two occupation zones.[4] The burgeoning
conflict swayed the decisions each side made, albeit to different degrees.[5] The
People's Council in the Soviet zone tended to react much more strongly to political events than the Western Parliamentary Council.

Second, female activists in both zones were instrumental in getting the
equality clauses added to the new constitutions of the GDR and the FRG.
While the debates were spearheaded by socialist and communist women,
centre-right women were ready to support their leftist counterparts on the
issue of "gender equality." Without this collective pressure on male council
members, women's rights in both Germanys would have remained suspended
at the level of the 1919 Weimar constitution. Given how much had changed
during and after the Second World War, the constitutions needed to present a
new model for equality between men and women. The new, broader equality
clauses would have significant long-term effects for men and women in both
states. The matching mandates encased in the 1949 provisional constitution
of the GDR and the Basic Law of the FRG would provide the legal foundation
for future reforms of the long-standing Civil Code (BGB) in the 1950s and
early 1960s.

Securing Gender Equality in the East German Constitution

Future German sovereignty and constitutional rights – and by extension,
equality for men and women – had been on the table from an early stage in
the Soviet zone. In July 1946, the SED approached the Soviets about writing a
national constitution that would cover all German territories.[6] Several events in
the preceding months precipitated this pitch. First, the CDU and the SPD had
fared much better than the KPD in local and regional elections in the American
zone, and this made the KPD and the Soviets uneasy.[7] The KPD responded in

April 1946 by forcing the SPD in the Soviet zone to merge with it to form the SED, in order to guarantee electoral gains. Second, at the end of June 1946, the Americans began writing constitutions for the *Länder* (i.e., states), a move that startled the SED and the Soviets.[8] When the United States rejected the idea of a centralized Germany at the Paris Conference in July 1946, pushing instead for a federal system, the Soviets balked and gave the SED permission to draft a national constitution.[9] Between 1946 and 1948, the international stakes of the constitutional debates in the Soviet zone changed drastically. By late 1948, the SED was under increasing pressure to outpace the Western zones, where a parallel discussion about a new constitution was taking place. It was not a given, however, that the new constitution would include women's equal rights. The final version of the East German constitution, passed in 1949, incorporated equal rights because of the efforts of female party activists and because of the rising competition with the Western occupation zones.

The inclusion of an equal rights clause in the 1949 constitution had its roots in earlier discussions in 1946 in the Soviet zone. The first constitutional draft, produced in August 1946, was not all-encompassing. It largely replicated the language of the old Weimar constitution, and in some ways it was even more limited than its predecessor. It did not, for instance, include any mention of equal rights for men and women. Moreover, the insular group selected to draft it was not especially diverse. In August 1946, a small, all-male commit-tee of SED members presented the Soviet Military Administration in Germany (SMAD) with the first draft of the "Constitution of the Democratic Republic of Germany."[10] Four of the five committee members – Wilhelm Pieck, Walter Ulbricht, Otto Grotewohl, and Max Fechner – were political leaders of the SED with little legal training but had displayed loyalty to the Soviet mission.[11] The fifth committee member, Karl Polak, had received his law degree in 1933 and had soon been dismissed from his civil service post under Nazi law because of his Jewish heritage. He went into exile in the Soviet Union, where he taught legal theory in Tashkent. He returned to Germany in 1946, joining the KPD/SED.[12] His law degree and time in exile teaching law in the Soviet Union qual-ified him to lead the constitutional reforms within the SED. When Polak pro-duced the first draft of an all-German constitution in August 1946, the Soviet authorities did not approve it, for unknown reasons.[13]

In September 1946, SED deputy chairman and former Communist Party leader Walter Ulbricht pressured SMAD to revisit the issue.[14] Ulbricht cited unity, both legal and political, as a major reason for pursuing reforms. Ulbricht insisted that publishing a draft of the national constitution would remind Germans that the Soviets and the SED intended to keep Germany united, un-like their Western counterparts. He also told the Soviets that it was no longer enough merely to criticize the Western zones – the SED needed to take action.[15] The SED's relative success in the October elections for the state legislature convinced the Soviets to relent and allow the SED to move forward with crafting the national and state constitutions for Germany.

In November 1946, the SED assembled a constitutional committee of sixteen members, in contrast to the insular group that had drafted the August 1946 version.[16] A key difference was that this time, the SED permitted women to participate. This decision had critical consequences for the constitution, for it led to the participation of Käthe Kern as the sole female delegate. The SED leadership had chosen Kern to represent women's interests. As the "token woman" on the SED constitutional committee, Kern lobbied for a separate and stronger equality clause.[17] Here, she was looking back to the 1919 Weimar constitution, which had included a weak equal rights clause that promised men and women "fundamentally the same rights and duties."[18] Now, she wanted a stronger formulation. The leader of the commission, former SPD chairman Otto Grotewohl, rejected her proposal.[19] Undeterred, Kern forwarded a written request for the amendment to the SED Central Office and SMAD. Perhaps motivated by their own constitutional guarantees of equal rights for men and women or seeing an opportunity to attract women to communism, the Soviets responded positively to Kern's appeal and ordered the SED to add the equality clause.[20]

Kern's initiative and Soviet intervention on her behalf undoubtedly altered the path of the German constitution in the Soviet zone. Had the Soviets approved Polak's version, married women would have experienced little change in their legal rights. The new version, published on 16 November 1946, instead significantly expanded civil rights for women. For example, Article 7 stated: "Men and women have equal rights." Additionally, Article 25 specified: "The family stands under special constitutional protection. Marriage derives from the equality of both sexes." Furthermore, Article 26 said: "Women are equal to men in all areas of civic, economic, and social life. All legal definitions that oppose the equal rights of women are overturned." Finally, the same clause promised equal wages for men and women and equal treatment of illegitimate children and their unwed mothers.[21] For the first time ever, a German constitution guaranteed men and women equality, stipulated equal wages, and established equal status among married and unmarried women and mothers.

The SED Politburo hid Kern's struggle with her male colleagues from the public. Instead, SED leaders used the Soviet zone press to present a positive, unified public image of its avowed support of women's legal equality. One strategy used by the Soviet zone media was to emphasize historic change. Several articles published in *Neues Deutschland* – the SED's official mouthpiece – praised the SED's draft for finally overcoming the shortcomings of the Weimar constitution.[22] As noted earlier, the latter had not granted women full equality in all areas. The SED played up the extent to which its new constitution was a progressive change from earlier eras in German history.

At the time, the occupation zones in the West were in the midst of creating state-level constitutions, many of which included their own equality clauses.[23] The Bizone (the British and US Occupation Zones, which had been combined on 1 January 1947), however, had not yet broached the subject of a constitution or equality on the national level. *Neues Deutschland* therefore presented the SED as the leader in the race with the Western zones for equal rights for women. One article, for example, featured an unidentified woman complaining about the proceedings in the Bavarian state constitutional committee. Some Bavarian representatives had opposed the inclusion of an equality clause because the Bible granted men authority over women.[24] The article ended by juxtaposing the Bavarian regional constitution with the SED draft and the Weimar constitution. In pointing out that only the SED would give women full legal equality for the very first time, the authors were clearly taking a dig at political leaders in the Western zones.[25]

This suggests that the SED wanted to use the issue of women's equality to discredit its rivals across the German–German border. But it served a second purpose as well: it undercut its political opponents in the Soviet zone, the Christian Democrats. In the recent October elections in Berlin, the East-CDU had beaten the Communists, with 454,202 to 405,992 votes.[26] For the SED, this margin was too close for comfort, even though the unified party had done much better outside of Berlin.[27] Given the CDU's electoral gains in recent local and regional elections, SED leaders looked for ways to undermine the opposing party. Equal rights served as one way to do that. One *Neues Deutschland* article emphasized how the issue of women's equality differentiated the SED from the East-CDU. The SED asserted here that equality of the sexes stood, alongside dispossession of large estates, the "conveyance of natural resources," and the punishment of former Nazis, as one of the four prerequisites "that promote progressive democratic development in Germany."[28] The message communicated to readers was that the CDU was failing to address important issues that were facing Germany. The impression the SED aimed to give readers was that it had altered the historic trajectory of women's rights – something their Christian conservative and Western counterparts were unable and unwilling to do.

The SED's media campaign for equality dropped off for much of 1947 as the wartime alliance between the Western Allies and the Soviets began to fall apart in the context of the developing Cold War. The quest for equal rights was then reinvigorated in March 1948 with the founding of the People's Council, which was tasked with writing a new constitution for Germany. Between December 1947 and February 1948, the SED had tried and failed to introduce direct democracy as a form of government for Germany. The Western Allies refused to latch onto that idea – indeed, they underscored their dissonance by not inviting the Soviets to the London Six-Power Conference in February 1948, where the "German question" was discussed. The Soviets and the SED interpreted their exclusion from that conference as a sign that the wartime alliance was ending. In response, the Soviets pulled out of the Allied Control Council. Meanwhile, the SED proposed a "provisional parliament."[29] The Soviets approved that idea, thus paving the way for the new parliament, dominated by the SED, to begin its work building a new socialist republic. That work began on 19 March 1948.[30] As the People's Council began its work, committee chair and SED leader Otto Grotewohl declared that "the principles of private life and the right to personal freedom should be seen as universal."[31] Interestingly, Grotewohl cited equal rights for men and women as a specific example: "It is self-evident that men and women must be treated equally in the constitution."[32] Kern's earlier stubbornness had paid off, leaving a permanent imprint on the constitutional debates from the earliest stages.

Grotewohl's defence of women's equality was a surprising reversal of his earlier disregard of Kern's proposals.[33] At the same time, much had changed in a year and a half. By the time the Constitutional Committee convened in June 1948, German division was almost inevitable because of the exclusion of the Soviets from the Six-Power Conference, their rapid departure from the ACC, and the announcement of the Truman Doctrine, the Marshall Plan, and the currency reform in the West German Bizone on 10 June 1948. Setting off on their own course offered many advantages to the Soviets and their German counterparts. For one thing, it allowed the SED and the Soviets to pursue their own version of basic rights without consideration of or fighting with the Western Allies. For another, the SED had already embraced a broad equality clause, having recognized the salience of equal rights as a discursive "Cold War weapon." Individual states in the Western zones, to different degrees, had granted women some level of equal rights in their state constitutions; the People's Council (and the SED) saw an opportunity to implement equality on a national level first.

It was one thing to support equality in principle, but another to work actively to address inequities. Many male People's Council representatives were reluctant to do the latter and waited for their female colleagues to do the heavy lifting for the constitutional convention. In the Constitutional Committee and the People's Council at large, female delegates like Hilde Benjamin, Käthe Kern, and Hildegard Heinze took the reins. Kern argued, as she had in November 1946, in favour of total equality and the overturning of all legal barriers to equality for women.[34] Benjamin, for her part, asserted that the People's Council's current guideline, which stated that "women are equal with men in all areas of constitutional, social, and economic life," was insufficient because it implied that men were always the measuring stick for women.[35] She insisted on adopting the formulation from the earlier SED draft, which stated: "Men and women have equal rights."[36]

Prominent female members of the People's Council recognized that the equality clause in itself was not enough. Women on the council argued that they needed to move from promises to enactment. Heinze observed that the concept of equal rights and its inclusion in the constitution were indisputable.[37] She contended that they could go further and demand and implement equality in all areas.[38] Heinze suggested, in fact, that the wording be changed from "to *be* overturned" to "opposing legal definitions *are* overturned."[39] This seemingly minor change in wording was critical. Immediate removal of the laws would close a temporary legal loophole, for it meant there would be no dispute between existing laws and the basic rights of citizens in the Soviet zone. As a specific example, Heinze cited the problem of the future viability of the Civil Code, which she argued demanded special attention. Similarly, in a separate address to the People's Council, Hilde Benjamin expressed concern that the current discourse had focused too much on women's economic equality and omitted civil equality for men and women.[40] In Benjamin's opinion, in order to move forward, Germany would have to enact equality in all spheres, including civil law. Benjamin's and Heinze's points demonstrated some departures from classical socialist thinking, which argued that the destruction of capitalism would heal other inequalities, such as gendered inequities. They seemed to understand that bourgeois law had traditionally played a special role in limiting women's rights in Germany and that there were multiple paths towards women's equality.

Besides focusing on historical precedent, female activists often used comparisons with the Western zones to present their own reforms in a better light. Kern, for instance, criticized the Weimar Republic and Western state constitutions for guaranteeing equality only "in principle" – an empty promise that perpetuated legal disadvantages for women.[41] As another example, Benjamin asserted that equality "is missing, as we can see in the Western part of Germany, in the area of constitutional equality." Furthermore, she averred that even if the Soviet zone had not yet achieved full equality in all areas, it had still done more than its Western counterparts.[42] Benjamin and Kern both identified the restrictions on female, and especially married, tenured civil servants as an example of flawed Western zone laws.[43] Kern noted that in Bavaria, married female doctors could still be dismissed from their jobs; this would be the case until 1953, when the Bundestag changed the civil service law.[44] Each of these examples demonstrated that the division with the Western zones was driving the inclusion of an equality clause.

Benjamin, Heinze, and Kern's stubborn support paid off. At its next meeting, in October 1948, the People's Council agreed to adopt the new constitution, complete with the equality clause and mandates for implementation. The only outstanding problem was that it was not yet legally binding. The constitution's future depended on the outcome of the Parliamentary Council and the fallout of the struggle between the United States and the Soviet Union. Indeed, between 1946 and 1948, constitutional equality in the Soviet zone was shaped by these growing tensions. Although SED leaders had originally followed the

Weimar template, they abandoned their first draft under pressure from female activists like Kern and from the Soviets; this led to their adoption of a broader equality clause. Having settled on this version, the SED argued that it was a vast improvement over the Weimar formulation: it was more progressive than the ones in the Western occupation zones, and it would facilitate the long-desired reforms of the Civil Code. Since the ruling party first broached the topic of a national constitution in 1946, however, the international stakes of the constitutional debates in the Soviet zone had changed dramatically. By late 1948, the SED was under increasing pressure to outpace the Western zones, where a concurrent discussion of a new constitution – and, by extension, women's equality with men –was occurring. Similar discourses over the constitutional equality of men and women unfolded in the Western Parliamentary Council in late 1948 and early 1949; in the end, however, different impulses shaped its decision to adopt a broader equality clause.

Protecting the Family in the West German Basic Law

By October 1948, the Western occupation zones had begun their own state and national constitutional reforms.[45] Their discussions would have important consequences for the trajectory of women's rights and family law reforms in the Federal Republic of Germany. The formation of the People's Council nearly a year before had forced the Western Allies into a tight spot: they could agree to the Eastern constitution, as the SED, Soviets, and West German KPD hoped in vain, or they could create a separate West German state.[46] The Western Allies chose the latter. They wanted, however, to preserve the possibility of reunification in the future and therefore officially pursued a "provisional" government and "Basic Law" rather than a constitution.[47] Regardless of the wording, the Parliamentary Council had a vital purpose: to define the basic structures and rights of (West) German citizens. As with the People's Council, one of the subjects the Parliamentary Council had to address within this framework was the constitutional equality of men and women.

On 1 September 1948, sixty-five delegates gathered in Bonn to compose the Basic Law of the Federal Republic of Germany. Ambivalence permeated the atmosphere of the opening sessions of the convention. Memories of the failed Weimar Republic, and of the catastrophe that had been the Nazi regime, created both a nation-wide anxiety and a certain sense of apathy about democracy.[48] Moreover, the Western delegates were aware of the developments in the Eastern People's Council. Most Germans had some hope for democracy, because "it offered an experiment, a pragmatic effort that could hardly be worse than the status quo," which remained politically, economically, and socially unstable.[49] It was up to the Parliamentary Council to make this experiment work so as to stabilize the West's precarious position. The delegates had their work cut out for them, especially because of various divisions in their ranks. The council leaned more to the right, with most of the liberal and conservative parties voting the same way as the CDU/CSU; only the Communists voted with the SPD.[50] Divisions on the council were not only political but also gendered. Only four of the sixty-five delegates (6 per cent) were women. The "four mothers of the Basic Law" – Elisabeth Selbert, Frieda Nadig, Helene Wessel, and Helene Weber – would spearhead the effort to include an equality clause in the new Basic Law.

While the "four mothers" later became the drivers of these debates, discussions over the concept of equal rights were kick-started by the Ausschuss für Grundsatzfragen und Grundrechte (Committee on Basic Matters and Rights; AGG). In late September 1948, the AGG enlisted committee member and Social Democrat Ludwig Bergsträsser to draft a Catalogue of Basic Rights as a starting point.[51] Bergsträsser's catalogue was significant because in it, he tried to set a new tone for the basic rights of citizens in the new republic. For instance, he began with a broad statement about equality (Gleichheit): "All people are equal before the law without consideration of sex, race, origin, religion, or political persuasion." The catalogue also guaranteed equal rights in employment and appointment to public offices. Finally, women and youth were to receive the same wages "for equal activity and equal accomplishment." All these stances were new; none had been present in the 1919 Weimar constitution. Equality in employment, wages, and public office had been long-time goals of the Social Democratic movement but had not been declared as such in recent German history, except in the constitutional draft in the Soviet zone across the border. However, Bergsträsser looked back to the Weimar Republic on some points. For example, he recycled some of the language of the Weimar constitution: "Men and women have the same fundamental civic rights and duties."[52] This limited phrasing would become a major point of contention among the council members.

As he set a new tone for the nascent republic, Bergsträsser omitted some parts of earlier discussions. One issue he did not address was family protection. As indicated in chapter 1, Article 119 of the Weimar constitution had included this family protection clause: "Marriage stands as the cornerstone of family life and the preservation and proliferation of the nation stand under special constitutional protection. These stem from the equality of the sexes."[53] The same clause further established that motherhood and the family were under special state protection. On some level, then, it was not surprising that some contemporaries pressed the Parliamentary Council to include a similar clause in the new Basic Law. Prompted by a series of petitions submitted by Catholic leaders, the CDU/CSU initiated a campaign to include a "family protection" clause in the Basic Law.[54]

In these deliberations over the family protection clause, CDU/CSU representatives were keen to leverage two international contexts to their advantage.

The CDU/CSU justified the clause's inclusion by citing the UN's not yet published Universal Declaration of Human Rights (UDHR). The UN was founded in 1945; the UN Human Rights Commission (HRC) followed in 1946. Led by Eleanor Roosevelt, the HRC was a mélange of representatives from around the globe. In January 1947, the new HRC began drafting the UDHR; on 10 December 1948, the UN formally proclaimed it. Article 16 of the UHDR stated: "Men and women of full age, without any limitation due to race, nationality or religion, have the right to marry and to found a family ... The family is the natural and fundamental group unit of society and is entitled to protection by society and the State."[55] Contemporaries acknowledged that the Second World War had contributed greatly to the destruction of families worldwide. In recognition of that crisis, the HRC had incorporated a family protection clause into the UDHR.

While the Americans never intervened the way the Soviets did in the early stages of the debates, the escalating Cold War competition between the United States and the Soviet Union had an impact. The contest between the two sides and their German proxies drove the actors on both sides to lean into the traditional family as a source of stability in a rapidly changing post-war environment. From the American perspective, "divisions in American society along racial, class, and gender lines threatened to weaken the society at home and damage its prestige in the world."[56] This fear drove Americans in the late 1940s to embrace domesticity and nuclear families. Meanwhile, the Soviet Union pursued a surprisingly similar path. In the 1930s, it began reversing course, abandoning a libertarian, individualist version of the family and reinforcing the "traditional" family through strong legal codes and an even stronger state.[57] The year 1944 saw the end of liberal divorce laws and a restigmatization of out-of-wedlock children, among other developments.[58] For slightly different reasons than the Americans – one side was for capitalism, the other for communism – the Soviets found themselves embracing the nuclear family much like their opponents did. These competing ideologies then trickled down to their counterparts on the Parliamentary Council.

Furthermore, the CDU/CSU sometimes combined the two contexts. One representative pointed out that the UDHR should prompt the council to "take leave of its strong contact with the East and its laws," especially regarding marriage and family, because "in Russia the relations are just different."[59] This comment was remarkably off the mark in a few ways. For one thing, the Soviet Union was a charter member of the UN, occupied a permanent seat on the Security Council, and had helped draft the UN Declaration. So "taking leave" of the Soviet Union and its influences was rather difficult. For another, as shown earlier, the everyday gender relations in Russia and the Soviet zone, the discourse, and the policies regarding "gender equality" were not that different at this stage. While the Soviet zone had implemented an equal wages policy, it still upheld the nuclear family as the norm. The SED even had its own "family protection" clause in its constitution, although it was equally committed to an expansive equal rights clause. When the CDU/CSU encouraged its compatriots to "take leave" of the East, it was with the intention of establishing the idea that the two sides were fundamentally different in regard to their policies on marriage and family.

In the end, the CDU/CSU persuaded the SPD to compromise and include a family protection clause. This was not the only source of contention on the Parliamentary Council. Another issue was Bergsträsser's proposal that equal rights for men and women be present when it came to electing women to public office. Some council representatives argued that it was superfluous if the constitution already promised equality, and they voted down the proposal.[60] With the issue of public offices settled, the council now turned to the subject of equal wages, an exceptionally contentious issue because of the Soviet zone's policies. The council's debates over equal wages, which stretched out for a full two months, reflected its members' ambivalence towards the issue. Most of the representatives initially agreed that men and women deserved equal wages if they performed equal work. Their debates often ran in circles as committee members offered different reasons for supporting or opposing equal wages. There was seemingly no resolution to these frequent impasses. Then, in November 1948, the KPD intervened, reigniting the debate by proposing a separate section of the constitution devoted to equal wages and other gender-related labour issues, such as maternity protection.[61] The KPD's suggestion resonated with many members of the council, even CDU members. The fact that some Western state constitutions (specifically those of Bavaria and Hessen) offered equal wages for equal work made some members more amenable to the clause. The Parliamentary Council seemed on track to approve an equal wages provision in the new constitution.

The politics of the looming Cold War inadvertently changed the course of the equal wages debate. One of the "four mothers," Frieda Nadig (SPD), offered her support for the KPD, observing that in the Soviet zone, the SED's draft went even further with its promises of full equality to women, equal wages, and special protection in labour contracts. Nadig here was trying to label the Western KPD's proposal as much more moderate and less threatening than that of its Eastern counterparts. Nadig's argument, however, had the unintended consequence of reminding the council of the SED's actions in the Soviet zone and that any support of the Western KPD might lead the new republic down the same path. Despite the council's initially positive – or at least, not outright negative – reaction to the KPD's proposal, it did not reach quorum. Enough centre-right and liberal members voted against the "equal wages" clause to ensure its omission from the final draft of the Basic Law.[62]

With few options left, in November 1948 the SPD proposed for the first time that the council adopt *this* broader formulation of the equal rights clause: "Men and women have equal rights."[63] By now, the SPD relied primarily on a juridical argument to support its proposal, and this ignited opposition on the council. Nadig (SPD) argued that such wording was necessary to ensure future reform of the Civil Code. As an example, she singled out the property rights of married women as a highly problematic section of civil law. She further noted that it was no longer uncommon for women to earn more than men or to have their own professions. She implied that it was ridiculous for a law to persist that relegated women's property to their husbands when, given the current social crisis, they were often the breadwinners in the family.[64] Helene Weber (CDU) supported the notion of altering the legal prohibitions encapsulated by the Civil Code. However, she expressed reticence towards the idea of completely changing women's roles. She claimed that there were cases where women's work forced them to "withdraw" from the family, a situation that was "good neither for the woman, her husband, or the children."[65] Meanwhile, several liberal and centre-right representatives outright opposed Nadig. One CDU representative argued that the non-discrimination clause should provide sufficient legal protection. Another opposed the SPD's proposal because it would make the Civil Code unconstitutional.[66] From the very start, the council was divided between those who recognized that the law had fallen behind the times and those who wanted to use the old law to craft the republic's future.

After several polarizing debates, the committee tabled the discussion indefinitely. A few factors were at play here. For one thing, CDU/CSU members employed a number of essentialist arguments to undercut the SPD.[67] One major figure in the party, Richard Thoma, asserted that it "is the task of the law ... to treat what is the same equally and what is different unequally, or 'handle it according to its nature.'"[68] Thoma's definition became the baseline for future party discourses. According to another CDU member, there were several situations – namely in employment – that demanded particular and different legal treatment of men and women. He furthermore pointed out the role of ethnic or racial differences in law, observing that groups such as Roma and Sinti and African Americans "had natural nuances that must lead to different regulations."[69] Such argumentation was especially striking given that racist and misogynist Nazi policies had ended only a few years before.

CDU members also tried to flip the discourse about women's rights on its head by employing an essentialist line of argument concerning masculinity and the rights of fathers. Some Christian conservative members claimed that the concept of equal rights would treat men unfairly. For instance, one representative argued that some legal protections regarding motherhood could not extend equally to men.[70] Council representatives in the opposition did not entirely disagree with him. Bergsträsser (SPD) called the idea of "manly motherhood" "absurd," indicating that he, too, was hesitant to embrace complete equality of the sexes.[71] In addition, Helene Weber (CDU) asserted her own position that "no equality exists among men either," pointing out to the council that drawing distinctions between men and women was arbitrary, since all individuals were different.[72] Some council members, then, tried to undermine support for women's equality by highlighting its detriments for men and arguing that no one was created equal. Their arguments were enough to shut the debates down.

Unwilling to let the matter go, the SPD in early December 1948 reintroduced the equality clause before the Steering Committee of the Parliamentary Council. The SPD went before that committee because it stood in a precarious position regarding equality. It had already suffered several defeats since the council had convened, the last one only four days earlier. This meeting was the SPD's last chance to change the minds of fellow council members. The Steering Committee was set to review the Catalogue of Basic Rights, which included an equality paragraph that stated:

1 All people are equal before the law. The law must treat what is equal as equal, it can treat what is different according to its nature. No one's basic rights may be violated.
2 Men and women have the same civic rights and duties.
3 No one may be discriminated against nor advantaged because of his sex, ancestry, race, language, homeland and origin, beliefs, religious, or political views.[73]

For a second time, the SPD recommended changing the second paragraph to read: "Men and women have equal rights."[74]

Once again, the SPD failed at this stage to get an equal rights clause added to the new Basic Law. That failure was a bit of a shock, because the party had employed a decided shift in strategy. Party leaders enlisted the help of Elisabeth Selbert, a women's rights activist and jurist. Selbert's path to politics had been anything but straightforward. Born to a "rural middle-class" family, she eventually became politically active in the Weimar Republic, joining the SPD and standing for local election. Meanwhile, she completed a dissertation on divorce rights and began to practise family law. Her work as a lawyer supported her family during the Second World War after the Nazis removed her husband (a longtime SPD leader) from his position for political reasons. After 1945, Selbert came to prominence again within the SPD, though her later attempts to join the Bundestag and the Federal Constitutional Court failed.[75]

At this stage, the SPD's success depended largely on Selbert's ability to convince the Steering Committee. She approached her speech from three different angles. First, she harped on historical precedents, declaring that it was "self-evident that today, one must go further than Weimar and that equality must be given to women in all areas." Second, she argued that women's sacrifices during the Second World War necessitated granting them full equality.

The non-discrimination clause (paragraph 3 of the above quote), she asserted, would do little to guarantee women the equality they deserved. Accordingly, she suggested that the council not only adopt the SPD's formulation but also add a statement guaranteeing its implementation in the Civil Code by 31 March 1953. Finally, she warned the council that if it did not comply, the "leading women in the entire public" would protest.[76]

The council did not comply. With a narrow margin of two "yeas," the committee voted to reject the SPD's proposal and adopt the CDU/CSU's formulation. The main reason for this outcome was the retreat of the FDP and KPD – reluctant allies of the Social Democrats – which undermined Selbert's campaign. Despite their many ideological differences, the FDP and KPD had found some common ground here. Both parties agreed, for instance, that the proposed 1953 deadline would prove ineffective and would only result in a repetition of the stalemates that had developed in Weimar. On other issues, the two parties differed. The FDP, for example, objected to the existing marital property structure but remained reluctant to change other aspects of family and marriage law that were "not equally applicable for both [spouses]."[77] One delegate, a liberal Protestant lawyer named Max Becker, asked the council rhetorically: "Should men and women take both names? Whose name will the child have, the man's, the woman's, or both? Who has legal authority over underage children, the man, woman, or both? Whose opinion comes first, if they don't agree with each other? You see, the practical implementation offers considerable difficulties."[78]

Meanwhile, the KPD called the SPD's formulation "empty" and insisted again, unsuccessfully, on the inclusion of an "equal wages" clause to substantiate women's claims to equality.[79] Heinz Renner, a KPD politician and former minister from North Rhine–Westphalia, argued: "The place that the BGB allots women is in my opinion simply a manifestation of the place that the bourgeois capitalist society gives women."[80] The solution, he asserted, was to ensure that women and men earned equal wages for equal work. By his logic, once women achieved economic independence, they would achieve emancipation elsewhere.

The FDP and KPD's abandonment of the SPD left the party without allies on the Parliamentary Council. The SPD was already facing criticism because of the burgeoning Cold War and the establishment of the SED, which had absorbed the former SPD in the Soviet zone. The precarity of the SPD gave the CDU/CSU a chance to seize upon its politically weak position. One way the CDU/CSU did so was by frequently raising essentialist notions of gender roles. Christian Democrats argued that the SPD's framing was unnecessary because the non-discrimination clause was there as a "security measure."[81] The exclusion of a wide-ranging equality clause was indeed a security measure, one designed to protect the notion that (perceived) biological difference determined legal status. The CDU/CSU attempted to demonstrate that the SPD shared these same essentialist sentiments by using the SPD's own words against it. One Christian Democrat quoted an article from the Social Democratic Party organ, *Neuer Vorwärts*, which expressed some apprehension about the "erasure" of sexual difference for working women in the Soviet Union.[82] If the SPD was nervous about erasing sexual difference, CDU/CSU logic went, then their members must not truly believe in equality of the sexes.

The CDU/CSU also tried to make juridical arguments. The SPD had argued earlier that the equality clause would set off a chain reaction and lead to more legal equality; the CDU/CSU now suggested the opposite here. According to one CDU member, it was best to focus on preventing discrimination based on sex, rather than enforcing complete equality. He claimed that the phrase "equal rights [Gleichberechtigung] does not capture what we actually want."[83] The CDU/CSU thus rebuffed Selbert's powerful arguments on the grounds of "legal consequences."[84] According to the CDU/CSU, the notion of women's equality with men was one thing, but "the legal consequences ... cannot be overlooked concerning the different definitions of civil law."[85] The speaking member qualified that they had specific concerns about family law, not necessarily marital property or marriage law. Both parties spoke of legal consequences, but only the CDU/CSU's arguments proved to be effective enough to prevent the SPD from succeeding.

Germans across both occupation zones learned about the SPD's defeat from newspapers and radio broadcasts. In the American-controlled zone, Munich Radio supported the SPD's position and communicated to its listeners that not all hope was lost: equality would come before the plenary again, and listeners could remain optimistic that "the real sense for the role of women in economic and public life will conquer prejudice."[86] The centre-right *Die Zeit* reported on the success of the Catholic and Protestant churches in getting a family protection clause, though it did not mention the SPD's defeat.[87] The SED newspaper *Neues Deutschland* reported that the Bonn "splinter constitution" paled in comparison to its own, which guaranteed full equality to the sexes.[88] As the public uproar demonstrated, many readers and listeners, regardless of political milieu, reacted to the news with discernible unease and with no clear consensus.

Selbert's earlier warnings came true: women in the Western zones began protesting. Within a week of the meeting, the Parliamentary Council began receiving petitions and telegrams from independent women's organizations, trade unions, and individuals objecting to the recent decision. Unlike the rest of the Parliamentary Council's debates, the one over gender equality generated an intense public reaction, and that captured the attention of council representatives.[89] It was more than just the volume (the petitions ultimately amounted to a little more than fifty) and the fervent nature of the responses – it was the very diversity of reactions that had a powerful impact on the council's later decisions. While the respondents were all indignant about the Parliamentary

Council's vote, they did not hold the same positions on the issue of equality. Their petitions laid out a range of opinions that stretched from complete support for the SPD to rejection of any of the parties' proposals.

As agents of change, female petitioners were all over the map. Some went for the bare minimum. The white-collar Female Civil Servants and Salaried Employees organization in Frankfurt urged the council to adopt only the following: "All people are equal before the law, without distinguishing between sex, race, origin, religious, or political persuasion."[90] Others, meanwhile, demanded a much stronger equality statement. The Free Trade Union of Hessen asserted that "as employed women, we know exactly and yes, experience daily, the equality of us women is not yet ensured in a paragraph of the constitution." They declared that they must fight for equality in practice in all areas of the economy and politics.[91]

Some openly and adamantly supported the SPD's formulation. The Industry Trade Union Metal for the British Zone and Bremen, representing 40,000 female metal workers, wrote to Adenauer personally to declare their support for the SPD's proposal for all women.[92] In addition, many of the petitions from individual associations within the German Women's Circle, for example, expressed support for the SPD's wording, even though many members did not support the party in general.[93] Erdmuthe von Falkenberg, a lawyer and leader of the Heidelberg Women's Association, expressed her association's "sharp protest against the denial of full equality in the constitution."[94] Other groups supported the SPD's phrasing, but with stipulations. Rather than merely agreeing, these members of society tried to build on the SPD's wording in hopes of improving and strengthening the language. There was no real consensus among women that the SPD's formulation was the only way to approach and guarantee women's equality, but they could agree that the language had to change.

Some went a step further, offering their own versions of the "equality clause." The independent, non-party South German Women's Circle of Nuremberg, for example, rejected the formulations of both the CDU and the SPD, stating that "men and women have equal constitutional and private rights and duties."[95] They stressed the urgency of constitutional protection as a response to major social changes. At the same time, they were clearly reluctant to embrace the word "equality [Gleichberechtigung]" and its so-called erasure of sexual difference. Their proposed phrase left out the term entirely; instead, it borrowed the words "rights and duties" from Weimar and the CDU/CSU, qualifying them, however, by adding "equal constitutional and private" and "absolute equal status." These independent associations exemplified the plethora of opinions among post-war women's associations. Support of equality did not automatically mean adherence to the SPD. These groups were attempting to find their own solutions to the issue of equal rights.[96]

For others, the key issue was not the principle of equality – nearly all petitioners could agree that women's equality was essential – but rather implementation and the 1953 deadline. Most petitioners feared the long wait between 1948 and a far-off deadline in the early 1950s. Trade union representatives sent letters to the council to protest the 1953 deadline. The women's committees of the trade unions representing Deutsche Dunlop Gummi Compagnie and W.C. Heraeus Platinschmelze, for instance, wrote to demand the implementation of equal rights even before the proposed 1953 deadline.[97] Similarly, several women's organizations argued that the new constitution needed to mandate that laws like the Civil Code were to be removed immediately (and not in 1954, as Selbert had originally suggested). For example, the Wuppertal branch of the German Women's Circle proposed adding the following phrase: "All existing opposing legal definitions are to be voided and immediately replaced."[98] These women wanted equality as soon as possible.

In other circumstances, such a diversity of opinions would have signalled that equality was a divisive issue. In this context, however, it represented a united front. Prior to 1933, socialist and bourgeois women had not seen eye to eye on most issues concerning women's rights or female emancipation. Even after 1945, their positions differed, and their petitions reflected the ideological bents of the various organizations. In some cases, independent groups supported the SPD when they would not have otherwise. Nevertheless, it is significant that the women of these trade unions and workers' councils were joining forces with the independent women's associations and white-collar women to urge the council to change its mind.

The fifty-plus petitions, representing diverse independent associations, trade unions, companies, state-level governments, and individuals, began to sway the council. Some members of the FDP became uncomfortable with the prospect of being on the losing side and started to shift allegiances. The FDP had no female delegates on the council, but Herta Ilk, a doctor of law who had been a member of the FDP party executive in Bavaria since 1948, worked behind the scenes to urge male FDP delegates to switch sides.[99] In early January 1949, she wrote to Thomas Dehler (FDP) with her own formulation of the equality clause, which read: "Men and women have equal rights in all areas of law. Exceptions can only be allowed in civil law, so far as it necessitates the preservation of the family."[100] Ilk was attempting to find a "third way" that would combine the SPD's broad promise of equal rights with the CDU/CSU's concerns about endangering the Civil Code. She argued that families' needs must not systematically come before women's equal rights. The FDP did not introduce the clause, but Ilk was nevertheless influential. Dehler changed his mind and threw his support behind the SPD in the next council vote on the issue.

On 18 January 1949, the council met again to review the basic rights of the Basic Law. This time, things went in the SPD's favour. By the end of the session, the council had unanimously voted in favour of the SPD's formulation ("Men and women have equal rights").[101] The FDP's shifting loyalties were one reason for this outcome. The other was the resounding public response, which the council members had heard. Without fundamentally changing their stance that natural gender differences existed and thus determined different roles and duties, CDU/CSU members began coming around to the idea that the equal rights clause was a reward for women taking on the "double burden" of employment and family life. For instance, Walter Strauß, a leading Hessian CDU representative, stated: "Most German women have now been employed for years, like men, but they have the additional tasks of the household and childrearing."[102] The framing of his argument suggests that he did not challenge the notion that women should be primary caretakers and that men played an ill-defined role as fathers and breadwinners. Rather, he was acknowledging the double burden placed on women.

Other members of the CDU offered similar interpretations. Helene Weber, for example, stressed the different natures of men and women. According to her, the council had to be careful to consider "the uniqueness and dignity of women and not a schematic equal status and rights."[103] Weber cited military service as an example of an area where "the nature of women should accomplish only a little of what we expect from men."[104] For Weber and many women of her generation, natural gender differences determined different duties of the two sexes in the economy, society, and politics. According to her, the military was a special arena in which women were unequal with men (a hypothetical point by this time, since Germany had been demilitarized after the war). Like her colleague Strauß, Weber never questioned the gendered division of labour or voiced any doubt that women alone had to deal with the double burden of work and nurturing, but she at least acknowledged that an expansive equality clause could help them better accomplish their duties in these roles.

Had it not been for Elisabeth Selbert, the debate might have remained mired in these ambivalent discourses. Selbert interjected to criticize Weber and Strauß, stating that the council, and the CDU/CSU especially, had to stop with the "yes, but" statements and commit to an "unconditional yes." She emphasized that the public supported the SPD position, citing several of the above-referenced letters, in particular those from the 40,000 trade union workers, the Women's Circle, the South German Women's Working Group, and the female delegates of all the state parliaments. She took a jab at the Bavarians, noting that they were the only state parliament without any female representatives. She attacked the council for fearing that Western equal rights would closely resemble Soviet zone equality. She even acknowledged her own stance that men and women were not inherently equal. At the same time, she argued that treating "equal rights" as "equalization" of the sexes was unsubstantiated.[105]

Image 2.1. Konrad Adenauer, president of the Parliamentary Council, proclaims
the Basic Law for the Federal Republic of Germany in the Pedagogical Academy of
Bonn (pictured, left–right: Helene Weber; Hermann Schäfer; Konrad Adenauer, Adolf
Schönfelder; Jean Stock) (23 May 1949). This photograph, taken by Georg Munker,
depicts the official proclamation of the new constitution of the Federal Republic. Image
courtesy of Bundesarchiv Berlin-Lichterfelde.

After these attacks, Selbert shifted her attention to the problem of the narrow
definition of equality. For her, the old slogan "equal rights and duties," which
the SPD had supported in the Weimar Republic, had wider implications. She
argued that such framing allowed marriage and marital property laws to continue to privilege men and oppress women in terms of alimony and inheritance,
because it assumed that men and women had different and particular duties in
these arenas. It also permitted the unequal treatment of housewives and working women, who both contributed in important ways to their households. As
a KPD member added, it also prevented equal wages for men, women, and
youth. Helene Wessel of the Center Party supported the SPD as well, stating
that she no longer saw "civic" duties – the formulation used in the Weimar
constitution – as an acceptable compromise for the millions of women who had

struggled throughout the war and its aftermath. Their arguments, coupled with the pressure of public opinion, were effective.

On 8 May 1949, the Parliamentary Council approved the final version of the Basic Law, which included the following provisions as part of Article 3:

1 All people are equal before the law.
2 Men and women have equal rights. The state supports the effective implementation of the equality of men and women and will act to remove disadvantages.
3 No one may be advantaged or disadvantaged due to gender, national origin, race, language, heritage, beliefs, and religious or political opinions. No one may discriminate based on disability.

This article, however, was hampered by Article 6, which stated that "marriage and family stand under special protection of the state." Finally, the Basic Law included Article 117, which stipulated that all laws contradicting Article 3, especially those in the German Civil Code that had been in place since 1900, had to be changed by 31 March 1953.

Over the course of five months, the Parliamentary Council's formal definition of "equal rights" had changed dramatically. At the beginning of the council, women had no civil equality before the law in any realm of economics, politics, or the domestic sphere. By the end of the council, women had full civil equality, no guarantee of equal wages, and a promise that the constitution protected marriage and the family. A combination of factors shaped this outcome. First, it became evident in their discourse that Parliamentary Council members wished to divorce themselves from the Weimar and Nazi pasts and, in the context of the rising Cold War conflict, from the Soviet zone. Second, female activists relied on the problematic and outdated Civil Code in their discourse as a reason to give women more constitutional equality. Finally, protests from society, especially women's organizations and the independent trade unions, played a significant role in swaying the Christian conservative coalition within the Parliamentary Council to adopt a broader equality clause.

Competing Interests in the Soviet Zone

As the Western Parliamentary Council concluded its proceedings, the Eastern People's Council was wrapping up its own debates. The SED had published the draft of the constitution in October 1948 but could not formally approve it until the next People's Congress, planned for May 1949. In the meantime, the West prepared to ratify its own Basic Law in May 1949. As late as March 1949, members of the People's Council continued to reach out to the West to settle the larger dispute over the constitution, but they were unsuccessful.[106] It was becoming increasingly clear by this point that the two sides would be unable to reconcile and pass a single, unified constitution.

In particular, the equality clause earned further attention from the People's Council in February 1949. As outlined earlier, in January 1949 the Parliamentary Council in the West had decided to adopt the SPD's proposal to change the Basic Law's equality clause to say: "Men and women have equal rights." The news soon reached the People's Council, which had been keeping close tabs on developments in the West and had constantly disparaged the Western Parliamentary Council's decisions. As shown earlier, the Soviet zone media had depicted the West as the losers in the debate over equal rights since 1946, even before the formal division of Germany.[107] The Western zones not only had beaten the Soviet zone to a new constitution but also had stolen one of the main arguments of the People's Council and the SED: that sexual equality was a hallmark of socialism, not capitalism or liberal democracy, which only served to oppress women.

Despite its public proclamations that the West had fallen behind in terms of women's rights, behind the scenes the People's Council was less confident. Internal protocols reveal the delegates' anxiety about and unwillingness to negotiate on the topic of equal rights with the West. By early February 1949, the People's Council possessed copies of the West German Basic Law.[108] Members of the constitutional committee responded with different degrees of consternation over the text because they had staked their legitimacy on their ability to pass a new constitution first. Some stressed that the very existence of the Basic Law was the major problem, because it undermined their claims to represent all of Germany. Committee chairman Otto Grotewohl assured the People's Council that their version was better, stressing the importance of socialism for Germany's future and asserting that socialism would win in the end.[109]

One of the most problematic areas, the delegates determined, was the Bonn constitution's treatment of equal rights. Their delegates clearly resented losing a battle they had set themselves up to win since late 1946. The committee designated three female members to work with the legal committee to determine how to implement the equal rights clause to ensure that "equality exists not only in constitutional text, but to stipulate concrete consequences" in additional documentation.[110] As the People's Council interpreted the situation, the Western sectors had swept the rug out from under them by using the same wording. They believed they had little choice but to look ahead to the next step: reforming the Civil Code as quickly as possible.

In the Soviet zone, in late 1948 and early 1949, even before the People's Council approved a new constitution, the People's Council and the German Justice Administration began discussing reforms of the Civil Code as part of these plans. In January 1949, the People's Council Legal Committee produced a series of proposals for future legislation, called the "Theses on the General Rules of Marriage."[111] Some old regulations remained, such as the guarantee of

Image 2.2. Are You in Agreement? Men and Women Have Equal Rights (1949). This placard, created by the administrative office of the People's Council, presents Article 7 of the draft of the constitution produced by the People's Council. Image courtesy of Bundesarchiv Berlin-Lichterfelde.

spousal obligation, but theoretically these would take on a new character under communism. For example, they would allow spouses the right to work and live separately; these were seen as necessities in a planned, production-driven economy.[112] At the same time, the "Theses" made several significant changes that undermined the masculine privilege embedded in the preceding legislation. For example, both spouses would have the right to determine important matters, a stark change from the old BGB's *Stichentscheid*, which allowed only men to make decisions.[113]

To be sure, the "Theses" only addressed parts of the family law and did not cover divorce or marital property. Still, the proposals hinted at the People's Council's – and, by extension, the SED's – desire to make family law more egalitarian. Two key personalities were responsible for the document: Hilde Benjamin and Hans Nathan. Benjamin had already made a name for herself as Director of the German Justice Administration and a founding member of the DFD; Hans Nathan had a less prominent public profile. Born in 1900, Nathan had served briefly in the military in 1918, earned a law degree, and worked as a public defender for the Communist-affiliated Rote Hilfe before joining the Weimar-era left-liberal German Democratic Party. In 1933, he fled to Prague, where he joined the Communist Party in 1938.[114] In October 1938, after the occupation of Czechoslovakia by Nazi Germany, he went into exile in England because of his Jewish ancestry and political activities. He returned to Berlin in 1946 and took up a position in the German Justice Administration and, later, at Humboldt University. He gained a more prominent public profile in the Soviet zone by serving on the People's Council Legal Committee alongside Benjamin and other well-known jurists. Benjamin and Nathan's ardent Communist convictions, memories of Weimar and the Third Reich, and work in the Soviet zone informed their approaches to the "Theses."

Benjamin and Nathan cited numerous reasons for their decisions regarding the "Theses." The imminent division of Germany influenced the thinking of both. At this stage, "the issue of separation from the West was of overriding concern to SED leaders," as evident in their discussions of family law.[115] On several occasions, Benjamin and Nathan referred to the possible effects of East and West German separation and the potential for reunification. At one point, responding to the commencement of the Western Parliamentary Council and recognizing how it might affect the legality of their own initiatives, Benjamin stated, "There must be ways to come quickly to a unified and more progressive structuring of this law."[116] At another point, Nathan asserted that it was important for the future GDR "that our new family law obtains legitimacy in all of Germany."[117] He called for the FRG to join these discussions, although West Germany never did.[118] The FRG's ambivalence at this time would set the tone for German debates going forward.

The earlier activities of women's committees and the German Justice Administration also left their imprint on the "Theses." As shown earlier, women's committees and the DFD had already generated proposals for the new Civil Code, to which Benjamin and Nathan attributed their ideas for the reforms.[119] These references illuminate the relationship between the DFD and the People's Council. As the women's mass organization in the Soviet zone and the GDR, the DFD's purpose was to represent women's interests. To some degree, the council's appropriation of the DFD's work can be read in a positive light: it valued women's contributions. At the same time, the council's heavy reliance on women's committees gave its members an easy out: they did not have to work out their own solutions, since the DFD did it for them. Either way, the ideas of the women's committees – likely mediated through Benjamin – were evident in the "Theses."

More distant, but no less significant, was the role of historic precedent, especially that of the Weimar Republic. Nathan emphasized that the People's Council had been inspired by the Weimar constitution's treatment of equal rights for women and equal legal status for out-of-wedlock births. As shown above, at an early stage, the People's Council had rejected Weimar, viewing it as an example of what *not* to do regarding women's rights. By now, the People's Council had largely moved beyond Weimar as an example. While Weimar would appear in media discourse from time to time, it increasingly lost significance as the Cold War struggle intensified and West Germany became the GDR's primary target. Similarly, Nathan refrained from mentioning the Third Reich, although it was almost certainly a second historical influence. There were reasons for this omission. The SED grounded its claims to be a legitimate communist state in antifascist struggle and refused to identify its new state as the successor to the Third Reich.[120]

The Eastern People's Council intentionally shaped its own future political moves in response to the Western Parliamentary Council's decision to adopt full equality for men and women as a constitutional right. The SED had always maintained that its socialist model would prevail. One way socialism would improve the future of Germany, they argued, was through its egalitarian treatment of men and women in all areas of society, politics, the economy, and home life, a promise that was validated by the constitution. In its public rhetoric, the ruling party had always set up the West as a foil, especially in terms of leading Christian conservatives' views on women's equal rights. After February 1949, having learned that the West had adopted a broadly worded equality clause, the SED and the People's Council stopped relying on mere rhetoric. Instead, they propelled forward reforms of the Civil Code as a direct response to the West's promise of equality to demonstrate that they led the more progressive German state.

From the beginning, the burgeoning Cold War drove debates about constitutional equality on both sides. Both constitutional conventions started out using the Weimar template for an equal rights clause and eventually abandoned it in response to women's activism. At the same time, the competition with the Western zones pushed the SED and the People's Council to embrace complete equal rights for men and women in the economy, politics, society, and marriage and the family. The same competition compelled Western politicians to reject the same model of equality in favour of the male breadwinner family model. The competing equality clauses became key markers of difference between the two occupation zones in the early Cold War. And this conflict was not solely discursive: it affected the negotiations on both sides, especially in the Soviet zone. When East German People's Council members realized the magnitude of their decision to adopt their own neutrality clause and its consequences for their own conception of equality, they pushed to overhaul the Civil Code in the East immediately.

The two Germanys were not alone. Across Eastern and Western Europe in the late 1940s, constitutional debates were taking place. Nearly all of these included some discussion of equal rights for men and women. In Western Europe, they also included compromises to placate conservative (mostly Catholic) political forces. In France, for instance, the provisional assembly adopted both an equality clause and an article protecting the family.[121] Across Eastern Europe, post-war constitutions also guaranteed women equality with men. In countries like Poland and Hungary, the new constitutions of the "people's republics" guaranteed men and women equal rights but framed the terms almost explicitly in the language of equality as workers.[122] Across Europe, women were key drivers of these changes to the new post-war constitutions.

In the broader context, considering that almost all European states adopted an equality clause of some type, the German debates may not stand out much. The German constitutional debates, however, were unique in many ways. For one thing, the two German constitutions were the only ones to state that "men and women have equal rights" without further qualification. All others, but especially those in the Eastern Bloc, stipulated that equality would be achieved through equal pay and other measures related to labour. For another, the German states were the only ones in competition with each other. No other states in Europe faced the unique situation of division. This competition forced East and West Germans to reconsider their equality clauses. Without it, contemporaries – especially men – would have felt satisfied merely resurrecting the Weimar constitution's wording. It was the nascent Cold War competition that convinced Germans to adopt a wider-ranging clause. The Cold War competition especially affected the decision-making of East Germans, who felt compelled to pass new legislation before the FRG.

Looking forward, the matching equality clauses had two significant outcomes for East and West Germany. First, the new equality clauses signified an important break with the past. The Weimar constitution had had an equality clause with limited wording. The clauses in the new German constitutions had much wider-ranging meanings that went beyond the mere recognition of "essential" differences. Second, the equality clauses mandated legal changes down the line for the two new German states. These stipulations were critical. Without the mandates, German politicians in both states would not have been compelled to alter the old Civil Code. As the next chapter shows, the constitutional mandates kicked off a complicated series of stalemates and near misses that ultimately led to reform in both states.

3 The Failed Reforms of Family Law in East and West Germany, 1949–1953

On 9 March 1950, the West German chancellor, Konrad Adenauer, received a letter from Frau C. of Cologne, North Rhine-Westphalia, who observed, "As of late, no one hears anymore if the law for the equality of women has been adopted or not."[1] On the other side of the Iron Curtain, a few months later, on 14 August 1950, Herr L. of Kretzschau, Saxony-Anhalt, asked the East German Ministry of Justice, "When will the new family law finally arrive?"[2] These letters from Herr L. and Frau C. hinted at similar problems in the two Germanys: new family laws had not yet appeared, despite the promises of their respective administrations. Herr L. and Frau C. were not the only curious citizens. In fact, their letters were part of a surge of correspondence from East and West Germans to their respective governments regarding the forthcoming reforms to the marriage and family law provisions of the Civil Code (Bürgerliches Gesetzbuch, BGB) and the 1946 Allied Control Council (ACC) law. Residents of both states wanted to know when the new laws would appear and how the provisions would affect them. In response, governmental representatives in both Germanys assured citizens that new laws to replace the old BGB and the 1946 marriage law were imminent.

When Herr L. and Frau C. wrote in 1950, politicians, society, and the media in both post-war German states were mired in discussions about new family laws. After all, the constitutions passed by both states in 1949 mandated reforms to the BGB. In the GDR, all legislation opposing equal rights was overturned immediately, meaning that a replacement law for the old Civil Code was necessary as soon as possible. Accordingly, in late 1949, the Ministry of Justice of the GDR (Justizministerium der DDR, MdJ) set to work drafting a new family law. Meanwhile, in the FRG, legislators had until 31 March 1953 to change the Civil Code. In late 1949, the Federal Ministry of Justice (Bundesministerium der Justiz, BdJ) of the FRG began formulating a new law as well. At this stage, both states seemed on track to pass the reforms by their constitutionally mandated deadlines. But despite positive momentum early on, the support of prominent women in the major parties and society, and new laws having been drafted by the end of 1952, neither state passed the legislation as originally planned. The GDR ended up with partial reforms that did not address major sections of the old law such as divorce regulations and property rights; the adjudication of these thus fell to the courts. Similarly, the FRG passed no reforms before its 31 March 1953 deadline, which left family law up to judges.

This chapter examines why family law reforms did not pass in East and West Germany between 1949 and 1953. In the case of the GDR, I argue that the ruling SED succumbed to conservative forces within both the party and society at large. As a result, the party prioritized short-term measures that immediately benefited the GDR while postponing more difficult matters that would have complicated the creation of a socialist state. This decision had important consequences for those East Germans whose lives depended on alimony and other provisions that remained unaddressed. In the FRG, meanwhile, the ruling CDU/CSU set its sights on the long-term restoration of the "traditional" family and chose not to address the short-term changes the FRG was facing. As a result, the CDU/CSU-led government faced resistance from society and within the federal government. This had significant consequences for West Germans' marital and familial partnerships.

These debates were not conducted in a vacuum; rather, they were shaped by the climate of the early Cold War years, when tensions were at their greatest, as were hopes for reunification. In the GDR, the ruling SED lauded itself for "beating" the FRG in the race for women's emancipation. However, anxieties about legal unity continued to mar the party's efforts to pass a more extensive law. In the FRG, political leaders expressed concerns about legal unity but ultimately swept these fears aside in favour of a more patriarchal law. By the end of 1953, no one had the laws they originally wanted. Policy-makers' inability to pass the reforms they desired created momentum later, in the 1950s and 1960s, when it became increasingly apparent to contemporaries that the Cold War division of the Germanys was more permanent than they had first assumed. In the pan-European context, the proposed reforms in each Germany stood out because of the swiftness with which the process began, but also the ways that the complex Cold War relationship intervened to halt the respective reforms.

Creating a New Family Law in the GDR, 1949–1952

Even before the formal approval of the parallel constitutions in 1949, officials in the two occupation zones had begun drawing blueprints for their future (if still hypothetical) states. At this stage, the future of occupied Germany was still officially in limbo, although the writing was on the wall. Over the preceding months, both German states had pursued constitutional reforms. Neither the People's Council nor the Parliamentary Council had officially approved their separate constitutions, but leading officials in both were preparing to found new states with competing agendas and new laws, in accordance with their ideological outlooks, that would govern Germans on both sides of the border. One of these laws would be a new civil law governing marriage and the family. Despite a promising start, spearheaded by female activists within the SED and driven by the Cold War competition with the FRG, the new GDR did not make the radical reforms it initially promised. The ruling party was ultimately too reticent to carry out the agenda it had originally set.

Initially, the SED thought it was in a strong position to carry out a socialist revolution. Former Social Democrat and Minister-President Otto Grotewohl and Communist and President Wilhelm Pieck nominally helmed the East German government, but SED chair Walter Ulbricht was the actual power behind the scenes. Ulbricht had long been on the rise to power. He had been an early convert to communism in 1920, had spent the war years in Moscow, and was one of the first German communists to return to Germany with the Red Army to set up a socialist state. Under Ulbricht, the SED "attached itself to extant currents in postwar Germany, such as antifascism, fear of war, and the desire for national unity"; those currents "provided the GDR with a mantle of legitimacy."[3] East and West Germany viewed each other as illegitimate. In the former, the ruling SED maintained that the FRG's separatism, rejection of East German constitutional proposals, approval of the Basic Law in May 1949, and policy of allowing former Nazis to join the new government were disqualifying. West German leaders, for their part, claimed that without free elections, the East was an imposter state.[4] Over the course of the early 1950s, Ulbricht steered the GDR towards a Stalinist model.[5] Like the Soviets, the SED aimed to be implementing a planned economy, which, according to communist thinking, would erase class and gender inequalities.

After the GDR was firmly established under Ulbricht's leadership, East Germany's SED-led government began to pursue legal reforms. Women's inequality was an important issue for the SED, which considered itself the leading force in "women's emancipation" in post-war Germany. SED leaders often cited their party program and constitutional mandate as evidence of the party's progressiveness.[6] At the same time, that mandate's immediate invalidation of family law posed certain obstacles for the ruling party and other members of the East German government. When Hilde Benjamin took up the post of Vice-President of the Supreme Court of the GDR in December 1949, it fell to Hans Nathan, as head of the Legislation Department of the GDR's new Ministry of Justice, to spearhead the Civil Code reforms. Drawing from the aforementioned "Theses," similar proposals from Benjamin, and the DFD's suggestions, Nathan finished writing the Bill for the Reordering of Family Law in early 1950.[7]

The proposed 1950 law restructured and replaced the old BGB regulations on marital unions, marital property, adoption, and the rights of children born in and out of wedlock.[8] The draft legislation departed from the Civil Code in stating that couples had the right to live separately if it advanced their education or careers.[9] Neither was permitted to abuse that right, and on major decisions, both were expected to come to a mutual agreement.[10] In addition, spouses were now permitted to agree on a family name, be it the man's, the woman's, or a hyphenated name.[11] Either spouse could work in the business of the other.[12] Both had the obligation to support the household income.[13] In cases where the spouses lived separately, each had the right and duty to support themselves unless one was incapable; then he or she could rely on the other for support.[14] Regarding marital property, the law proposed that property inherited before and after marriage remain under the authority of the receiving spouse, albeit subject to adjustment.[15]

Nathan and the ministry promoted some major changes to the BGB, but they also saw practical and political reasons for retaining parts of existing laws. The first paragraph, for example, stated that "spouses are obligated to one another in matrimony" – phrasing lifted straight from the old Civil Code.[16] This clause bound both spouses to remain faithful and to take actions designed to promote marital union. As another example, all provisions regarding engagement would remain because they were "practical" and there was no reason to remove them.[17] Additionally, they argued that the structure of the custody court needed to be simplified to reflect the economic changes since 1900, but they did not call for its complete overhaul.

In addition to transforming the old Civil Code into a law that would work in a socialist state, Nathan and the Ministry of Justice also had to consider the shared history of the divided Germanys and the larger Cold War context. Thus, they used discourse about unity with the FRG to justify their suggestions for family law. For one thing, they saw no urgent reason to change the 1946 Allied Control Council law, for "the legal unity between the GDR and West Germany must remain undisturbed."[18] As noted earlier, however, the 1946 law reified parts of the old BGB, which meant that the old Civil Code was technically still in effect in the GDR after all. Despite the SED's blustery rhetoric, Nathan's decision here indicated that legal unity, in the case of future reconciliation, remained an obstacle for the new GDR.

Throughout early 1950, the SED disseminated information about the new family law through its mass media, particularly the radio and the national newspapers *Neues Deutschland* and *Berliner Zeitung*, which served as venues for the regime to exercise its "opinion monopoly."[19] The print media and radio broadcasts propagated the law to readers and listeners.[20] As authors editorialized, they drew on several common themes, such as comparison with the FRG. Hans Nathan, for instance, penned an article for *Neues Deutschland* in April 1950 that insisted that a new family law was necessary in the GDR because the old one "corresponded to a primitive economic order" and because the FRG had not moved past Weimar – indeed, it *would* not do so.[21] Yet as outlined earlier, the FRG had in fact begun to move past Weimar by rejecting it as a template for constitutional equality. As another example, the *Berliner Zeitung* criticized the "forces in West Germany" that worked to keep women at home, unlike in the GDR, where women worked full-time in much higher numbers.[22] In both articles, the East German editors framed West Germany, especially its capitalist system and outdated notions of rights, as perpetuating gendered inequalities.

The SED's media campaign prompted many individuals, interest group representatives, and members of state-level ministries to write to the Ministry of Justice to inquire about the forthcoming legislation. The degree of engagement displayed by East Germans is interesting, given that they were living in a system in which an independent public sphere did not exist and petitions were only possible through a government-moderated system. Nevertheless, many East Germans felt compelled to articulate their views on the potential law to the SED-led government. Some expressed their ardent support. In January 1950, for instance, a branch of the DFD forwarded a resolution in favour of the law.[23] Other respondents were clearly more ambivalent about what elevating women's equality would mean for men's rights. Herr R. of Brandenburg, for example, indicated in response to a radio broadcast that while he supported women's choice to keep their maiden names, he wanted to see equality elsewhere too, such as with regard to alimony payments, where, he argued, it discriminated against men.[24] Some respondents were strongly against an expansion of women's rights. As one example, Herr J. of Mecklenburg-Vorpommern explained that, as a man who had been married four times, he would find it confusing if each of his children took both parents' names: "A woman who does absolutely not want to submit herself to the will of the husband should remain single and not establish an unhappy family, then she [best] serves all of humanity!"[25] These types of responses gave the SED some insight into the population's varied reactions to the draft legislation. Many more citizens never wrote to the ministry or the media, which suggests they may have feared the ruling party or were indifferent. Nevertheless, the SED used all this feedback to monitor its progress and adjust its promotion of the proposed law.

As it happened, the law never passed.[26] As Cold War competition intensified in early 1949, Nathan's draft fell by the wayside, for it came into conflict with other regime priorities, namely enticing women into full-time work. At the time, the SED and several ministries were pursuing other policies that affected women, especially mothers, in the workplace. The GDR already theoretically promised equal wages for men and women, a policy set down by the Soviets in 1946 and encased in the 1949 constitution as a basic right in the new socialist state. In addition, on 19 April 1950, the Volkskammer passed a new labour law that guaranteed every citizen the right to work "according to his capabilities."[27] The same law was intended to promote the empowerment and training of women, though its provisions on this front were rather scant, except to state that age and gender were not supposed to impede equal wages for equal work (and studies of practice show that gender often did interfere).[28] Additionally, one part offered pregnant women time off before and after giving birth. Finally, the law did not regulate health codes for women or youth – they only guaranteed that such definitions would soon follow.

Because the new labour law did not stipulate health codes for women and young people, female functionaries in the GDR set their sights on passing a separate law that covered women and maternity protection in the workplace. A legislative bill had been in the works since late 1949 under the watchful eye of SED functionary and DFD leader Käthe Kern, who led the Mother and Child Department of the Ministry of Labor and Health.[29] Such a law was not an innovation on the part of the SED. Maternity protection laws dated back to the late nineteenth century, a result of the labour movement and Chancellor Otto von Bismarck's social welfare reforms.[30] Over the years, the imperial, Weimar, and Nazi governments made critical changes to the legislation, reducing women's work hours, increasing their wages, and upping maternity leave.[31] In the immediate post-war period, the Allies suspended these benefits for working mothers, having decided that the new German government could determine what regulations it preferred.[32] Now that Germany was divided, GDR politicians chose to reinstate welfare provisions in order to entice their largely female population into the workplace and the socialist planned economy.

Outside the government ministries, the DFD propagated its own version of a law for women's rights at home and in the workplace. On 7 March 1950, at the International Women's Day celebration, the DFD met with Minister-President Otto Grotewohl to offer proposals for the new Women's Law (Frauengesetz). Above all, the DFD wanted to work towards the "strengthened inclusion of women in economic life"; this, they argued, would require increasing the numbers of employed women and offering them the chance to earn higher qualifications in fields such as optics and engineering.[33] Women would also need to receive better benefits and protection in the workplace. They furthermore called for greater civic participation of women. Finally, they stated that family law would have to be reformed. Not long after this meeting, on 18 April 1950, the Politbüro of the SED issued a statement that it would pursue a law meeting the DFD's demands.[34]

Publicly, the SED was very much in favour of the Frauengesetz; after all, the party touted itself as the deliverer of women's emancipation. Behind the scenes, however, the DFD faced an uphill struggle because male SED leaders felt threatened by the outspokenness of female party members. On 8 June 1950, Grotewohl met with several leading DFD members (who were also members of the SED Central Committee), the Minister of Justice, and other prominent SED officials. He reported that the Soviet Control Commission

Image 3.1. Käthe Kern delivers a presentation during the anniversary of the founding of the German Democratic Republic (6 October 1951). This photograph, taken by Illus Schack, portrays Kern delivering a presentation during the celebration of the anniversary of the founding of the German Democratic Republic. Image courtesy of the Bundesarchiv Berlin-Lichterfelde.

refused to allow the law as it was, claiming that it was "a declaration, not concrete provisions."[35] Moreover, he asserted, the SED had to contend with changing notions of socialism and women's equality.[36] This statement was in line with contemporary Soviet thinking, which had initially favoured women's liberation before reversing course in the 1930s to support traditional family structures, hence re-outlawing abortion, making divorce more difficult, and again requiring legal registration of marriage. Then, during and after the Second World War, the Soviet Union introduced a pro-natalist policy to address the vast population losses.[37]

In the end, Grotewohl, the DFD, and SED members decided to rework the law under the auspices of the State Administration Department of the Politbüro of the SED. In the interim, the SED settled on a compromise measure: merging the Mutterschutzgesetz, the Frauengesetz, and parts of the proposed family law, which is how elements of each piece of legislation ended up in the final version of the Law for the Protection of Motherhood and Children and for the Equality of Women. Presenting the legislation this way allowed the SED to take credit for emancipating women in the GDR while also knocking out several pieces affecting women in one fell swoop.

On 21 September 1950, the Ministers' Council – the executive branch of the GDR – sent to the Volkskammer the Law for the Protection of Motherhood and Children and for the Equality of Women (Mutterschutzgesetz), a catch-all law designed to ameliorate "the triple burden" of work, housework, and political activity.[38] The law was progressive in certain ways. It provided state aid to working mothers, gave women more rights in their partnerships and families, and opened doors to them in politics and the workplace. Most significantly for this book, it also reformed parts of the old BGB. The new law explicitly overturned the man's right to decide and mandated couples to make decisions together. Furthermore, marital status could no longer prevent women from pursuing employment. Both parents would be expected to care for the children. Finally, illegitimate children would no longer be considered stigmatized or have a different legal status. At the same time, the new law was not especially progressive. It did not change marital property regulations, divorce, or any number of other provisions that restricted women's equality. It also recriminalized abortion.

A few intersecting reasons grounded the law's passage at this moment and in this form. Most immediately, the central point of the law was to provide social aid to working mothers in order to incentivize and support their work under the Five-Year Plan. Because of the disproportionately high losses of male labour as a result of the war, the GDR had to find ways to draw in women. On a deeper level, however, the party's reticence to adopt more progressive reforms at this stage hinted at its internal ideological conflicts and growing pains as it began to establish a socialist state in place of an old, bourgeois state. Party leaders still functioned with a specific heteronormative model of families, partnerships, and marital property in mind. It was easy for the SED to reform provisions that did not require accountability – for example, by telling men to help with childrearing. By contrast, divorce (or, more realistically, alimony) and reconfiguring marital property schemes required material sacrifices from men. The only real revision they were willing to accept was adding female earners to the equation, which would not fundamentally alter family structures or require men to give up all that much. The legislation promised that the Ministry of Justice would produce a corresponding and expansive law by the end of the year.[39]

When the bill went before the Volkskammer, members of the National Front – the coalition of Communist and non-Communist parties and mass organizations – voiced their support in myriad ways. They praised the Soviet Union as a model of pro-natalist population policy, disparaged the Nazi model of the previous decade, and emphasized that the patriarchal West German model across the border dangerously limited women's emancipation.[40] At the end of the meeting, the Volkskammer voted unanimously to adopt the law. At first glance, this result seems to have been a logical consequence of the communist dictatorship.[41] The SED-controlled Ministry of Justice and the Volkskammer had been able to create and pass legislation with the unanimous support of around 466 representatives. Digging deeper, it becomes evident that female activists in the DFD and various ministries were instrumental in bringing the legislation to the government's attention in the first place. Without their prodding, the Mutterschutzgesetz would not have emerged when it did.

The SED recognized that media propagation was crucial to the success of the 1950 legislation. After the Volkskammer passed the Mutterschutzgesetz in September 1950, all of the major papers printed the law for all East Germans to read, declaring that "women [were] finally equal" in the GDR.[42] Evincing this claim, *Neues Deutschland* later ran an article explaining how working women at the synthetic fibre factory in Premnitz benefited from the law's mandated "social facilities" – in this case, a laundry, a kindergarten, and a children's clinic, among other things.[43] In addition, *Berliner Zeitung* (BZ) emphasized the law's efforts to expand the role of women in social and cultural life and balance out the surplus of women to men.[44] Furthermore, BZ used women's voices to argue that the law would have a sure-fire impact on West Germany. One BZ article quoted a female trade union representative as saying that the Mutterschutzgesetz would show West German women "how to fight for such profits."[45] These examples exhibited a clear strategy by the paper's editors to show that the GDR was more progressive than the FRG and West Berlin, whose citizens would learn from their model.

The BZ editors also tapped the voices of men to push male readers to adopt more progressive positions on women's rights in marriage and the family. On 7 October 1950, for instance, the paper ran an article quoting East German men who openly supported the law and West Berlin men who opposed it. One man described how his wife went to a DFD meeting and came back "crazed" about the Mutterschutzgesetz in the GDR.[46] With excerpts like these, the East German media contrasted "more civilized" East German men with less sympathetic West German men. Additionally, editors showcased the reactions of married men to the new legislation. Another article relayed the story of a "Herr Wegner," who attempted to exercise his right to a final decision on his teenage son's education. The paper reported that his wife stepped in with a copy of the morning edition and pointed out to him that his legal rights had changed and that he subsequently altered his perspective.[47] A BZ cartoon from the same date depicted a man taken out on a stretcher by medical orderlies. The caption explains that he had opposed his wife's right to work, and now she was his superior at work, which had shocked him.[48] These articles collectively worked to convince East German men that they wanted to support their wives' equal status, although many of them ultimately clung to their old notions of gender roles.

The media presented the law as a victory for women's economic and civil rights. Hoping that this argument would entice female voters in the upcoming elections in October 1950, the SED leadership pressed for the law's quick passage. Elections in the GDR generally served "as a means of mass mobilization, presenting candidates and issues to the public, and advertising policies which had already been decided upon elsewhere."[49] This observation also applied to the new family law and the *Mutterschutz*. The ruling party had already decided on the parameters of the law and was using its incentives for working women and mothers to attract their votes in the upcoming elections.

According to the Mutterschutzgesetz, the Ministry of Justice was slated to pass broader family law reforms by the end of 1950, but it did not. One key factor was that the 1950 Mutterschutzgesetz had already removed some of the most controversial regulations of the former family law, such as the husband's right to make decisions for his wife and to restrict her right to work.[50] A second factor was that at the time, the legislation did not really have a champion within the ministry. Benjamin had largely stepped out of the picture because of her role on the Supreme Court. She oversaw a series of show trials between 1950 and 1952.[51] Under her watch, roughly 78,000 people were convicted of crimes in 1950 alone.[52] Hans Nathan, meanwhile, was dividing his time between the ministry and Humboldt University. Finally, building socialism – a process that included abolishing states within the GDR, enforcing a version of *Gleichschaltung* of the educational and judicial systems and religious groups, and cracking down on political dissent – was beginning to occupy much of the SED's attention.[53] With the most urgent provisions of family law taken care of in the *Mutterschutzgesetz* and the attention of the SED functionaries in the Ministry of Justice diverted elsewhere, family law reforms were delayed.

The ministry set aside the reforms until July 1952, when the SED Party Congress resurrected the matter of the old Civil Code as part of its forthcoming "building socialism" initiative.[54] To create a new socialist family law, the Ministry of Justice convened a Legislative Commission in December 1952.[55] By this point, the stakes had changed so that it was more urgent to alter the law. For one thing, West Germany had begun its own reforms. For another, legal uncertainty stemming from issues unaddressed by the Mutterschutzgesetz was becoming more evident in the GDR. Benjamin asserted to the commission that the work set out before them was no longer just about women, but about the "entire complex of family law, including divorce, custody, and so forth."[56] Letters to the Ministry of Justice and recent court decisions underscored this point. One correspondent explained that he had been separated from his wife for twenty years and divorced for ten yet was still paying her alimony. He wanted to know how long this would continue in the GDR, given that the 1950 legislation did not address divorce.[57] By correcting the entire law, the new socialist state would ameliorate problems plaguing both men and women.

Court decisions also highlighted the ongoing dilemma of having no single, cohesive family law. Without a law, judges had to rely on the "equality principle" to guide their decisions, and that principle was open to interpretation, depending on the issue. Regarding property, for instance, the decision was straightforward: women were entitled to their own.[58] Other issues presented more complex problems. In the case of divorce, because men and women were granted the equal right to work, "the right to alimony was negated."[59] At the same time, courts had to take into account what women contributed to the home in cases where they did not work. After all, in the early 1950s, it was not unusual for women to leave the workforce as men returned from POW camps.[60] It was also not uncommon in the early years of the GDR for remnants of the pre-socialist bourgeois society to exist. As one example, women (especially older women) often remained homemakers as they had been for several decades. Thus, one outcome of the "legal chaos" of this time was that communist judges became so focused on creating parity between men and women in divorce settlements that they overlooked how the removal of alimony would disadvantage women, especially housewives who were unable to adjust to the new, socialist system.

In response to these issues, the Legislative Commission finally tackled these legal provisions. In contrast to the unified and enthusiastic front the SED put on for the public, the internal work was sometimes contentious. More often, though, it was tedious. While some topics attracted little attention – no one disagreed, for example, that incest and bigamy should be outlawed – others proved more controversial and demonstrated the difficulties communists faced in implementing socialism. The family surname was one. The commission had to decide whether to prioritize unifying the family under one name or upholding a woman's individual right and claim to self-identity (especially in professional life). In the end, it was left it to the marrying partners to choose their surname. Property posed another challenge for the SED.[61] If one of the spouses purchased something with money he or she earned *before* marrying, did it become communal marital property? Did entitlement to communal marital property change if a woman stayed home and contributed no income, but offered her domestic labour instead? For a state that resolved to erase bourgeois notions of individual property, marital property law presented a complex dilemma. It was up to the Legislative Commission to figure out how to balance the conflicting priorities of the SED regime with the realities facing East German citizens.[62]

Their efforts eventually resulted in a new legislative draft; however, its approval was pushed aside in favour of other more pressing issues for the regime and the Ministry of Justice, such as reforming the judicial system and clamping down on political opposition.[63] Moreover, in March 1953, the death of Joseph Stalin, the de-Stalinization of East Germany, and then the uprisings of 17 June 1953 shook up the GDR and consumed the SED's attention. Family law fell by the wayside as the SED regrouped and reorganized its ranks in the wake of the dramatic civil unrest.

Throughout the early 1950s, the official discourse on family law in the GDR presented the draft legislation as a symbol of progress. SED officials within the government and those in charge of the East German media presented the law as a victory over Weimar- and Nazi-era restrictions on women's rights. Moreover, they situated their legislation, in many ways, as modelled on the Soviets'. Finally, they depicted the law as the "winner" in the contest with West Germany for women's emancipation. At the same time, SED leaders like Nathan and Benjamin confronted objections from citizens, the misgivings of members of the ruling party, and uncertainty in court rulings. Furthermore, over the course of these debates, the Ministry of Justice shifted its attention elsewhere. As a result, while family law took a few steps forward during this period, it was ultimately hindered by the SED's reticence about pursuing radical reforms. For all its claims about being revolutionary, the SED was unwilling to upend some "traditional" gender roles.

Inciting Controversy over a New Civil Code in West Germany, 1949–1950

The East German Ministry of Justice had made a head start on family law reforms, but the West German government and legislature were not far behind. Like their Eastern counterparts, Western Parliamentary Council members had begun planning for a future Germany without the *other* zone. Indeed, female activists had already raised the issue of a new Civil Code with the Parliamentary Council, and women's newspapers had already begun elucidating the problems of following the outdated law in the post-war world. The fraught implementation process spurred activists' and politicians' commitment to either loosen the law or, conversely, reify its most rigid components. The issues surrounding family law could not gain traction, however, until after the FRG was declared and the first Bundestag elections were held on 14 August 1949. In that election, the CDU/CSU eked out a narrow victory with 31 per cent of the vote to the SPD's 29.2 per cent.[64] As the plurality in the Bundestag, the Christian Democrats then rejected a grand coalition with the SPD in favour of an alliance with the FDP and DP.[65]

That decision would critically shape politics in the FRG for the next two decades, not least because it delivered the federal government into the hands of CDU chairman Konrad Adenauer, a pro-Western Catholic. On 15 September 1949, by a narrow margin, the Bundestag selected Adenauer as chancellor over his opponent, Social Democratic leader Kurt Schumacher. A few days later, in a speech to the Bundestag, Adenauer laid out his agenda for the Federal Republic. To start, he embraced the social market economic system, in contrast to the planned economy Schumacher wanted and that the Soviets already had.[66] Currency reform, the introduction of the US Marshall Plan, and the creation of a social market economy by British zone Minister of Economics Ludwig Erhard in 1948 had provided a vital boost for the faltering economy of the Western zone.[67] As Adenauer's Minister of Economics from 1949 to 1963, Erhard carried out these policies, which contemporaries credited for West Germany's "economic miracle" during those years.[68] Adenauer and Erhard also believed in Western integration (the "transatlantic alliance" with the United States) and opposed reunification with East Germany.[69]

Besides embracing pro-Western and anti-Communist policies, Adenauer planned to transform Germany through social policy. For the CDU/CSU, the guiding principle behind all (or most) social policy within the Federal Republic was re-Christianization, which included the restoration of the family.[70] To that end, Adenauer promoted an idealized vision of the "traditional" male-bread-winner/female-homemaker (and later female part-time worker) family.[71] This image stood directly counter to the social reality of the 3 million or so "surplus women," which Adenauer attributed to the "consequences of war and the displacement of men."[72] Politicians attempted early on to respond to the ongoing "crisis of the family" through legislation aimed at re-creating the "traditional" male-breadwinner family model. In an address to the Bundestag, Adenauer called for the creation of jobs and training opportunities for women as one solution to their "unavoidable spinsterhood."[73] Without men, Adenauer implied, women had no choice but to work, and the CDU/CSU would support them as necessary until the FRG's "surplus of women" righted itself. In the meantime, if a conflict arose between women's rights and family protection, Adenauer and

Image 3.2. Konrad Adenauer delivers a speech during the first session of the newly elected Bundestag on 15 September 1949. This photograph was taken by George Munker. Image courtesy of the Bundesarchiv Berlin-Lichterfelde.

his party would defer to the latter.[74] He promised that the federal government would establish a "women's department" (*Frauenreferat*) to address the problems facing women, who were entering the workforce in larger numbers while simultaneously caring for their families.

Many West Germans seemed less hung up on traditional marital and family structures than Adenauer and the CDU/CSU. The Allensbach public opinion polls offered important insights into how West Germans viewed the status of marriage and the family in relation to the Civil Code reforms.[75] To a certain degree, interviewees longed for social order. For instance, when asked in September 1949 whether they viewed marriage as a necessary institution, 89 per cent of (West) Germans indicated that they did. Even more women than men – 90 per cent versus 87 per cent – responded that they found it necessary.[76] If marriage was a foundational institution for which they longed in an unstable post-war era, then the question was what that would look like.

As much as West Germans longed for marriage, they also desired an easier release from its bonds, and they pushed back against traditional family structures. Under the old Civil Code, divorce rested on the guilt principle and could only be pursued under certain conditions (such as adultery or abuse by one party).[77] The stigma of divorce, especially for the parties deemed guilty, could therefore have long-lasting consequences for men and women. The polls suggested that in post-war Germany, divorce did not carry the same shame it had at the turn of the century. In 1949, when asked whether they approved of divorce, 78 per cent of men and 79 per cent of women responded that they did.[78] In addition to this, unmarried mothers and out-of-wedlock children had long endured legal and social discrimination in Germany. Many West Germans, however, indicated that they either supported (33%) or were ambivalent about (41%) unmarried women having children.[79] Given the rising numbers of unmarried women with children in the immediate post-war years, greater open-mindedness on the part of West Germans was no surprise.

The momentum for reform was present in West Germany. Yet despite its promises to pay attention to women's issues, Adenauer's administration dragged its feet. The parties in opposition, the SPD and KPD, seized the opportunity to act. In November 1949, the two parties badgered the Bundestag to implement "equal rights" in all legislation, create a women's department within the federal government, and ensure equal wages for equal work.[80] This last suggestion from the KPD gained no more traction in the Bundestag than it had in the Parliamentary Council. In fact, from this point forward, the CDU/CSU, FDP, and SPD excluded the KPD from internal ministry discussions of Civil Code reforms and other legislation because of strong anticommunist sentiments in the West that limited the political space available for it.[81] The federal government established a "women's department" within the Ministry of the Interior in the fall of 1950; thereafter, the Bundestag did not engage in further discussion of women's rights. The SPD/KPD's proposal from November 1949 to incorporate "equal rights" in all legislation remained in limbo. In debates on 1 and 2 December 1949, representatives from the CDU/CSU made their position clear: "equal rights" meant equal *but different*, and any radical legal changes would interfere with – as Protestant lawyer and CDU member Robert Lehr put it – the "God-willed order of creation."[82]

Despite warnings from Christian conservatives that its proposals might disturb "natural" gender roles, the SPD persisted. Frieda Nadig – selected by her party to speak because of her strident advocacy on the Parliamentary Council – asserted that the Bundestag must restructure all areas of the economy, politics, and society to include equal rights.[83] She assured the Bundestag that the huge undertaking before them was necessary, given that men were still patriarchs of the family and that women still had the property rights of "patronized children."[84] For Nadig and the SPD, equality did not override the importance of marriage and the family, but rather deserved incorporation into these institutions.

Outside the Bundestag and the federal government, the West German media provided myriad perspectives on the forthcoming law. At times, editors were openly critical of the old law. The new liberal/conservative daily, the *Frankfurter Allgemeine Zeitung*, for example, used "rights" in scare quotes as they discussed limits on marital property – an indication that the editors doubted that the BGB's treatment of women should continue.[85] The liberal newspaper *Die Zeit*, meanwhile, ran an article in January 1950 that featured anecdotes intended to demonstrate the complexity of the current legal situation for married couples. For example, there had been cases of men and women remarrying, under the impression that their spouses had died in battle, only to learn later that they were alive. To whom, then, were they legally married?[86] On some occasions, the West German media informed readers about developments in the GDR. In March 1950, for example, the *Frankfurter Allgemeine Zeitung* reported that earlier provisions of family law relating, for example, to surnames and marital property were to be changed in the GDR.[87] These examples demonstrate that at an early stage, West German newspaper editors mediated debates about family law by offering readers a variety of perspectives.

The Bundestag decided to assign the matter of family law to the Federal Ministry of Justice, where a lower-level official named Maria Hagemeyer took on the reforms. Hagemeyer had studied law in Bonn and, after a brief stint in the Berlin Ministry of Justice, had become the first female judge in Germany in 1927.[88] After 1945, she was a district attorney in Bonn before being appointed to the federal ministry.[89] In 1951, she published a memorandum (*Denkschrift*) with proposals for new family law provisions in the BGB and the 1946 Allied Control Council marriage law. Her memo placed family law reforms back on the public radar. Although she emphasized reform above all, she also contended that parts of the old law did not conflict with the Basic Law. She stated, for example, that the age of marriage could remain different for men and women because "women mature earlier than men" and different ages did not present a legal disadvantage.[90] She also supported keeping the clause that "obligated spouses to a marital life community."[91] And she retained the paternal family name because it was important that children have the same name as the parents, but she offered hyphenation for mothers as an option.[92]

Hagemeyer determined, however, that other provisions prioritizing male authority did not align with the principle of equality. She stated that the man's right to decide (*Stichentscheid*), for instance, must be replaced with a clause that guaranteed equal decision-making, but she acknowledged the possibility of indecision and need for third-party intervention.[93] Relatedly, she argued that the clause that forced women to live with their spouses must be overturned.[94] Furthermore, she asserted that the BGB's prescription that women were the household heads contravened the Basic Law. Regarding legal transactions, spouses would have the same obligations to each other, except in "circumstances when the matter should not be handled equally in the name of the other spouse."[95] Only those who abused their rights would have them removed by the Guardians' Court. A spouse who lived apart was obligated to support the other. In some regards, Hagemeyer's proposals were significant departures from the old BGB, in that they enforced egalitarian relations between spouses. In fact, her suggestions were often tightly aligned with Nathan's suggestions in the GDR. In other areas, though, she adhered more closely to the old Civil Code, provided its regulations did not overtly contradict Article 3 of the Basic Law.

To some degree, Hagemeyer's somewhat discordant proposals were a product of the two predominant juridical interpretations of the equality clause. Discussions of how to interpret that clause had arisen over the previous year in legal journals and important meetings of the judicial profession, such as the 1950 Jurists' Congress in the West.[96] The first strain of thought, derived from texts by several liberal and SPD legal experts, maintained that Article 3 of the Basic Law "normalized complete equality of women and that biological sexual difference allows no differential treatment in legal relations."[97] The second view, held by Christian conservative legal experts, was that "an 'equalization' cannot be in the essence of Article 3, but rather the physiological and functional differences of the sexes must be observed."[98] Hagemeyer posited that the cause of these prevailing differences of opinion was that the Basic Law did not define "equal rights." This circumstance had arisen, she asserted, because of the history of the Weimar constitution's equality clause, the discussions in the Parliamentary Council, and the constitutions of individual states within the FRG that had adopted their own equality clauses.[99] The consequence, she implied, was that the concept remained open to interpretation and offered little guidance going forward.

Hagemeyer also turned to contemporary comparative law to point out possible paths for the FRG to take.[100] As a low-profile ministry official and legal expert, Hagemeyer was not bound by the politics of the ruling CDU/CSU or other parties and therefore could appropriate or consider ideas from other legal traditions as she saw fit. At times, for instance, she cited and extolled the laws of other Western states, such as France, Belgium, Spain, and Sweden, as well as "Eastern" states such as the Soviet Union and China.[101] Her examples ranged from among the most conservative in Europe (Spain) to the most liberal (Sweden). In the former, divorce reform would not happen until the 1980s; in the latter, it had been in place since 1915.[102] Clearly, Hagemeyer was trying to situate the West German case in a pan-European context and determine the best solutions for the FRG, given its history and location.

Hagemeyer recognized the special circumstances of the German–German context. First, she explained that individual state constitutions as well as the constitution of the GDR guaranteed that "men and women have equal rights." Second, she noted that in stark contrast to the FRG, "in the Eastern zone, as far as one can see, [there are] no differences of opinion over the meaning and the extent of the concept of equality."[103] She also compared the Soviet Union's 1936 constitution with Article 7 of the GDR's 1949 constitution in order to draw correlations between the two texts. Finally, she observed that the East German constitution's immediate overhaul of all laws opposing equality in the GDR and Article 117's deadline of 31 March 1953 deadline posed potential "legal insecurity," because beyond that date the two states would no longer follow the same laws.[104] Each of these statements engaged the issue of equality and family law in the Eastern Bloc in its own way. On the one hand, Hagemeyer was implying that women's equality did not have to be that contentious – after all, many Germans across all four occupation zones had already settled on it. On the other, she warned readers that the GDR was veering too close to the Soviet model, which could jeopardize German unity. (Incidentally, the idea of Germany's reunification had also arisen in Nathan's assessment of the GDR's new law.) Her points added up to one larger argument: there were potential long- and short-term legal consequences for married men and women and their families on both sides of the German–German border. However, she did not offer any proposals for a solution.

As a memorandum, Hagemeyer's *Denkschrift* was somewhat limited because it was not legally binding. It did, though, serve the important function of stimulating discussion in society, which in turn helped the Ministry of Justice gauge reactions on the ground level. Throughout 1951, the Ministry of Justice sent out copies to the major political parties, their women's committees, and independent women's associations, requesting their opinions on the text.[105] Some, mainly the political parties and groups that already supported reforms to the Civil Code, responded favourably. Various independent women's associations, other professional organizations, some major political parties, and even some regional church leaders agreed with the spirit of the *Denkschrift* but offered their own suggestions for different provisions.[106]

Picking up on Hagemeyer's points about East Germany and the Soviet Union, some individuals harnessed similar language in their letters. Some correspondents used reluctant praise of the Eastern Bloc and the Soviet Union to pressure the ministry to alter certain regulations. Herr M., for example, lauded the Soviet Union's removal of alimony payments to support his own case, with the qualification, though, that he was "*no* [emphasis original] Communist!"[107] Others noticed the problem of legal unity. Another correspondent remarked that "legal development in the other half of Germany has progressed further than in the Federal Republic."[108] This person urged the ministry to move quickly with the reforms in order to keep pace with the GDR. Both writers were pointing to the progress in East Germany and the Soviet Union in order to pressure the West German federal government to pursue expansive reforms.

In their correspondence with the ministry, social organizations had focused primarily on the wording or legality of specific provisions. Individuals, by contrast, homed in on other issues, often based on personal experiences and anecdotal evidence. For example, Herr G. wrote in February 1952 to ask about the right of spouses to inherit the property of the other, indicating that he supported a more extensive version of marital property schemes.[109] Some wanted to see more equality because the old law had forced them into difficult financial and personal positions. Herr M., a rector from Bavaria, wrote to the ministry in March 1952, elucidating his own story. Pronounced the guilty party in his divorce proceedings because his former spouse was unable to support herself, he had been paying her alimony, even though he had remarried and was supporting another woman. Their children were grown. How could it happen, he asked, "that a woman *never never* must rise up for her own support?"[110] From his perspective, the Civil Code was most harmful to men, not women.

Women, especially those who had tried to divorce their spouses, often wrote to the ministry to describe the detrimental effects of the Civil Code on their lives. Frau W. from Frankfurt am Main wrote that her husband of twenty-eight years had been "tormenting her mercilessly" because she refused to hand over half of her property in a divorce.[111] Similarly, a recently divorced woman from Rottorf am Winsen, who had had trouble getting alimony from her ex-husband, pleaded with the ministry to pass a law that would protect the family, not leave it to "a man to allow a family to go into misery and destitution."[112] Yet another, Frau M., expressed that she found it shameful that as a married woman she had no rights to property, her own bank account, or even her name.

Moreover, she found it ridiculous to argue that the circumstances of the BGB were different, when women had always worked in agriculture, industry, and the home. She encouraged the ministry "to listen to *women* [emphasis in original], not churches."[113]

The churches were the thorn in Hagemeyer's side. Catholic and Protestant church leaders, who represented 43 per cent and 51 per cent of the population respectively, exerted significant pressure on her.[114] In February 1952, Catholic bishops warned Adenauer and the federal government that they had "serious concerns" about Hagemeyer's memorandum.[115] Protestant leaders took a slightly softer line but nevertheless had reservations about her proposals. In March 1952, for instance, Otto Dibelius, the chairman of the Council of the Protestant Church in Germany, told Hagemeyer in correspondence that he agreed with her on some points, such as allowing married women to control their own property. Still, he emphasized that his first priority was to ensure that "the new rules of the subjective rights of men and women" did not maintain the "presently endangered institutions of marriage and the family."[116] Protestant leaders like Dibelius supported the retention of measures that helped the family, such as the paternal surname and the *Stichentscheid* in cases of indecision. Their stances continued to shape the ministry's responses going forward.

The West German Ministry of Justice now embarked on the next stage of its reforms. In March 1952, the Federal Minister of Justice, Thomas Dehler, debuted a new legislative draft based on Hagemeyer's memorandum, the responses to it from churches and women's organizations, and opinions from other federal ministries.[117] Dehler's personal experiences and his convictions as a liberal politician in a new, Western-oriented government informed his approach to the new legislation. Dehler, born in 1897, had fought in the First World War before earning a law degree and joining the liberal German Democratic Party in 1920. After 1945, he became a district attorney in Bamberg; later, he represented the American zone in the Parliamentary Council as an FDP member. When Adenauer took office as chancellor, he named Dehler the Minister of Justice.[118]

Dehler was less conservative than Adenauer and approached the new law with a different set of concerns. First, he wanted "to adapt the current law to the principle of equal rights of the sexes" – a goal, incidentally, that superficially resembled that of the GDR's family law. However, the very concept of equality was more contested in the FRG. Furthermore, he stated that the ministry's second goal was to "restore legal unity in the area of family law."[119] The East Germans emphasized all-German unification; by contrast, West German politicians focused not on legal unity with East Germany, but rather on the "entire federal territory," meaning all of the Western zones.[120] This approach allowed them to avoid legitimizing the GDR and at the same time to promote German unification in the early years of the Federal Republic.

Dehler contended that his proposed law promoted equality and unity; in fact, it amounted to an ambivalent compromise. In some regards, his legislative draft did not fundamentally change the old Civil Code. For instance, he retained the BGB's guarantee of equal obligation to the matrimonial community. His draft also kept the paternal family name but allowed women to hyphenate with their maiden names.[121] Dehler maintained that while women must have the right to work, they must also uphold their domestic duties.[122] At the same time, his version changed many parts of the old law. He decided that the *Schlüsselgewalt*, formerly the right of women only, had to extend to both spouses.[123] In addition, his version allowed both parents (not just the father) to determine when a child was of age.[124] The age of marriage – to which mothers *and* fathers had to consent – would be eighteen for both men and women.[125] In addition, out-of-wedlock children no longer had to live with their fathers (assuming the child's paternity was acknowledged) and would be able to share either parent's domicile.[126] Dehler determined that spouses no longer had to live together, a provision that had previously disadvantaged women.[127] Under the new regulations, men and women would both be responsible for support of the household and family.[128] He furthermore overhauled the old marital property system, proposing that spouses have control over their own property, manage shared property together, and benefit from an "equalization of gains" clause.[129] Regarding parental rights, Dehler stated that the old BGB's regulations were decidedly against equality and therefore parents had to share authority over the children, including the right to make decisions.[130] Finally, he removed the *Stichentscheid* unequivocally.

The elimination of the *Stichentscheid* plunged Dehler into dangerous waters with Protestant and Catholic church leaders and the Christian conservative Adenauer administration, even though he had the support of women's organizations and female party representatives. Among all the provisions, religious leaders were most hung up on the *Stichentscheid*. At a meeting in April and May 1952, pastors, bishops, and other Catholic and Protestant public figures made it clear to Dehler that they did not believe individual rights should be allowed to endanger the familial community.[131] The Catholic faction took an especially hard line on this issue, supporting the retention of the *Stichentscheid* in spousal *and* parental relations. Protestants took a softer line on this front: they supported the removal of the *Stichentscheid* in marriage, but not parental authority. To please his opponents, Dehler chose the middle road, siding with the Protestant leaders.

Compromise, as Dehler soon discovered, was not the correct solution in the eyes of the Adenauer administration. He confronted discord when he met with the federal cabinet on 27 June 1952. Most of the cabinet agreed that men and women were mutually obligated to contribute to the marital community, but they also favoured the retention of measures that reinforced male authority, such as the *Stichentscheid*, which Dehler had removed from his bill.[132] Echoing the position of the churches, Adenauer and his supporters argued that Articles 3 and 6 of the Basic Law could not be interpreted in isolation of each other. Dehler and Adenauer agreed that a man could have the final decision in cases regarding the children, but they stood at odds over the place of the *Stichentscheid* in marriage. Dehler defended himself by noting that his draft had garnered approval from most Catholic and Protestant leaders, but it was not enough to convince the other Christian conservative cabinet members.

Dehler tried to push back against the federal cabinet, and he reinstated the controversial *Stichentscheid* provision only after being pressured by the chancellor and other ministers.[133] His opponents argued that Article 3's guarantee of equality did not apply to measures such as the *Stichentscheid*. He also agreed to change other regulations, now allowing, for example, that a women could work only if it was "reconcilable with her duties in marriage and the family."[134] Furthermore, under this version of the law, a woman would contribute to the household via domestic labour and would only seek employment outside the home if her husband's income was insufficient. To drive these points home even more, Adenauer wrote to Dehler on 2 September 1952 to remind him that prohibiting women from following decisions that went against their well-being would only endanger the marriage and that he therefore opposed the goals of the federal cabinet.[135]

The federal government's prescriptions for what was best for the family ultimately divided society. On one side were Christian conservatives, who largely supported the Adenauer administration, albeit to different degrees. Catholic leaders fell completely into line with the federal cabinet, supporting a family model in which men still made major decisions for their wives and families, controlled all marital property, used the patriarchal family name, and relied on female caretakers in the home. One Catholic publication justified its position by arguing that "wives and mothers are the center of the home, which is an inviolable foundation of Judeo-Christian family order."[136] Protestants took a more moderate position but nevertheless stressed their commitment to "God's order."[137] They continued to support a family model in which women took their husbands' surnames and men could still make all decisions for the children; however, they rejected male authority in marital decision-making and male control over marital property.

The conservative press toed the CDU/CSU line. The *Münchner Merkur* call equality "satire" and compared the Civil Code reforms to the aftermath of the French Revolution, stating that then, the "sacramental character" of marriage was "robbed" and "degraded to a bourgeois legal contract."[138] The conservative *Frankfurter Neue Presse* warned readers that the reforms were the work of "a minority" and that women could not be expected to serve in the military or work in mines or furnaces – veiled references to East Germany and the Soviet Union, which employed women in industrial jobs in much higher numbers than in the West.[139] Finally, others focused on the draft's passage through the government. The CDU organ *Union in Deutschland* alluded vaguely to the controversies over the law, stating simply that Dehler's version "did not find the full agreement of the federal cabinet."[140] All of these articles attempted to undermine Dehler's proposals and support the Adenauer administration's alterations to the law.

These Christian conservative positions differed from those of the Bundesrat, independent women's associations, trade unions, and professional organizations. The Bundesrat, the representation of the *Länder* at the national level, opposed the federal government on issues such as the *Stichentscheid* in marriage.[141] In addition, groups such as the Deutscher Frauenring, the Deutscher Gewerkschaftsbund, and the Deutscher Anwaltverein petitioned the federal government, laying out their visions of future German families. What they imagined, in contrast to the old BGB and the Adenauer administration's proposals, were marriages in which women had mutual say in important decisions, could retain some individual identity by hyphenating their surnames, were no longer the legally designated caretakers, had the right to work outside the home without the husband's permission, and could control their own property.[142] This reimagined family model, while elevating the status of married women, necessarily took certain key rights away from married men, which is why it was so unpopular in some circles.

Left-leaning and liberal media pundits in West German society were vocal in their opposition. For instance, *Die Neue Zeitung*, which was run by the Western Allies, bluntly reported that the removal of "the dictatorial capabilities of the husband" had caused strife in the federal cabinet.[143] A popular national newspaper, the liberal/conservative *Frankfurter Allgemeine Zeitung*, emphasized that the Bundestag was reticent about granting primacy to men in matters of decision-making, a matter they labelled "undoubtedly legally unclear."[144] The *Frankfurter Allgemeine Zeitung*'s main competitor, the left-liberal *Frankfurter Rundschau*, meanwhile, praised the "wisdom" of the Bundesrat but noted the uncertainty that its proposals would remain.[145] Each of these newspapers alluded to the problematic nature of the federal cabinet's draft and the infighting among government officials as a way of expressing their disdain for the Adenauer administration's draft legislation, or at least their reticence about it.

By October 1952, after the onslaught of correspondence and the media coverage, Adenauer and his cabinet were well aware that they had little support from the Bundesrat, non-party women's organizations, party-affiliated women's committees, trade unions, other independent professional associations, and interested individuals. Even women in their own party could not agree on the fate of controversial regulations such as the *Stichentscheid*. Catholic women, for instance, butted heads over the provision's removal, while Protestant women expressed their dissent to bishops like Dibelius.[146] Still, the Adenauer administration disregarded all of its opposition and honoured only the opinions of the male Catholic and Protestant church leaders.

On 23 October 1952, the federal government sent to the Bundestag the final version of its Law about the Equal Rights of Men and Women in the Area of Civil Law and Restoring Legal Unity in the Area of Family Law. This draft offered several minor changes from the original BGB but still reified the male-breadwinner/female-homemaker family model. Regarding the *Stichentscheid*, for example, the federal government proposed to give the man the right to decide in cases where an agreement could not be reached, and decisions made without consultation with the wife or that opposed her interests were not considered valid. Regarding surnames, women would still be required to take their husbands' names, but they could hyphenate with their maiden names. Women could work if it was "reconcilable with their duties in marriage and family."[147] Both spouses were considered responsible for supporting the family, though the court could intervene in cases of abuse of that right. Women could fulfil their obligations through domestic work and were only required to work if their husbands' salaries alone could not support the family. In cases of separation, if one spouse was unable to support him- or her-self, the spouse could demand a monthly support payment from the other.[148]

A month later, on 27 November 1952, the Bundestag met to discuss and vote on the law. By now, parliamentarians were aware of the societal opposition to the law. They also realized that the 31 March 1953 deadline was fast approaching. Dehler pushed the Bundestag towards compromise. While calling for cooperation, he expressed his reluctance to keep certain provisions such as the *Stichentscheid*, or the husband's right to decide. He acknowledged that with children, there were several issues – names, confession, education, and medical emergencies – that necessitated decisions that were beyond the scope of a court ruling. In these matters, he agreed that a man's right to decide should be upheld, though with careful consideration of the mother's side, and she would be given the right to appeal to the courts. In matters affecting only the spouses, however – in a public display of dissent against the ruling CDU/CSU government – he called for the dismissal of the *Stichentscheid*. He also advocated giving women equal rights in household support, and he supported the legal separation of their property from their husbands'.[149]

The Bundestag's ensuing debate over family law displayed several coexisting discourses. First, these were conflicts over gender roles and the partial redistribution of rights from men to their wives. Christian conservatives resisted efforts to change the status quo of unequal rights between men and women in marriage and the family.[150] Second, each side justified its interpretations of marriage and the family by referring to social crisis and change. To be sure, their differing interpretations of the post-war social crisis did not denote absolute positions on either side. Even the SPD recognized that many women, if given the choice, would choose motherhood over the alternative of paid work outside the home.[151] For the time being, however, when many women had to bear the double burden of breadwinning and raising the family, the SPD maintained that the law had to change to fit the contemporary situation. Helene Wessel of the Center Party, the Catholic social worker who had supported women's equality as one of the four "Mothers of the Basic Law," supported the SPD's proposals for a more egalitarian marriage and family law.[152] So did select members of the FDP, despite earlier support during the Parliamentary Council for the CDU/CSU.

The discussions also reflected broader queries about state intervention in private life and the relationship of the church to the state.[153] To some degree, these issues far predated the founding of the Federal Republic. Catholics had been fighting the state regulation of marriage and the family since the nineteenth century, and the shattering events of the early twentieth century only exacerbated these tensions. After all, state intervention in marriage and the family had been a pillar of Nazi racial policy. "Racially unfit" individuals such as Jews, Roma/Sinti, and mentally or physically disabled had been barred from marriage, forced to divorce their "Aryan" partners, and sterilized to prevent reproduction. This recent history no doubt informed their understanding of the power of the BGB.

While state intervention was obviously a point of contention among Christian conservatives and their socialist opposition, the November 1952 debate revealed a critical omission: the Third Reich's treatment of marriage and family policies and laws. For all their talk of the Kaiserreich, the Weimar Republic, both world wars, and the changing status of women, the Bundestag rarely mentioned the Nazis overtly. The Third Reich was no doubt an implicit guiding force; the Bundestag's thorough debates over state intervention and the dangers of totalitarianism hinted at anxieties about repeating a difficult past. At the same time, the parliamentarians steered away from explicitly mentioning the Third Reich, which indicated that they were as reticent to associate themselves with the Nazis as they were with the communist dictatorship in East Germany.

While the Bundestag rarely mentioned the Third Reich, its members did discuss the *other* prominent German dictatorship – the one next door. The CDU/CSU held up the GDR as an example of what not to do, while the Communist faction extolled the East German legal system for its treatment of women's rights.[154] But it was the SPD that brought up the elephant in the room: this particular law held the potential to further divide the two states. The thought of permanent, physical partition would have been fresh on contemporaries' minds. The year 1952 had witnessed a flare-up of tensions over the topic of German reunification. The decision to strengthen the border followed a series of conflicts between the two Germanys, the Soviet Union, and the Western Allies. Up to this point, the two states officially advocated reunification. In March 1952, Stalin offered the "Stalin Note," a proposal for German reunification that was eventually rebuffed by Adenauer and other Western leaders. The Western Allies responded by granting more sovereignty for West Germany in May 1952.[155] Shortly thereafter, East Germany began to fortify the border between the two sides.[156]

Undoubtedly, the recent border conflicts shaped the Bundestag's discourse on family law reforms. Frieda Nadig (SPD) argued that adopting this version of the law would create "greater legal insecurity and inequality and would deepen the rift between East and West."[157] The Adenauer administration had already made its anticommunist stance clear, and even the SPD was unwilling to venture as far as the SED had with its Mutterschutzgesetz. Furthermore, by this point, the SPD's Bundestag representatives were willing to employ rhetoric that placed them firmly in the pro-Western camp. Walter Menzel (SPD), for instance, attempted to steer the conversation away from comparisons with the GDR and towards the West. This tactic appealed to the proponents of Western integration in the Bundestag and diverted accusations that the SPD wanted the FRG to resemble the GDR.[158] The issue of legal unity, however, was more potent. New laws on both sides of the Iron Curtain had the potential to leave indelible marks on German legal history, and, more importantly, on Germans themselves, who had to navigate the complex legal situation of the divided state.

With all these considerations in mind, the SPD proffered several changes to the government's draft.[159] In the end, however, the Bundestag did not come to an agreement on the law. The CDU/CSU insisted that the parliament "had gone as far as possible with equal rights already" and should pass the law and move on. They also stated that the CDU/CSU would work with the parliament to revise the law before the 31 March deadline. To the CDU/CSU's outrage, the SPD, the KPD, and some FDP members refused to approve the legislation.[160] The Bundestag elected instead to send the law to a special parliamentary committee, which would revise it before the deadline.

Meanwhile, the West German media saw the writing on the wall. A few weeks before the Bundestag met, the *Deutsche Zeitung* ran an article titled "Family Law between Two Fires," which delineated how the law changed the entire structure of marriage and the family.[161] After the debate, the conservative/liberal *Frankfurter Allgemeine Zeitung* reported that the law had received an "honorable burial" in the first round of Bundestag debates. The same article remarked that the CDU/CSU had "gone too far" while the SPD/FDP had gone "too little."[162] The conservative *General-Anzeiger* reported

that the debate had displayed conflicts not among parties but rather between men and women. The author warned readers that although men and
women were legally equal, they were also "essentially different by nature ...
and must have different duties and rights."[163] The American-backed *Neue
Zeitung* was more neutral, offering a play-by-play of the meeting with little
editorializing.[164]

With the March deadline looming, a parliamentary committee took on the
law; however, its work ended in a political stalemate. The CDU/CSU now proposed extending the deadline another two years, which meant that the Civil
Code would stay in place and the constitutional guarantee of equality would
remain compromised.[165] The SPD, the FDP, and numerous women's organizations protested, successfully defeating the extension. The absence of a new law
before 31 March 1953 presented the risk of *Rechtschaos*, or legal chaos, but it
also meant that West Germans, especially married women and mothers, could
finally claim their constitutional right to equality in court cases concerning
marriage and family law.

The West German media quickly spread the news that the Civil Code had expired. For instance, the women's magazine *Constanze* cynically asked its readers
in April 1953: "Do you look at your husband – if you have one – differently
than before? No? ... Do you find that hardly anything has changed since 31
March 1953 at midnight, when you became equal with your husband and all
other men according to the Basic Law?"[166] For many couples, little had changed
on 1 April 1953. Sociological surveys and public opinion polls indicated that
many citizens barely adhered to the old Civil Code. Over the years, many Germans had found their own solutions, demonstrating the limits of the old law's
enforcement.

Sociological studies – all employing slightly different methodologies and sur-
veying different populations – came to a remarkably similar conclusions: most
families in (West) Germany barely followed the old prescriptions of the Civil
Code.[167] Of course, it depended on the section of the law. One study suggested
that most men did not exercise their right to decide much. This study's author
claimed that "in no class does a husband make important decisions without
consulting his wife."[168] The law also pushed couples to establish a mutually ben-
eficial marital community. One interviewee said that before the war, he had
held views that were more traditional, but now he wanted a more egalitarian
household.[169] Another man, Herr P., remarked that his first marriage – wartime
nuptials that ended in divorce – had convinced him that it was vital to establish
a mutual matrimonial communion.[170] One couple noted that their reason for
pursuing a companionate marriage was ideological: they had long been part of
the SPD.[171]

Another contentious part of the former law was its stipulations about work
for married women (and mothers). Under the Civil Code, a married woman

would not have been able to work without her husband's permission. Various studies, however, indicated that many couples did not adhere to these rules. In the case of the couple T., they reversed roles after the war. She wanted to continue running their business, which she had taken over in his absence, and he enjoyed the tranquillity of household work.[172] Another couple, the Q's, declared that they believed in equality – indeed, so much that they even dabbled in an open marriage, and she pursued her own career.[173] Other examples showed that a fusion of law with family life was possible. The P. family ran a business together. Under the old Civil Code, Frau P. would have been legally obligated to help her husband. Now, instead, they divided the work in their shop equally and made all decisions mutually.[174] Rather than adhering to the patriarchal structures prescribed by the law, West Germans were developing their own rules and norms.

At the same time, the studies highlighted that some Germans willingly followed the social, religious, and legal prescriptions presented to them in the Civil Code. Many families followed patriarchal authority as outlined in the law. Frau A., a religious woman, left important decisions to her husband. She had taken over these responsibilities in his absence during the war, but they reverted to this pattern of behaviour once he returned.[175] Another survey captured the dynamics of the H. family, whose members were seemingly ruled by the authority of Herr H. A hard worker, Herr H. was frugal, strict with his two daughters, and occasionally abusive.[176] Some women preferred this type of family. One woman expressed that she "had no interest in the independence of the wife. For [her], it was more important that the husband support [her] and the children."[177] Another family suggested that despite constitutional prescriptions for equality – added to the 1949 Basic Law of the FRG – they preferred to stick to the "time immemorial Christian household."[178] For these couples and families, the expiration of the 1900 Civil Code at the end of March 1953 meant they had no legal backing for their day-to-day practices.

Patriarchal authority often varied in its levels of implementation; other areas of law did not. The gendered division of labour in the home was one area where both legal prescription and societal practice were evident among many families. Even in the chaotic post-war years, men often worked outside the home while their wives cared for the family full-time. For instance, Frau I. indicated that she "essentially oversees the household alone," with some help from her children.[179] Similarly, Frau K. received some help from her eldest son and mother.[180] Another woman, Frau F., reported that she spent ten to twelve hours a day doing housework and rearing her three children.[181] Even families without children tended to follow this pattern. For instance, one childless couple reported that the wife "oversees their household alone," while the husband convalesced in bed and read.[182]

Women's employment outside the home was another area in which the old law's provisions often were practised. Under the old Civil Code, a woman could only work outside the home if she had her husband's permission. In addition, under former laws such as the civil service law (Beamtengesetz), married women could only work until the age of thirty-five.[183] In the immediate postwar years, this standard remained in place for many married women. Whether couples followed this pattern because of the law or because of deeply ingrained cultural mindsets, it was clear that marital status played an important role in decisions to work outside the home. Frau L., for instance, worked as her father's secretary until she married.[184] Similarly, Frau N. trained and worked as a social worker until her marriage at twenty-nine.[185] Meanwhile, Frau M. did not pursue any higher education and stopped working when she married at the age of twenty-two.[186] In these cases, marital status determined women's continued employment.

At times, marital status appeared to play less of a role in determining women's work outside the home. Thus, Frau O. went back to work as a seamstress during the war, after her husband was drafted. When her sewing machine was destroyed in a bombing raid, she took up work as a night-time cleaning woman at a local officers' club.[187] Frau Q. opted to sell goods on the black market to supplement the family income and, in particular, to support her newfound smoking addiction.[188] Frau R. stopped working when she married but began volunteering with various women's associations. She eventually curtailed her involvement when the voluntary work took her away from her housework.[189] In the latter two cases, however, the distinction between legal paid and below-the-table unpaid labour is significant. Frau Q's black market activities and Frau R's voluntarism would not have been formally recognized as paid labour, meaning they would have flown under the radar of the law. In these cases, marital status did not always serve as an obstacle to employment or activities outside the home, even if the law technically dictated it.

Many Germans reported to anthropologists and sociologists that their daily lives did not follow the old Civil Code perfectly. Other West Germans noted that their lives closely matched the law's prescriptions and that they had chosen to remain in such an arrangement for a variety of social, economic, and cultural reasons. If Germans were more or less doing as they wished, then why did the reforms matter? They mattered because if marital disputes brought the couples before a court of law, judges would be forced to rule in line with the old Civil Code, which was decidedly out of line with the Basic Law. Until the law was overturned on 31 March 1953, married men and women and their families were still under the jurisdiction of the old Civil Code and the ACC law.

The 31 March expiration therefore represented a significant turning point, because after 1 April 1953, interpretations of marriage and family law were

turned over to the courts. After that date, the fate of average Germans ultimately rested on local judges' personal interpretations of equality and the
place of the family. Judges sometimes did adjudicate according to the principle of equality. Thus, one refugee from East Germany was told that he could
not, by West *or* East German law, force his wife to join him by claiming a
right to the *Stichentscheid*.[190] Had he attempted to do so in the FRG before
31 March 1953, he might have succeeded. He would have faced problems
pressing the case in the GDR, however, because the 1950 Mutterschutzgesetz
had removed the *Stichentscheid* unequivocally. In other cases, the courts continued to privilege men and fathers. One Catholic woman tried to baptize her
child in her faith without the permission of the child's Protestant father. The
judges declared that she had no right to claim equality and ruled in favour of
the father.[191] After several months of conflicting court decisions, the Federal
Constitutional Court, the highest in the FRG, ordered the federal government to draft a new law.[192]

It was never a foregone conclusion that the Federal Republic would adopt
a male-breadwinner/female-homemaker family model. In fact, initially,
when Dehler and the Ministry of Justice drafted a new law, they rejected
that model. Dehler, however, buckled under pressure from the Catholic and
Protestant churches and the Christian conservative government and changed
the draft legislation to reflect their views. This enraged party-based and
non-party women's organizations, trade unions, and individuals, who petitioned the federal government to change its mind. The Adenauer administration ignored their pleas and pushed through its version to the Bundestag,
demonstrating the pseudo-authoritarian nature of the Christian conservative
government in the early 1950s. The Adenauer government and its parliamentary arm maintained that listening to women and workers on the left would
destroy the natural order and bring the GDR's law dangerously close to the
SED's Mutterschutzgesetz. During the Bundestag debates, it was clear that
other forces were at play as well – namely memory of Germany's legal treatment of women before 1945 and legal reforms in the GDR. The combination
of social activism within the FRG and the problem of the GDR ultimately
prevented the Bundestag from passing the legislation by its constitutionally
mandated deadline of 31 March 1953.

Between 1949 and 1953, the parallel family law reforms in the GDR and FRG
were driven by two impulses. First, both states were spurred by the Cold War
competition. This was especially the case in the GDR. Throughout early debates, the SED, the Ministry of Justice, and the media disparaged the perceived

lack of progress in the FRG over women's equal rights in the economy and at home. West German politicians made fewer overt references to the GDR but still at times expressed reservations about resembling the other Germany or creating legal confusion between the two Germanys. Second, debates on both sides were driven by female activists. In the GDR, these women used their positions within the party or the DFD to push for reforms. In the FRG, it was women within the major parties and government as well as women outside official political channels who called for new legislation. Despite these driving forces, other obstacles – the SED's own reticence, West German churches – stood in the way of reforms.

The two Germanys were not alone in trying to respond to changing gender roles after the Second World War and shape them going forward. Across Europe, the early 1950s were an important time of gender role transformation. On some fronts, women's rights expanded significantly. Between 1944 and 1952, women in Italy, France, Belgium, and Greece acquired suffrage for the first time.[193] On other fronts, women's rights had not changed dramatically and women had to press for more equality. Only in Britain and Scandinavia had patriarchal marriage and family laws been significantly altered before the Second World War.[194] Everywhere else, family laws remained as paternalistic as they had been a half-century before. Throughout the 1950s, France, Italy, Portugal, and Spain still had patriarchal family laws on the books (albeit to different degrees). Christian conservatives in Western Europe were eager to keep these laws intact, arguing that a return to the traditional family was vital to post-war reconstruction. In the Eastern Bloc, "gender integration" policies to encourage female participation in the workplace and political spaces were more common than in Western Europe.[195] In most of the East, the communist governments overturned patriarchal family and marriage laws in the 1950s but did not provide a viable alternative to address structural inequalities in housework and childrearing.[196]

What stood out about the German cases in the early 1950s? For one thing, unlike the rest of Western Europe, the two Germanys pursued family law reforms immediately. France, for instance, avoided the issue until the 1960s.[197] A driving force here was the demographic imbalance in the two Germanys, which remained sharper than in the rest of Western and Central Europe. The population crisis was especially dire in the GDR, which faced a labour shortage as East Germans fled to the West in the early 1950s. Perhaps as a result, East and West German attitudes towards motherhood, families, and out-of-wedlock children were different from those in the rest of Europe. Both states encouraged the traditional family, but East Germans made more exceptions for non-traditional families and discouraged abortions more than other neighbouring states. In addition, Germans had the Nazi past to cope with. As their debates in the Bundestag and the Volkskammer showed, the legacies of Nazism and its policies on reproduction and parenthood continued to directly inform legal reforms in the two Germanys in ways that were not found in the rest of Europe. Finally, the two Germanys were the most directly steered by the Cold War competition, with the result that both states kept reforms of the Civil Code on their agendas in the early 1950s. Neither state achieved the reforms for which it had hoped in 1950; even so, the discussions laid important groundwork for the most critical stages of debate in the mid- to late 1950s. Those were the years that would make or break family law reforms in East and West Germany.

4 A Series of Stalemates in East and West Germany, 1953–1957

On 15 December 1954, Herr M. of Stuttgart, West Germany (FRG), wrote to the Ministry of Justice of the German Democratic Republic (GDR, East Germany) to ask about the status of the proposed East German Family Code (FGB). He explained that his ex-wife and child lived in the GDR. He had been paying forty German marks a month into a savings account in West Germany for his child. He wanted to know how he could pay the child support to an account in the GDR. The approval of the forthcoming law mattered to him because he needed to know what changes to expect regarding alimony and child support. A ministry official replied that Herr M. could not send the money, because "on principle, Western currency cannot be introduced into the GDR."[1] Moreover, the Family Code did not cover cross-border relationships. Herr M.'s story exemplified the complex and unique legal situation regarding marriage and divorce in the divided Germanys. He could correspond with his ex-wife and child, but he could not make his monthly payments because the two states had largely severed financial and diplomatic ties.

Without new family laws in either state, and given the deteriorating diplomatic relations, it remained unclear what citizens like Herr M. were supposed to do. In West Germany, the ruling Christian Democrats (CDU/CSU) hoped to address this uncertainty with a new, conservative family law that would reinforce the old patriarchal family model comprised of a male breadwinner and a female homemaker. The CDU/CSU also expected to have the broad support it needed to quickly push through family law reforms and related social policies. The CDU/CSU had entered a new legislative period at the end of 1953, riding high off the successful "economic miracle." Coupled with the anticommunist campaign of the Adenauer administration in the mid-1950s, designed to pare down political opposition from the left, and the backing of the major Protestant and Catholic churches, the CDU/CSU anticipated a swift victory. Instead, the ruling party found itself mired in a series of stalemates between 1954 and 1957, when the Bundestag chose to pass a compromise solution: the Equal Rights Act.

Herr M.'s letter arrived in the GDR at a time when several months of intense public debate over the new family law were dying down. Six months earlier, in June 1954, the East German Ministry of Justice, under the leadership of the Socialist Unity Party (SED), had debuted a new Family Code. The new law would replace the old, patriarchal Civil Code with new, egalitarian, socialist regulations on marriage, divorce, marital property, and parental authority. The SED expected widespread praise for its new legislation, but instead it received an overwhelmingly negative response from the populace, especially Protestants and Catholics. Without a word to East Germans, the SED abandoned the legislative changes in November 1954. Instead, the one-party state chose to pass some incremental reforms in 1955. It then repeatedly delayed addressing the issue until 1963.

This chapter examines how and why legislators in the FRG finally passed the 1957 Equal Rights Act while the GDR struggled to push through its own reforms in the mid- to late 1950s. In both states, the ruling regimes expected to pass new legislation by the end of 1954 but faced harsh opposition from society that ultimately delayed passage of the new laws. This resistance resulted in paradoxical outcomes for the two Germanys. I argue that in West Germany, the ruling party was unable to overcome opposition within its own ranks, the Bundestag, and society at large, especially women's organizations, whereas in East Germany, opponents of the communist regime, such as religious leaders, appropriated Cold War rhetoric – with great success – as a means to halt the regime's progress. Opposition in the latter was compounded by petitions from ordinary East Germans, who demanded to know how the law would affect them and who pointed out its potential pitfalls. As a result, neither ruling government got the laws their leaders set out to make: a patriarchal family law in West Germany, and a radically egalitarian socialist law in East Germany.

This chapter also explores how and why the changing "entangled but demarcated" Cold War relationship between the two Germanys shaped family law reforms on both sides. In particular, it argues that the Cold War context adversely affected the GDR's reforms. Divorcing the FRG from the GDR freed West German politicians to pursue their own reforms; meanwhile, the GDR – and, much to the ire of the SED, not a few of its citizens – remained stuck on the issue of German unity. In other words, during the 1950s, East Germans inhabited a political imaginary in which German reunification was imminent. Furthermore, structural links between the two sides complicated reform processes. All these issues and obstacles contributed to the SED's failure to pass the East German Family Code in 1954 as originally planned, while West Germany forged ahead and approved its own 1957 Equal Rights Act.

The passage of the 1957 Equal Rights Act in West Germany had a significant impact on both German states and across Europe broadly. In the GDR, the stinging failure to pass reforms and the knowledge that the FRG had approved its own law kept the matter on the SED's agenda. In the FRG, the law signified an important albeit limited step towards legal equality of men and women. The law removed, for example, men's right to make all decisions for their wives, but it also permitted women to do paid work outside the home *only* if it was reconcilable with their "obligations" to the household and family.[2] These conflicting provisions marked the 1957 Equal Rights Act as a political compromise designed to protect the dominant ideal of the male-breadwinner family that was at the heart of Christian-conservative policies. In a broader pan-European context, the 1957 Equal Rights Act was significant because it was among the first of its kind in post-war Europe.

Contesting the Family in the Federal Republic, 1954–1957

The preceding round of debates between 1949 and early 1953 left the CDU/CSU painfully aware that the SPD, FDP, numerous social organizations, and some newspaper editors opposed its plans for marriage and family law. Then the Civil Code expired on 31 March 1953, plunging West Germany into a state of "legal chaos." Recognizing the instability in the FRG, the Federal Constitutional Court ordered the Bundestag to settle family law once and for all. The reignited discussions between 1954 and 1957, however, did little at first to solve these problems. Bundestag politicians found themselves rehashing the same tired arguments about natural law and order, women's double burden, totalitarianism, and masculine authority and duties that they had presented in 1952. Moreover, the CDU/CSU tried to leverage the Cold War competition with the GDR to its advantage by removing political opponents on the left and playing up the problems facing the dictatorship next door. The Bundestag finally budged and changed the law in 1957. This was for two reasons. First, the new rounds of debates had exposed cracks in the CDU/CSU's veneer that were undercutting the ruling party's patriarchal family law. Second, societal resistance, especially among women's organizations, pushed legislators to compromise.

The CDU/CSU should have been in a strong enough position to push through a conservative version of marriage and family law. After all, the balance of power in the Bundestag had tipped strongly in the CDU/CSU's favour after the September 1953 election, moving the Christian Democrats from 31 per cent to 45.2 per cent of the seats. The "economic miracle" engineered by Ludwig Erhard had begun to pay off for many West Germans. In fact, the FRG's economy was growing by 8.2 per cent annually in the 1950s.[3] Moreover, the

West German public had become more amenable to the "Western integration" policies of Adenauer's administration than they were in 1949.[4] The 17 June 1953 uprisings in East Germany further cemented voters' confidence in Adenauer's decision to abandon German reunification and focus on the transatlantic alliance.[5] Voters' satisfaction with the rapidly strengthening economy and the positive outlook on the Western alliance effectively delivered the 1953 election to the CDU/CSU.

Moreover, the 1953 election saw some of Adenauer's political opposition suffer strong hits as a result of Adenauer's anticommunist campaigns in the early 1950s. The Adenauer government had begun persecuting communist and leftist critics earlier than that. In September 1950, for instance, the CDU/CSU-controlled government adopted the "Adenauer-Decree." This order requested loyalty to the West German Basic Law from all employees in public service and barred them from membership in any organization that was perceived as disloyal to the constitution. Many KPD members lost their positions in public service as a result. Increasingly, all West German parties and their supporters (except for the KPD) officially rejected everything coming from SED-controlled Germany on other side of the Iron Curtain. These consistent efforts resulted in the KPD gaining only 2.2 per cent of the vote in the 1953 Bundestag election – below the minimum 5 per cent it needed for representation in the Bundestag. The Adenauer government's concerted effort to persecute the KPD and its members, supporters, and "sympathizers" had the effect of removing potential allies for the SPD, including those who would have advocated a more egalitarian family law and related policies.

Confident that its electoral win and the removal of political opposition would ensure its success, the CDU/CSU decided to tackle family law reforms from two directions. First, the CDU/CSU leveraged its control of the executive branch and legislature to expand the federal government, a decision that directly shaped family law reforms. In October 1953, for example, Adenauer created the Federal Ministry of Family Matters. In and of itself, creating a new ministry did not have to signal doom for those who wanted a more progressive family law. It quickly became evident, however, that Adenauer intended the ministry to serve as a vessel for elevating political Catholicism when he named the conservative Catholic Franz-Josef Wuermeling as its first minister.[6] Born in 1900 in Berlin, Wuermeling served in the German navy near the end of the First World War before pursuing a law degree. In 1945, he joined the CDU, representing Rhineland Palatinate in the Bundestag.[7]

Wuermeling's selection solidified the growing influence of political Catholicism on the federal government. Two mutually reinforcing impulses comprised the core of political Catholicism.[8] First, its proponents argued that the state had a responsibility to protect religious belief. When it came to family law, most conservative Catholics argued that any changes to the Civil Code would undermine the traditional Christian family and parents' rights to raise their children and therefore violated state religious protections.[9] Second, there was the idea, disseminated by Pope Pius XI in the 1930s, that Catholics must use the state to pursue Catholic social teaching.[10] This idea became popular again among Catholic clergy and lay organizations in the late 1940s and 1950s. Their adoption of this stance was a response to their memories of the Nazi regime's persecution of Catholic clergy who opposed Hitler. It was also a reaction to the increasing secularization of the East German state next door. In other words, Christian conservatives viewed secular communism and the way it employed women outside the home as a threat to the homeostasis of the Christian family, which they identified as the cornerstone of (West) German society.

By choosing Wuermeling, Adenauer could be almost certain that the new ministry would become a front for political Catholicism. Wuermeling's nomination was also meant to undercut the Women's Department, housed in the Ministry of the Interior. Founded in February 1950, that department was supposed to research and advise the federal government on issues relating to women and gender, but it suffered from underfunding and understaffing.[11] News of the new ministry and Wuermeling's appointment shook women's organizations, which argued that a Family Ministry was unnecessary, given that there was already a Women's Department within the Ministry of the Interior.[12] Adenauer persisted. Without adequate funding or staffing, and with little support from Adenauer, the Women's Department found itself subordinated to the new ministry, at least when it came to family law. Tellingly, Wuermeling, in his role as Family Minister and a parliamentarian, was invited to deliver speeches to the Bundestag; Women's Department representatives were not.

Because Adenauer and the CDU/CSU had won one battle by establishing the Family Ministry, they thought they could quickly push through family law reforms on their own terms. As it turned out, they could not, largely due to female activists outside the Bundestag who voiced their opposition. Even so, because of its electoral victory and control of the government, the CDU/CSU recognized that power in numbers was on its side. So in the fall of 1953, the Christian conservative coalition in the Bundestag reintroduced an earlier defeated proposal to extend the constitutional deadline to 31 March 1955. This time, the strength of the CDU/CSU and its smaller allied parties in the Bundestag gave the Christian Democrats the two-thirds majority they needed to approve the extension.[13] Yet even though it had won the vote, the CDU/CSU did not succeed in extending the deadline. Independent women's groups, trade unions, the SPD, the FDP, and their respective constituencies immediately fought the proposal.[14] Then the Federal Constitutional Court in Karlsruhe rejected the postponement and ordered the federal government to address the issue.[15] The

CDU/CSU-led government had little choice but to surrender and reopen the debate over family law in January 1954.

On 12 February 1954, the Bundestag gathered to discuss the three competing legislative drafts submitted by the federal government (in effect, the CDU/CSU), the SPD, and the liberal FDP. The major parties' legislative proposals made it clear that they still envisioned the family quite differently. The CDU/CSU's version privileged male authority at the expense of women's equal rights. It imagined a family structure in which women took their husbands' surnames (though they could hyphenate), a husband made all decisions for his wife and family (on the grounds that marital strife would arise from indecision), and the household was the domain of the wife (who could work only if it was reconcilable with her domestic duties).[16] The FDP's version largely aligned with that of the CDU/CSU, though it was more liberal in certain regards – for example, it favoured overturning the husband's right to decide in marriage (while upholding it for children) as well as designating both spouses as supporters of the household.[17] In contrast to the CDU/CSU and FDP, the SPD supported an egalitarian marital and familial model. Its version would give both spouses the right to come to a mutual agreement on important matters and permit either spouse to take the other's name or hyphenate. It would not designate women head of the household or restrict their right to work outside the home and gain economic independence. It would also identify both spouses as responsible for supporting the household.[18]

Though fundamentally dissimilar in some ways, the CDU/CSU, FDP, and SPD's respective proposals overlapped on several issues. For one thing, all the major parties supported abolishing the right of the husband to control his wife's property, agreeing instead to allow the separation of marital property, although the CDU/CSU qualified that it was "in the interest of the family" not to divide property holdings.[19] Additionally, all parties agreed that men could no longer terminate their wives' legal contracts. Finally, all the major parties agreed to overturn the regulation that forced a woman to share a domicile with her husband.[20] Although the major political parties were divided on some issues, they found common ground on others, namely matters that did not stem from beliefs about sexual difference. Their proposals also made it clear that these discussions were, above all, about married women's rights in marriage and the family and did not pertain to other large groups of women in post-war West Germany, such as unmarried or widowed women and mothers.

The fault lines in the Bundestag had changed little since 1952. CDU/CSU and SPD members still disagreed on basic issues. For instance, the two sides could not find common ground regarding whose rights – the husband's or the wife's – took precedence within a marriage and/or family. The CDU/CSU and some FDP members stood by the husband as the final word in complicated matters but framed their arguments in language about the entire partnership.

For instance, Karl Weber, a CDU representative and Catholic lawyer from Koblenz, stated, "There are things in marriage that cannot remain undecided."[21] In response, Frieda Nadig (SPD) pointed out that a woman could press the case in court but had no way to fight the judge's decision and therefore risked taking on "the role as destroyer" in her marriage.[22] Nadig also observed that it was impractical for a man to be given such a right when it was typically the mother who made these decisions every day, especially in the post-war years.[23] While the CDU/CSU framed its argument in terms of "marriage" as a whole, the party representatives were ultimately making a case for the husband's authority over his wife.

Another issue over which the two sides had not budged was church–state relations. The CDU/CSU relied on the theological and political backing of the Protestant and Catholic churches to undergird its position. Karl Weber and Wuermeling, the Family Minister, for instance, cited earlier letters from Catholic and Protestant leaders that opposed the expansion of women's rights.[24] Furthermore, the CDU/CSU used notions of natural law drawn from Catholic and Protestant theology to defend its support of provisions such as the man's right to decide. The CDU/CSU and some liberals argued that in "healthy, normal marriages, such a regulation is hardly necessary."[25] The CDU/CSU not only emphasized theological arguments about "natural" and God-given gender roles but also tapped the major churches' support in order to threaten its opponents and display its political power in the FRG.

Despite pressure from the CDU/CSU, other members of the Bundestag did not find the ire of the churches or religious doctrine convincing enough reasons to abandon reforms. Thomas Dehler (FDP), a parliamentarian and the former Minister of Justice, told the assembly: "The legislator does not govern the Christian, godly world, he does not disturb it, he only rules the material world through law."[26] Furthermore, Social Democrat Ludwig Metzger, a Protestant lawyer from Darmstadt, reminded the Bundestag that not all Christians – including himself and the Protestant Women's Aid Organization – followed such rhetoric.[27] Elisabeth Schwarzhaupt, a CDU member and prominent leader of a Protestant women's group, supported Metzger by professing her own opposition to her party's proposed legislation.[28]

While some of these discourses and positions had not changed dramatically, other political circumstances and discursive points had shifted enough to make a difference. For one thing, the composition of the Bundestag had changed just enough to tip the scales away from the CDU/CSU on the issue of family law. The 1953 election cycle had brought a new CDU member into the Bundestag: Schwarzhaupt. Born in 1901 to two teachers, she had earned her law degree in 1930 in Frankfurt am Main and joined the liberal German People's Party. An active opponent of the Nazis during the Third Reich, she found employment as a legal aide in the Protestant Church of Germany in Berlin, where she continued to work after the war. After 1945, she joined the CDU and led the re-established Protestant Women's Association until 1953, when she entered the Bundestag.[29] Schwarzhaupt's presence mattered because she was one of the few CDU/CSU members who willingly and openly opposed her own party.

The CDU/CSU also began to politicize issues that it had not emphasized as strongly before, in 1952. A point that was politicized in 1954 that had largely been absent in 1952 was the social situation on the ground. Throughout the late 1940s and early 1950s, sociologists had been publishing studies recording the day-to-day lives of West German families. As the preceding chapter showed, Germans were all over the place in terms of following the law's prescriptions. This did not stop CDU/CSU representatives from politicizing the work of sociologists. Wuermeling, for instance, played up the findings of well-known sociologist Helmut Schelsky's book to justify the CDU/CSU's version of the law. Schelsky was a former NSDAP member who had moved to the University of Hamburg in 1953.[30] He had concluded in his study of expellee families that the family should be the bedrock of future social policy.[31] According to Wuermeling, the "obvious research finding" was that "as before, today, the authority in the family lies with the husband."[32] Yet Wuermeling never referred to similar studies – such as those conducted by Schelsky's assistant, Gerhard Wurzbacher – that found that most Germans were not strongly patriarchal. Clearly, Wuermeling was trying to draw attention to Schelsky's work because its assumptions supported the Christian conservative agenda.

Other CDU/CSU members, however, interpreted Schelsky's and other sociologists' studies differently, exposing some cracks in the CDU/CSU's façade. For instance, Wuermeling's peer, Elisabeth Schwarzhaupt, cited the works of Wurzbacher *and* Schelsky, imploring her colleagues to ask themselves what they could learn from them.[33] Schwarzhaupt's opposition was especially powerful given her position straddling the CDU/CSU and the women's movement. From that location, she put her experience as an activist to use, calling out her peers within her party, such as Wuermeling. At another point in the debate, Schwarzhaupt again professed her opposition to her party's proposed legislation.[34] She now found herself in opposition to her chosen party, telling them that "it is neither confessional difference ... nor is it sexual difference ... nor generational"; rather, it was the Bundestag members' willingness to cooperate that mattered most for women's rights.[35]

Christian conservatives also resurrected concerns that the new law would destroy masculinity. At one point, Wuermeling acknowledged that "an orderly society is not possible without authority."[36] He argued that just as states did not have to have total control over their populations, neither did fathers – but the ability to wield authority was always there.[37] Authority, he asserted, was "care and responsibility for the welfare of the family, and surely more of a duty than a right."[38] He implied that it was, to some degree, a burden *and* a duty, and that without some form of control, society would falter. In short, Wuermeling was attempting to turn the discussion on its head. Instead of focusing on women's rights, he made the debate about masculine duty and privilege, constructing an image of *men* as the overburdened members of post-war West German society. In the post-war years, in the wake of Nazi militarism and the humiliation of defeat, it was important to reconstruct masculinity, and debates over that paralleled discussions about reinterpreting women's roles. In post-war Germany, men had to relearn how to be peaceful providers for their families and re-create themselves as consumers and citizens.[39]

In an effort to sway Bundestag members who were on the fence, the CDU/ CSU also revived the spectre of totalitarianism. In the 1952 debates, Bundestag members had largely shied away from open discussion of the Third Reich and its legacies. In 1954, CDU/CSU members mentioned the Nazis but framed their discourse within a broader comparative discussion of totalitarianism so that they could harp on the Soviet Union and its satellite-states. Wuermeling, for instance, cautioned the Bundestag against the abuse of the individual for the purposes of "state socialism" and "the goals of the omnipotent state."[40] Here, he was referencing the conscription of young women into the Bund Deutscher Mädel and the labour force under the Third Reich, although these policies had little to do with family law.[41] On the surface, Wuermeling's comments appeared to reject the Nazi past. The real purpose of Wuermeling's citation of the Third Reich was to draw comparisons to the totalitarian policies of the Soviet Union. Almost immediately, he jumped to the Soviet Union, arguing that its evolving family policies demonstrated the danger of too much state intervention. Under Stalin, women were entering the workforce in much higher numbers and had access to day care, which facilitated their work. Christian conservatives in the West viewed such state aid as contributing strongly to the destruction of the family.[42]

Wuermeling also pointed to the East German dictatorship next door as evidence. Earlier, Bundestag politicians, especially those from the SPD, had been concerned about legal disunity if they passed a new law. Now, however, all mention of the GDR was coming from the other end of the political spectrum and the problem of legal unity was off the table. The CDU/CSU emphasized the need to pursue a radically different and more conservative form of the law. Wuermeling cited verbatim the 1950 Law for the Protection of Motherhood in the GDR as an example of legislation that had gone too far in expanding women's rights, especially in the workforce, to a point of abusing the principle of equality. He stated that the law's emphasis on bringing women into production and industry "is an equality which has necessary consequences, if one understands the equality of men and women as isolated from the worth and essence of women and from the natural order of marriage and the family."[43] Each case he mentioned suggested that drawing women out of the home ultimately harmed the family, because it separated children from their parents and indoctrinated them with particular agendas.

The opposition in the Bundestag was just strong enough to prevent approval of the CDU/CSU's version of the law in 1954. In the end, the Bundestag sent the three competing drafts from the CDU/CSU, the FDP, and the SPD to the Committee on Legal and Constitutional Matters, which would make the ultimate decisions regarding marital property, spousal relations, and parental authority.[44] As the Bundestag committee began its proceedings, the West German press updated the public on the new family law. The West German press coverage reflected the growing fault lines within the Bundestag, especially among the Christian Democrats. Even the more conservative papers, which typically interpreted such debates as favouring the Christian Democrats, were forced to concede to their readers that there were some divisions among CDU members.[45] Similarly, while the conservative *Frankfurter Allgemeine Zeitung* (FAZ) typically supported the CDU/CSU, its editors occasionally drew attention to readers' ambivalence about the ruling party. One letter to the editor of that paper stated that since men were the ones who typically harmed women, it made no sense for the administration to uphold a law giving them more authority.[46]

More liberal and left-leaning newspapers seized the moment to reinforce the left's commitment to women's equality with men. Several articles in SPD-run newspapers called the Bundestag's decision an "overdue change" and assured readers that "the SPD has never vacillated in its ninety-year existence from the issue of the equality of men and women."[47] Yet even liberal papers, like the weekly *Die Zeit*, were critical of both parties' positions. In October 1955, one author warned readers that no matter what form of marriage the parliament chose – "partner-like" or "patriarchal" – "the other [form of marriage] is placed in opposition to the law."[48] Across the political spectrum, the media were communicating to readers that fault lines were widening, no matter which side they ultimately supported.

The committee worked through 1956 and finalized its work in April 1957. On several issues, it found common ground. On marital property, for example, the members agreed that men and women should have the right to control their own belongings.[49] All members were willing to grant surviving spouses a greater share of inheritance. Regarding the husband's right to decide, however, the committee remained divided. On 15 November 1956, by one vote, its members narrowly overturned the right of husbands to decide, replacing it with a provision that promised equal decision-making by both partners.[50] On 12 December 1956, however, by a margin of two votes (fifteen to thirteen), the committee opted to keep the "final decision" with the father. This severely undercut the prior removal of the husband's right to make all decisions for his wife, because it gave her few rights over the children and forced her hand in cases where she might oppose her husband's thinking with regard to her children's welfare. The conflicting messages embedded in these two decisions set the parameters for subsequent discussions of family law in civil society, the media, and finally the Bundestag, where oppositional factions openly stated their reservations about the committee's proposals.

The inconsistent messages stirred members of society to protest the decision of the Bundestag committee. A multitude of women's associations, for example, proposed in statements in January 1957 that both parents should have a hand in decision-making, not just the father. That same month, Women's Work, a Protestant organization, offered the alternative of allowing a court to step in when parents could not come to an agreement. Other women's groups argued that denying women equal parental rights made no sense because they spent more time with their children. Finally, a local-level Social Democratic women's committee argued that it was the "harsh wartime and crisis years of our century" that had granted "women and mothers their equality with men."[51] Whether the subject was broached from a juridical, Christian, or retributive perspective, women's associations had reached a consensus: the parental right to decide unfairly favoured men.

Women's associations, other professional organizations, and individuals conducted letter-writing campaigns targeting Bundestag members, especially FDP and CDU/CSU representatives. The CDU/CSU's staunch opposition to women's equality provoked women to write its members. Thus, Frau C. of Karlsruhe wrote to her CDU parliamentarian Eduard Wahl to explain that she was "deeply disappointed" and "alienated" by the Bundestag legal committee's decision to retain the father's right to decide.[52] In later correspondence, she told Wahl that keeping such a provision was something the Nazi state would have done.[53] Similarly, Frau H. compared and contrasted wartime and peacetime, asserting that the wars had proved women were fully capable of making decisions for the family on their own.[54] Finally, Frau Dr. C. expressed disdain for the decision, because it "opposes Article 3, gives men 'blank' authority without proving themselves," and forced women, but not men, to pursue remedies in the courts.[55]

Perhaps the most striking letter came from Frau K. On 12 March 1957, Frau K. sent a letter to Eduard Wahl, a Christian Democratic member of the West German Bundestag, from Heidelberg. In it, she described the circumstances of her seventeen-year-old son's death.[56] In 1941, her husband signed the boy's enlistment papers for the German navy. Not long after their son went off to war, his submarine was sunk off the coast of Scotland. In her letter, Frau K. did not fault Nazi warmongering or Allied troops for her son's early demise. Rather, she blamed her husband, who by exercising his right under the German Civil Code to make all decisions for his wife and children sent their only son to an early grave. She did not include any more identifying information in her letter. It was clear, however, that Frau K. believed that the root of the problem was the discrimination against mothers and wives embedded in the Civil Code. Had the laws been different, had they given mothers the same rights over their children, she argued, her son might have lived.[57]

FDP members too found themselves on the receiving end of irate letters from voters. Women feared that the ambivalence and factionalism within the FDP would lead its representatives to side with the CDU/CSU. One female FDP member, for example, explained that when her husband was in a Russian POW camp, she had made all the decisions, and she resented having that right taken back.[58] Another wrote Dehler that she believed the *Stichentscheid* turned men into bullies. One female FDP member threatened to leave the party if "just one member votes" in favour of the *Stichentscheid*.[59]

Beyond letter-writing, there were other ways for women to display their irritation with the Bundestag's decision. The Deutscher Frauenrat and the Informationsdienst für Frauenfragen used the newsletter *Information for Women* (IfF) to communicate to its readers the existing dissent in society. Up until now, individual women's organizations, the two major churches, trade unions, and other professional organizations had petitioned the Ministry of Justice separately. The editor of IfF, Annelise Glaser, now reprinted their petitions and opinion pieces together in the pages of the newsletter.[60] Publishing all the petitions side-by-side was a way of spreading information about the opposition to and support for the law. Furthermore, it allowed readers to see how widespread and united their protests were. The IfF continued this practice until the final decision of the Bundestag about the Equal Rights Act.

On 3 May 1957, the Bundestag convened for the final time to discuss the Equal Rights Act. The bill's compromise nature provoked Bundestag members to make a last-ditch attempt to persuade the others to move towards the right or left on particular provisions in the legislation. Karl Weber (CDU) reintroduced the husband's right to decide, for instance, in hopes of getting the Bundestag to reverse its decision.[61] He cited legal uncertainties, tradition, sexual differences, and masculine duty as reasons to reinstate the husband's right to decide. Once again, the SPD and the FDP (and a few sympathetic CDU members, such as Schwarzhaupt) refuted these arguments on several grounds, but mainly on the ground that legislators had no right to impose a patriarchal structure on families, nor was it sensible in the post-war era, which was dominated by women.[62] Women's petitions had made this point clear enough to legislators.

These arguments, however, did not prove compelling enough to sway most of the Bundestag one way or the other. By a narrow margin, the Bundestag voted to keep the committee's recommended law as it was. Its final version, which the Bundestag approved on 18 June 1957, and which went into effect on 1 July 1958, therefore can be viewed as a series of compromises. On the one hand, it made fundamental changes to the old law. It entirely removed the man's right to decide in marriage, with no replacement provision. Also, men could no longer make decisions on their own about the marital home or whether their wives worked. If spouses separated, women would be forced to take on employment only if they would otherwise be expected to contribute income to the household. Marital property changed from a "marital property scheme" to a "community of accrued gain," meaning that property held by each spouse before or acquired separately during marriage remained their personal property.[63] Management of the other's property could only be undertaken with express permission.[64]

On the other hand, the law reinforced paternal authority and the gendered division of labour. Men reserved the right to make decisions about their children, without input from their wives. Women still retained responsibility over household affairs, although men were now legally required to assist and legally represent them. The new law maintained the *Schlüsselgewalt* – the right of the other spouse to take on dealings regarding the household with a third party – as the prerogative of the woman (in contrast to giving it to both partners). The idea behind this provision was that the "power of the keys" should remain the woman's responsibility because the household was her domain. In addition, married women could now hyphenate their married and maiden names, though they still had to adopt the husband's surname. Furthermore, both spouses were now viewed as contributors to the household: women's domestic labour counted as their half, while men's work outside the home counted as their half. Finally, women could work outside the home, but only when it was reconcilable with their household work and only when it was necessary to supplement an insufficient male wage.[65]

Equal Opportunities in the GDR, 1954–1957

While West German debates were unfolding, East Germans continued to reexamine their own legislative proposals. At the end of 1949 and the beginning of 1950, the SED-led government appeared to be on the fast track to passing a new family law. By mid-1950, however, the party had opted to take a different tack, folding the most pertinent points of the legislation into the catch-all Mutterschutzgesetz. This legislation, however, did not cover all relevant points of family law. Like West Germans, East Germans found themselves facing inconsistent judicial rulings and uncertainty over nuances of the law. The SED responded by forming a new legislative commission; soon after, though, it sidelined family law reforms in favour of other regime priorities. By 1954, just as the SED seemed ready to pass the new law, it encountered an unexpected obstacle: resistance from society.

The strength of societal resistance came as a surprise to the SED because by the end of 1953, the ruling party believed it had secured complete control over the government. In July 1952, following a Soviet initiative, SED party chairman Walter Ulbricht announced at the Second Party Congress that the party's priority was "building socialism [*Aufbau des Sozialismus*]," which would require the complete "power of the state."[66] "Building socialism" ushered in several changes for East Germany. The government reorganized the GDR into new districts, granted collectives special privileges, brought educational institutions into line, and fortified the border with West Germany with the aid of the Barracked People's Police, the precursor to the National People's Army.[67] In addition to securing its borders against potential foreign invasion, the SED prepared itself to combat insurrection within the GDR. To that end, the SED heightened its persecution of potential or perceived political dissidents as well as anyone who might oppose socialism. Liberal-minded judges, jurists, Christians, and independent business owners, for example, fell into these categories.[68] Only then did the SED place more radical family law reforms on its agenda. These initiatives were meant to place socialism front and centre and undermine the influence of subversive non-socialist forces such as religion and, more generally, West Germans.

Joseph Stalin's death in March 1953 disrupted the SED's plans for installing socialism and, by extension, changing family law. Immediately after the Soviet leader's death, the leading members of the Soviet Union's Communist Party Central Committee and Stalin's successors, Nikita Khrushchev, Lavrenti Beria, and Georgi Malenkov, proclaimed the New Course, a plan to increase the supply of consumer goods, repeal terror, and reduce industrial production.[69] When the SED did not remove the productivity quotas as promised, however, workers began leading demonstrations on 17 June 1953, first in Berlin and then across the GDR. Around 40,000 workers in Berlin, and thousands more around the GDR, took to the streets.[70] Under orders from the SED, the People's Police and the Soviet Red Army violently suppressed the protests. The ruling party asserted that the uprisings were the work of Western spies and infiltrators. In the months following the 17 June uprisings, to quash dissidence, party leaders clamped down on potential dissent, monitoring East German citizens and, especially, uncooperative party officials even more closely.[71] Where necessary, the SED dismissed known anti-Ulbricht members such as DFD leader Elli Schmidt and Max Fechner from their positions.[72] Fechner, a former Social Democrat, had served as Minister of Justice from 1949 to 1953. His public apprehension about Ulbricht's handling of the June 1953 uprisings and the persecution of political dissidents during and after led to his removal from office and expulsion from the SED in July 1953.[73]

Image 4.1. Celebration of Max Fechner's sixtieth birthday (27 July 1952). This photograph, taken by an unknown photographer, depicts Hilde Benjamin and Ernst Melsheimer standing with Max Fechner, demonstrating that just a year before the 1953 uprisings, members of the Ministry of Justice had been close and collegial. Image courtesy of the Bundesarchiv Berlin-Lichterfelde.

Fechner's dismissal had especially profound consequences for family law because it led to the appointment of Hilde Benjamin, then Vice-President of the Supreme Court of the GDR, as the new Minister of Justice in July 1953.[74] By the time Benjamin took over that ministry, family law reforms had long been on her personal agenda. Since 1946, as a leader of the Central Women's Committee, founding member of the DFD, and a People's Council representative, she had conducted many discussions herself regarding future legal reforms. In the meantime, she presided over a series of show trials in the GDR. Benjamin was responsible for bringing family law to the fore again as a part of the SED's "building socialism" program, which the leading party reiterated during its Fourth Party Congress in March 1954.[75] The June 1953 uprisings, even though they failed, persuaded Benjamin to orchestrate the legislation's public debut in June 1954 very carefully.

On 30 June 1954, the Ministry of Justice under Benjamin published drafts of the law, as well as commentary on its major provisions, in the major newspapers and legal journals.[76] The new Family Code's most tangible changes included fixing the age of majority at eighteen, replacing the guilt principle in divorce, giving women greater independence to work or live away from their spouses, and allowing partners to choose which surname they preferred.[77] The preamble to the Family Code outlined the ideological motivations behind these changes. The new law, for instance, emphasized the need for women to be equal to men both in marriage and in society. In addition, it would govern relationships between spouses, parents, children, and other relatives "for the development and stabilization of the family and upbringing of children in the spirit of democracy, socialism, patriotism, and friendship between nations."[78] Finally, the text asserted that raising children was the duty not only of parents but also of the state (as represented by youth organizations and schools).[79] The introduction to the Family Code (Familiengesetzbuch, FGB) demonstrated the SED's dual commitment to fostering equality and building strong, properly socialist families, albeit with greater amounts of state intervention.

In the weeks leading up to and following the legislation's debut, the SED and its partners in the National Front publicized the law through the mass media. The East German media suggested, through a series of editorialized synopses of the legislation, that East Germans could expect historically unprecedented and more egalitarian family structures once the Family Code was approved.[80] In addition to providing overviews of the impending legal provisions, the media emphasized that the legal changes were meant to ensure citizens' privacy and individual rights. On 15 June 1954, for instance, Hilde Benjamin asserted in a *Neues Deutschland* article that the forthcoming law was a response not only to women's complaints and court rulings but also to the changing currents of SED policy. She noted that by adopting the New Course, the SED was trying to "actually ensure the personal lives and personal interests of citizens, especially before the law."[81] It is more likely, though, that the 17 June uprising and its aftermath, not merely the introduction of the New Course, is what had spurred the SED to take an interest in protecting its citizens' private lives. Benjamin tried to steer readers towards a positive image of the SED and the GDR by depicting the new Family Code as a response to contemporary political developments and citizens' wishes.

Another strategy the East German media employed was allowing public – albeit carefully vetted – displays of differing opinions, to demonstrate that it was a true "people's democracy." *Berliner Zeitung* printed excerpts from readers' letters, for example, that covered a range of opinions on subjects such as the marrying age and the guilt clause in divorce. Regarding the age of majority, one older woman stated that sixteen was too young for a girl "to make such an important decision for her life," but if a girl was pregnant, then she should be allowed to marry.[82] Other readers opposed the removal of the guilt clause in divorce, arguing that without it, men would commit adultery uninhibited, "the number of unhappy and destroyed marriages would rise," and women would be disadvantaged.[83] In this way, the East German media presented the SED's reforms as improvements over past conditions. At the same time, these measures revealed a certain amount of traditionalism among readers, arguably a strategy on the part of *Neues Deutschland* and *Berliner Zeitung* to make the SED's position seem even more progressive.

The SED also conducted public forums to court GDR citizens. The Ministry of Justice set up several "Justice Conversation Evenings" in localities across East Germany. In these public spaces, citizens could pose questions and comment on the law to ministry functionaries or members of mass organizations such as the DFD. Occasionally, prominent figures from the ministry were invited to speak at public venues.[84] A typical Justice Conversation Evening consisted of a presentation delivered by an official from the local District Court, the Ministry of Justice, the National Front, or a mass organization such as the DFD. These evenings attracted anywhere from 50 to 1,000 participants at a time. By October 1954, the ministry had held 6,117 of these evenings, in which 313,538 GDR citizens participated.[85]

In a typical session, SED representatives walked the participants through each part of the law. For instance, at a meeting in Saxony, the chief justice of the nearest district court led the discussion. He spoke primarily about indemnity claims during the breaking of engagements, whether or not medical certificates were required for marriage, and the consequences for children of having parents who held different last names.[86] Participants showed special concern about the state's intervention in childrearing, especially the role of youth organizations like the Free German Youth (Freie Deutsche Jugend, FDJ).[87] In these spaces, the SED facilitated the debates, with the participants – often recalling the limits of their power during the Third Reich – raising their objections and attempting to negotiate with the party.

The presenters often underscored the "pan-German [*gesamtdeutsch*] meaning of the legislative draft."[88] There were both ideological and practical reasons for employing this argument. First, the SED had always proclaimed itself the protector of German unity, in contrast to the "divisive" West. Second, the inter-German borders were still open, and many Germans harboured fantasies of reunification.[89] Third, the 1946 Allied Control Council marriage law still technically governed both Germanys. Highlighting the pan-German implications of the law allowed the SED to portray itself as the German state that united German families in opposition to its Western counterpart. At the same time, the pan-German argument demonstrated that the SED was fully aware of the looming consequences of the law's imminent approval and that it was seeking to head off accusations that it was setting out to divide Germany.

Predictably, the East German mass media presented the public discussions in a positive light, but this belied a more complicated reality.[90] The SED quickly found that its public forums, designed and carefully controlled to reinforce the party's aims, were turning into spaces for voicing complaints about the new law's provisions. In addition, the correspondence from private citizens to the Ministry of Justice made it clear that the populace was at best confused by and at worst strongly discontented with the proposed family law. Over the course of the summer of 1954, the Ministry of Justice received hundreds of letters and petitions from curious and dissatisfied citizens on all types of issues related to the Family Code. For the most part, writers emphasized problems related to property and inheritance rights, alimony for spouses and children, family names, the legitimacy of children, women's working rights, adultery, and divorce. Typically, writers inquired about circumstances unanticipated by the SED as it attempted to transition East Germany from bourgeois norms to socialism. They saw their petitions as "an instrument for solving conflicts," which in this case stemmed largely from differing conceptions of marriage and the family.[91]

Property and inheritance rights were one area that provoked much confusion among East Germans. The law's provisions stated that any property acquired during the marriage for the support of the family was to be divided equally in divorce. As one case from Thuringia demonstrated, such regulations were not easily enforced. A local lawyer wrote in on behalf of his clients, a divorcing couple whose assets were invested primarily in livestock, extracted from both spouses' money but primarily the husband's livelihood. To make it more difficult, the animals had reproduced.[92] The couple and their lawyer wanted to know how the proposed law handled such situations. In other words, which way were they to cut the cows? This example demonstrated to the Ministry of Justice that equality in property rights was simple in theory but difficult to apply in a state that was still transitioning from a bourgeois to a socialist society and economy.

Another common complaint from correspondents had to do with the equal treatment of illegitimate children. The 1949 constitution and the 1950 maternity protection law already safeguarded the rights of out-of-wedlock children. The 1954 Family Code's reiteration of the SED's stance on illegitimacy nevertheless attracted hostility from those citizens who spotted its potential to disrupt their families and personal lives. For instance, Frau F. from Saxony-Anhalt explained that in her town, there was a young woman who seduced a married man, became pregnant, and attempted to ruin the family. In her opinion, the woman had no right to demand money from the man and his family.[93] Another writer, Herr M., proposed refusing out-of-wedlock children the right to inherit, because "females are the origin of illegitimate children ... If illegitimate children are given inheritance rights, it will just encourage sinful women."[94]

The regime routinely ignored these pleas because under socialism, birth status was not an impediment to social or economic status. In pursuing this path, the SED not only elevated the legal status of out-of-wedlock children and mothers (a long-time demand of the women's movement and something the FRG did not do until the 1960s) but also diminished the right of the alleged fathers to distance themselves from and disinherit their illegitimate children.[95] Still, overcoming the social norms that had long privileged men and disadvantaged their mistresses and out-of-wedlock progeny was a serious challenge for the ruling party.

Another point of controversy, as indicated by the petitions, was family surnames. The proposed law stated that the spouses could keep their own names, or they could take the other's name. The children would have to take the name of one or the other, but all offspring had to have the same name. This provision was designed to allow both spouses individual identities, especially in their careers, but also to foster some sense of familial unity, which was still important to many leading communists. In some petitions, citizens did not necessarily oppose the provision but offered exceptions or expansions to the text. One woman asked why, after leaving an abusive husband and father, it was not possible for her child to take her maiden name.[96] Men were especially keen to find out if they could change their surnames, but typically only if the last name was especially embarrassing. One man, a Herr Ficker, requested that men with embarrassing surnames be able to change them.[97] Other writers opposed the SED's proposals altogether on the grounds of protecting the family and preventing adultery.[98] One woman argued that with different names, no one would know who was married to whom, which "would lead to much unpleasantness."[99] The petitions regarding surnames exposed the SED to a wide variety of opinions from their citizens that ranged from mostly positive to outright opposition.

Another major issue for petition writers was alimony after divorce. Removing the guilt principle meant that alimony would no longer be tied to the spouse responsible for the marital breakdown. One subscriber to the women's magazine *Die Frau von heute*, Frau K., wrote that a guilt clause was necessary because "it would definitely no longer be a problem for the men's world then, to still look at their 'marriage' as complete."[100] Another respondent stated that she saw guilt as a consequence of the actions of both spouses and that women who sought to blame their husbands for leaving did not reflect enough on their own damaging actions.[101] A male reader called Frau G. "anti-man" and stated that he saw both sides as responsible for the breakdown of a marriage.[102]

Some correspondents referred to Germany's division when crafting their arguments. Some writers were quite literal-minded. In July 1954, for instance, a lawyer from Rostock urged the ministry "not to range too far from the Germans west of the Elbe" in terms of the new law, especially since "the approaching unity of our Fatherland is in motion."[103] Other writers used Germany's division as a metaphor. One male writer used the analogy of German reunification to make a point about individual surnames, stating that for spouses to have separate names "is as wrong as wanting to call both halves of Germany the GDR and the Federal Republic after reunification."[104] These writers invoked the FRG as a way of conveying their anxieties about individual provisions as well as the greater international consequences of passing the new Family Code.

The above correspondence offers several insights into citizens' responses to the new legislation. For one thing, it highlighted specific controversial issues stemming from the draft legislation, namely property rights, naming rights, and the fallout from adultery and divorce. The 1950 Mutterschutzgesetz had already removed many of the provisions (such as the right of men to make all decisions) that women's rights activists had long opposed (and were still fighting against in the FRG). But the new laws and policies did not cover every area of marriage and family law. Thus, correspondents, who were often less versed in socialist theory than the functionaries drafting the legislation, focused on how outstanding problems, such as divorce and property law, affected their daily lives.

In addition, these petitions hint at the persistence of more conservative understandings of gender and the family in the GDR. For instance, many writers blamed women for marital breakdown, illicit trysts, and unexpected pregnancies. These writers, especially men, were unwilling to trade the privileges granted by marital status to ensure equality for unmarried mothers. Others were willing to forgo individual identities for the sake of the family's integrity. It is important to note, however, the silence of others. Those who wrote did so to find solutions to their own problems or to sway the SED. Many more, however, chose not to correspond with the SED, indicating apathy, contentment with the draft, or, at the other extreme, perhaps fear of outing themselves to the regime.

Besides the provisions themselves, the issue of German unity quickly developed into a major point in the 1954 Family Code public discussions, during which the SED stressed the pan-German nature of the law. German unity became a rallying cry for the SED's strongest opponents: members of the Protestant and Catholic churches. The SED had been implementing "de-Christianizing" measures for years, but it still recognized the influence of the churches. In fact, SED leaders courted and attained the Protestant leadership's favourable opinion on the new family law in March 1954, months before the ministry debuted the draft of the Family Code.[105] Still, Christians on the local level started to protest the law in the summer of 1954. In addition to making arguments about their religious rights, they often buttressed their assertions about gender, the family, and religious freedom with arguments about German reunification, and they often invoked the West to undermine the SED.[106]

Picking up on the unrest of their parishioners, the governing body of the Eastern churches, the Ecclesiastical Eastern Conference of the Protestant

Church in Germany, issued an official opinion to the Ministry of Justice on 1 September 1954. Their statement employed a distinct rhetorical change from an earlier resolution, which had emphasized that in Christianity, "marriage and parenthood are endowed by God."[107] The Ecclesiastical Eastern Conference now added another compelling reason to stymie the FGB: the parallel developments in the FRG. They called on the SED to halt the passage of the law on the basis that it was creating "an artificial cleft in cultural cohesion."[108] The law, they asserted, must be considered for and by all Germans, especially in the event of future reconciliation.[109] With such arguments, the conference simultaneously appropriated the SED's own rhetoric about desiring a unified Germany and criticized the East German government's efforts to keep their nation divided based on marriage, family, and culture.

In its weekly newsletter *Die Kirche*, the Protestant Church of Germany (EKD) disseminated its message that the new FGB endangered both Christian beliefs and all-German unity. Drawing parallels between the East German constitution and the West German Basic Law, the author encouraged readers to avoid anything that created "an artificial rift in unified German cultural relations." The author then explained that the law opposed the Christian idea that marriage came from God and that parents had the right to raise their children in the church (i.e., not under socialist indoctrination). It ended by reminding readers that their strength lay in numbers and that they belonged to a unified Christian community despite the Iron Curtain.[110]

Protestants in the GDR clearly took this call seriously; their petitions flowed into the Ministry of Justice between September 1954 and February 1955.[111] Many of these petitions broached the issue of pan-German unity. One writer, for instance, stated emphatically that "what aggravates a reunification of Germany is to be avoided on all sides."[112] For other protesters, Christian belief and legal unity were indivisible. At an illegal meeting of a Protestant congregation in Saxony on 8 November 1954, the pastor spoke to around 450 participants about the issue of legal unity.[113] He observed that both German states had made a mutual commitment to equality between men and women in 1949, yet neither side had passed new legislation, though the GDR was close to doing so. He condemned the SED for deepening the rift between East and West on a legal *and* spiritual basis. He called on Christians to dissent by honouring God's law above the man-made laws of the regime.[114]

Though the majority of the petitions came from Protestant ministers and their parishes, the Catholic Church formally opposed the new Family Code as well.[115] Its impact on the SED, however, was largely inconsequential because of low numbers.[116] Protestants comprised roughly 80 per cent of the GDR's population in the 1950s; Catholics were only about 12 per cent.[117] Grassroots mobilization among Catholics was also lacking. Both factors contributed to the Catholic Church's relatively minor role. In her internal correspondence,

Benjamin always paid much more attention to the Protestant protests.[118] It was the Protestants who had impactful strategies, as well as sufficient numbers to rile up Benjamin and the SED in a way that Catholics did not.

Benjamin's consternation over Christians indicated that she knew early on that she was facing a formidable opponent. In fact, a few days after the EKD issued its official opinion, the SED drew up an anonymous report responding to the churches. The report lamented that the church leadership had developed many useful avenues for critiquing the law's provisions and offering alternative proposals. The SED could have opened itself to these suggestions. Instead, the author expressed indignation that the churches had chosen to point out the consequences of reunification: "The church must expect, that everything [in the law] that can deepen the cleft between both parts of Germany is omitted." [119] The dogmatic rifts between communism and Christianity – revolving largely around the aforementioned issue of state intervention in the family and childrearing – did not appear to cause the writer much concern. Nor would have proposals for new provisions. The SED brushed off the churches' criticism by claiming that reunification was not much of an issue, even though the party itself had introduced this very strain of argument.

Developments in the FRG compounded the SED's anxieties about internal dissent. At the time, the Federal Republic was formulating its own reforms to family law, and Benjamin and the East German Ministry of Justice were aware of them. Benjamin realized that the two nascent laws were deeply entwined and sought to engage the FRG on the parallel reforms. On 26 July 1954, Benjamin reached out to her West German counterpart, Fritz Neumayer (FDP), with a proposal that politicians and legal experts from East and West meet for an Academic Conference on Questions of Family Law in Germany, to be held in Leipzig on 13–14 November 1954. In August 1954, Benjamin and Neumayer engaged in a brief tussle over the invitation, which ended when Neumayer issued a press release condemning Benjamin and the FGB for only deepening the divide between West and East Germany through its thorough societal restructuring.[120] In its newspapers, the SED seized the opportunity to declare Neumayer the divisive party, but the damage had been done.[121] Aware that Neumayer's rejection would generate problems in the public forums, Benjamin warned the courts and regional justice administrations to emphasize the importance of "the implementation of the principle of equality in all of Germany."[122] The FRG's rejection of the SED's Family Code signified more than just ideological disagreement over the status of women and the family. Indeed, it was a spurn of the highest degree: the West German government would not legitimize the GDR's existence by engaging with its political leaders and foremost legal experts on the topic of family law.

This dispute between Benjamin and Neumayer – which the East German government may have resented more – illustrates a deeper engagement in

West Germany with the issue than previously acknowledged. The official West German line was non-recognition, and that stance that would be entrenched a year later in 1955 with the Hallstein Doctrine. Even so, the West German federal government, major political parties, and the media kept close tabs on the debut of the new Family Code in the GDR. Neumayer's reticence trickled down to supportive organizations in West Germany. The Anti-Communist People's League for Peace and Freedom, founded in 1950 in Hamburg as an anti-GDR propaganda and news organization, contacted all jurists in the FRG to warn them against participating in the conference. According to the league, the SED would be using the attendance of Westerners as propaganda.[123] The extent to which Western lawyers were convinced by this particular argument is unclear, but in the climate of heated Cold War anticommunism and fear of persecution, Neumayer and the league got their wishes – fewer than twenty Westerners attended the conference.[124] Those who did, such as Waldemar and Hildegard Wolle-Egenolf, a married Social Democratic couple who practised family law and had published a booklet on West German family law reforms in 1952, tended to have left-leaning independent positions or sympathized with the GDR.[125] But most legal experts in the West simply ignored the event. The tone set by Neumayer's ministry thus played a significant role in cutting off further intellectual exchange between the two sides.

The Adenauer government attempted to create distance between the two German states when it came to gender and the family. They found it difficult, however, to cleave apart organizations that had representation on both sides of the German–German border. The Protestant Church of Germany (EKD) was one prominent example: it was one of few organizations that remained structurally unified across the border in the 1950s and 1960s. Protestant leaders on both sides corresponded about family law throughout 1955.[126] In addition to that, the Protestant press produced articles on the competing legislative drafts in the FRG and the GDR. In February 1956, for example, Elisabeth Schwarzhaupt published an article comparing the two drafts. She emphasized that the FRG honoured "familial community" whereas the GDR "placed individual freedom … in the foreground."[127] Schwarzhaupt intended to demonstrate that the GDR's new family law would harm, not help, German families.

Meanwhile, the major political parties in the West kept a close eye on developments in family law reform in the GDR. The SPD Ostbüro – a department within the party aimed at helping Eastern refugees and staying informed about former SPD members in East Germany – produced a report on the public debates in the GDR in the summer of 1954.[128] Unnamed "sources" provided the SPD with insights into the public forums. They reported that a law "seldom has … aroused so much feeling as the one presented by the Ministry of Justice and put forward for discussion."[129] The other political parties had their own Ostbüros, which were active in spreading information about the East, and gathering it. For example, the CDU's Ostbüro, based in West Berlin, had organized the Christian Democratic expellees and refugees from the GDR. It published the newspaper *Der Tag*, which was smuggled into the GDR to inform dissidents there. In the early 1950s, one prominent issue addressed by *Der Tag* was the family law reforms in the GDR and the opposition against them.[130]

The West German and West Berlin media also monitored developments in East Berlin. For instance, the local West Berlin newspaper *Spandauer Volksblatt* reported on the controversial decision of the Protestant Church in Germany to withdraw its support for the GDR's Family Code. Initially, Protestant leaders had backed the SED's law. Six months later, however, they reversed their decision. The article stressed that Protestant leaders had revoked its earlier statements because the SED "used the marital and family life of citizens 'to posit definite political goals.'"[131] On 14 September 1954, *Frankfurter Allgemeine Zeitung* published an article titled "Critics of Family Policy in the Zone" that reported on the Protestant Church of Germany's recent rejection of the East German Family Code.[132] Its depiction of the EKD focused similarly on the church leaders' reticence about the law, because of its highly politicized nature and its threat to destroy distinct gender roles. It notably did not mention German unification, though the EKD had raised this as a separate issue in other papers.[133] In an earlier article, from 16 June 1954, the FAZ had taken a more neutral tone when presenting the key points of the East German Family Code, emphasizing in its final sentence that "political circles in Berlin have labelled the law as a new hit against the legal unity of Germany."[134] Such a statement was designed to steer West German readers away from positive impressions of the law. Meanwhile, more liberal and left-leaning media outlets criticized the suggested new GDR Family Code and the family policies underpinning it as antidemocratic and totalitarian. *Der Spiegel*, in a 15 September 1954 profile of the new Family Minister Franz-Josef Wuermeling, called the policies of the Soviet Union (and by extension, the GDR) "similar to those of the National Socialist regime in Germany."[135] However, *Der Spiegel's* article also criticized the CDU family policy and described Wuermeling as a "papal guard."

Whether she was aware of the West Germans' surveillance or not, the problem of the West's reforms continued to haunt Benjamin in other ways. For example, on 5 October 1954, in a letter to the State Administration department of the SED Central Committee, she expressed some apprehension that the West German Bundestag would pass its own family law reforms before East and West German jurists had a chance to meet to discuss the laws.[136] The press release that accompanied her letter portrayed West Germany as uncooperative and as preventing its own citizens from discussing the laws: "Neither the rejection of the Bonn Minister of Justice Neumeier [sic] to meet with the Justice Minister of the GDR, Dr. Benjamin, nor the lies and attempts at destruction can prevent [the fact] that numerous citizens and jurists in West Germany recognized the meaning of the draft and were prepared [to join] the pan-German conversation in the area of law in the manifestation of its different forms."[137] The language of the press release relied on the image of willing and eager West Germans to depict the West German government as the problem. The letter, however, demonstrated that Benjamin saw herself in a bind. If the West went forward with its reforms and completely ignored the East, it would look like the GDR had failed.

In August and October 1954, the East German Ministry of Justice paused to take stock of the public forums and protests.[138] The ministry praised the public for its positive responses to the laws.[139] Still, the public forums had exposed the SED to direct criticisms from East German citizens. In their correspondence, when reproached, ministry representatives bristled and did not hesitate to tell writers they were wrong.[140] In internal meetings, the Ministry of Justice dismissed most of these critiques as the consequences of "an insufficient understanding of [the laws'] practical effects."[141] In addition, ministry bureaucrats accused the West German press of propagating falsehoods.[142] Criticism from the public only pushed the SED to clarify its goals for the law and to remind its own cadres to toe the SED line.[143] Achieving unity among those cadres, however, sometimes proved difficult for the SED. For months, letters from regional-level functionaries communicated the desires of their constituents. This fostered further disunity among party leaders, which is precisely what Benjamin and other higher officials hoped to avoid.[144]

Furthermore, the SED faced opposition from West German Protestant church leaders. On 20 November 1954, Gustav Heinemann wrote a letter to Otto Grotewohl, the Minister-President of the GDR. Heinemann, born in 1899, had gotten a law degree, joined the anti-Nazi Confessing Church during the Third Reich, and eventually became mayor of Essen under the British occupation. After 1949, he became leader of the Synod of the Protestant Church in Germany.[145] He argued to Grotewohl that the GDR's reforms would "intervene in the personal relations" of citizens and disrupt the "basis of order that was already valid in Germany and will be continued in its Western part."[146] West German women's rights activists alleged that that order amounted to a continuation of the old, bourgeois, patriarchal Civil Code. Given that Heinemann was the leader of the EKD, his words carried extra weight. While based in the West, his reach extended into the East. When he indicted the SED for deepening the rift between the two Germanys based on women and the family, he did so as a representative of German Christian interests whom the SED could not touch.

The petitions and public forums, the protests of East German churches, the rejection by the Western government, and the intervention of West German religious leaders shook Benjamin and other Ministry of Justice officials. In November 1954, the ruling party closed discussion of the FGB. In January and again in April 1955, Benjamin forwarded petitions from the churches to

Lieutenant-General Erich Mielke, second-in-command of the Stasi.[147] Her letters did not explicitly ask the secret police to watch and inform on church members, but one can infer that this was her intent. It is not clear exactly which steps the Stasi took to observe the leaders and members of the protesting churches; more obvious is what conclusions they drew from their efforts. In 1956, the Stasi produced an internal report chronicling its activities between 1 September 1954 (the same date the EKD issued its opinion piece) and 1 September 1955. The report labelled the churches' work as reflecting West Germany's "policy of aggression." In particular, the author singled out Otto Dibelius, a leading Protestant bishop in Berlin, as "opposing the democratic institutions of our republic ... against the regulations of our government, for example against the Law of Equal Rights of Women, against the youth confirmation, against the family law, etc."[148] The Stasi's report ultimately blamed West Germany for the churches' rebellion over women's legal rights and the family.

The disappearance of the Family Code did not escape public notice. Throughout 1955 and early 1956, the Ministry of Justice continued to receive petitions and letters from East Germans inquiring about the status of the law, requesting advice for their personal situations, and offering scepticism about the law's prospects.[149] The ministry answered their petitions, but at the same time, the SED-backed media stopped reporting on the law. By the end of the 1950s, family law had drifted to the margins of the SED's agenda and the public's attention. The SED's muted propagation of the Family Code in 1955 coincided with major changes in economic and foreign policy that had unintentional consequences for the law. West Germany gained its sovereignty from the Western occupation powers, rearmed itself, and joined the North Atlantic Treaty Organization (NATO) in 1955.[150] In response, in May 1955, the GDR joined the Warsaw Pact, the Soviet Union's answer to NATO, and formed its own National People's Army (already in the works since 1950 with the founding of the Volkspolizei). The Soviet Union declared the GDR a sovereign state on 20 September 1955, marking a sea change in GDR–USSR relations. The nominal withdrawal of Soviet influence meant that the ACC laws no longer had to be enforced, though the Soviet Union had to be consulted about overturning the legislation.

Leading GDR officials like Benjamin took advantage of the dissolution of the ACC laws. Unable to make the Family Code the SED's priority or overcome public discontent with the proposed reforms, she aimed for partial solutions. With the permission of the Soviet Union, the SED sought to replace the 1946 ACC law.[151] Benjamin, reflecting on this decision later, stated that the GDR simply needed to change divorce regulations.[152] On 24 November 1955, the Ministry of Justice released the Decree on Marriage and Dissolution of Marriage.[153] The following year, it updated the previous decree with new divorce and adoption decrees, which signalled incremental steps towards regulating aspects of family law.[154]

Image 4.2. Poster for the International Women's Day from the Democratic Women's League of Germany advertising opposition to nuclear rearmament (1955). The poster depicts a woman protecting her family and states that the DFD opposes atomic weapons and remilitarization. Image courtesy of Bundesarchiv Berlin-Lichterfelde.

While the debate over family law was dying down in East Germany, the West German federal government, specifically the Inner-German Ministry, continued to publicly disparage the GDR's Family Code. For example, in 1955 it published a brochure by Maria Hagemeyer – the same Ministry of Justice associate who had provided proposals for the new West German family law – titled *Regarding Family Law in the Soviet Zone*.[155] The bulk of Hagemeyer's brochure was an in-depth and incisive critique of the East German Family Code, covering topics such as family names, alimony, marital property, and illegitimacy. According to Hagemeyer, every provision that the SED contended was a path to women's emancipation would in fact destroy women's chances at equality and endanger the family. For example, the SED believed that women's full-time work eliminated the need for alimony, a lingering form of economic dependence on former husbands. Hagemeyer countered that removing the right to alimony would "lead to an obvious worsening of the position of women under the cloak of equality."[156] There was also the issue of marital property. Under the SED's purview, couples needed to combine their assets in a show of setting aside individual desires. Hagemeyer disapproved of the GDR's shared marital property scheme, claiming that it would further disadvantage women if their husbands were permitted to use common property for their own purposes.[157] Finally, she cited the right to independent surnames, claiming that the GDR did not value familial unity.[158]

Beyond trying to convince readers that women's equality did not truly exist in the GDR, Hagemeyer's brochure had a second purpose: to undermine the SED's assertions about German unity. She criticized Benjamin's opinion that "the draft of the Family Code has a pan-German meaning," and she praised the response of her West German counterpart Fritz Neumayer, who had bluntly rejected an all-German debate about family law. For Hagemeyer, the GDR draft "endangered the structure of the German family," and the law and the 1955 relaxation of divorce regulations in the GDR would "lead to the dissolution of the family."[159] These sentiments reverberated around the Federal Republic at a number of meetings. Hagemeyer presented her position to the public as often as possible. At a conference in Stein near Nürnberg, presenters supported Hagemeyer's rhetoric, calling the "difference of juridical formulations" a "huge danger" for reunification.[160] Another event, held in March 1956, had the telling title "Women's Equality as a Principle of Construction or Destruction"; there, Hagemeyer concluded in her keynote that women's equality and family law would hinder German reunification.[161]

All-German unity had been a persistent theme during the 1954 debates in East Germany. First introduced by the SED as a form of criticism of West Germany and a form of praise for its own proposals, the term had been co-opted by the opposition – the churches – and used against the SED. On top of this, West German leaders were spying on the protests in the GDR and making similar arguments about the problems East German laws would cause for all German families. The way the churches and other opponents of the communist regime employed this rhetoric against the ruling party riled East German leaders and led to the momentary end of family law reforms in the mid-1950s.

When East and West German leaders picked up family law reforms again in 1953, they thought there would be new family laws by the end of 1954. By 1953, West Germany had established a semi-functioning liberal democracy – albeit one defined by Adenauer's "authoritarian power politics" – and the "economic miracle" had practically handed the 1953 election to the CDU/CSU.[162] Christian conservatives were at the peak of their power. Meanwhile, in East Germany, the ruling SED was convinced that its power as a one-party dictatorship was secure. "Building socialism" was under way, ensuring that various sectors of society – churches, educational institutions, and courts, among others – were brought into line with socialist teaching. Despite some delays between 1949 and 1954, both German states seemed poised to push through reforms in 1954. Yet in neither state was the ruling party entirely successful. Resistance within the parties and in society made it difficult for East and West German political leaders to achieve the laws they had set out to create.

Across Europe, as in the earlier half of the decade, there was little traction in the late 1950s for making changes to family laws. France and Italy would remain in a holding pattern until the 1960s and 1970s. Spain and Portugal – deeply Catholic dictatorships – would not address reforms to family law until the 1980s.[163] Most Eastern European countries had already ditched their patriarchal laws to reflect Soviet policies. Even the more conservative parts of Europe, like Romania, had altered their family laws in 1954. But by changing their laws, communist governments had not necessarily established welfare states. Still set on properly building socialism and carrying out the goals of their Five-Year Plans, the Eastern Bloc states overall did not devote much attention to expanding infrastructure and access to consumer goods so as to achieve their productive and reproductive goals.

The two Germanys were the only European countries in which critical discussions of family law had significant outcomes in the late 1950s. For the first time, however, the two states diverged significantly. They had largely kept pace with each other in the late 1940s and early 1950s. Now, at last, West Germany was pulling ahead, having passed the 1957 Equal Rights Act while East German debates languished. In both states, activists on the ground and Cold War divisions played significant roles in alternately pushing and halting reforms. Had it not leaned into anticommunist sentiments, the CDU/CSU would have had an even more difficult time passing the Equal Rights Act. As it was, resistance in society and within the party kept the CDU/CSU at bay. In the GDR, activists employed rhetoric about German unity to their advantage to halt the reforms. In the end, both states ended up with uneasy, incomplete solutions to their family law problems. It was only in the 1960s and 1970s that wide-ranging reforms would come to fruition.

5 Achieving Equality in East and West Germany, 1957–1976

The Equal Rights Act came into force on 1 July 1958, signalling a sea change for West German women like Frau B. In 1948, Frau B. married. She then worked as a teacher while her husband pursued a graduate degree in law. When he was hired as a clerk at a law firm, she was forced to give up her job, for the law at the time forbade two full-time breadwinners. The family then moved around West Germany, following the husband's career. Frau B. described a difficult and alienating daily existence, with few friends and little help with raising the children on her own. As Frau B. told her story, her husband did not consult her about major life changes – he simply decided that they would move for new job opportunities, without regard for family upheaval. Until 1957, when the Equal Rights Act passed, he would have had the legal right to do so, with little input from Frau B. She could have pressed the case in court, but a judge might rule against her and in favour of her husband.

For women like Frau B., the 1957 Equal Rights Act was an important step towards achieving some equity within marriage. At the same time, the law was woefully incomplete. In fact, almost immediately, West Germans began identifying problems with the new law. While men could no longer make all decisions for their wives, they could still make decisions for their children, thus leaving their spouses in a bind. This provision would go before the Federal Constitutional Court in 1959. Furthermore, the law did not address areas such as divorce. For a woman like Frau B., then, the 1957 law was both a blessing and a curse. It was not until the 1970s, when the children were old enough, that she could return to school and divorce her husband.[1] For Frau B. to get a divorce prior to the late 1970s, either she or her spouse would have had to be formally declared the "guilty" party. Until the next round of reforms in 1976, the notion of divorce on grounds of "irreconcilable differences" did not exist in West Germany.

Meanwhile, in the GDR, legal reforms had stalled out by 1957. Petitions, public forums, and mainly Protestants had convinced the SED regime to hold off on passing a new family law in the mid-1950s. In the meantime, the SED laid low on family law as it pursued new initiatives in collectivization and nationalization of key industries in the GDR. These new policies drove even more East Germans across the German–German border. Facing a labour drainage and a confusing border situation, the SED placed family law back on its agenda. This time, the SED was successful. At the end of 1965, the Volkskammer finally passed the new Family Code, which went into effect in 1966. A few years later, in 1968, the GDR passed a new constitution with an even stronger equal rights clause. By the mid-1970s, the GDR had a welfare state in the works and was preparing to revise the original Family Code.

This chapter examines the final stages of legal reforms in East and West Germany from the late 1950s to the early 1970s. I argue that in East Germany, the regime had become savvier since the early 1950s. This time around, unwilling to succumb to the same societal pressures that had doomed the family law reforms in 1954, the SED clamped down on churches. In the end, the SED-led regime was able to pass much more extensive reforms than its West German counterpart. I argue that in West Germany, the incomplete reforms of the 1950s set in motion a new stage of discussions over women, gender, and the family in the 1960s. The new SPD-led government, aided by the New Women's Movement, then became the primary drivers of the reforms that went into effect in the 1970s.

These final stages of discussions marched hand in hand with the Cold War struggle between the two Germanys. For East Germany, the Cold War was the main stimulus for the reforms. For one thing, its government was confronting the mass exodus of its citizens to the West, and this led the SED to fortify the German–German border, culminating in the construction of the Berlin Wall in August 1961. With East German citizens contained, the SED turned its attention to social reforms via avenues such as family law. In West Germany, Cold War competition was less obvious but still present. In the 1970s, as the Cold War thawed in the face of *Ostpolitik*, West German politicians still referenced the East German Family Code and seemed cognizant of its potential effects on their own laws.

The approval of the 1965 Family Code in the GDR left a significant imprint on the two Germanys and the rest of Europe. The new law introduced no-fault divorce, provided state infrastructure for childcare, dictated equal childrearing and marital community between partners and parents, and allowed either spouse to take the other's surname, among other provisions. Though still largely heteronormative in nature, the new legislation nevertheless introduced some innovative changes in German law. West Germans took notice of the changes across the border. They also began to reassess their own family law, specifically as it related to divorce, and this resulted in major reforms in 1976. The East German Family Code's passage in 1965 and the West German First Law in 1976 would remain the laws of the separate lands until German reunification in 1990.

Incremental Steps towards Approving the 1965 Family Code

In the decade that followed the Family Code's failure to pass, the SED pursued several paths towards a new family law. In 1955 and 1956, the Ministry of Justice created some decrees to regulate divorce and adoption. Also, ministry officials continued to discuss potential revisions to the Family Code, demonstrating that the issue never completely disappeared from the party's agenda. Throughout the various debates, the FRG loomed large in the SED's language. The ever-tightening border controls were evidence that the GDR wanted little to do with its bourgeois, capitalist neighbour. Once the FRG passed its own law and the Berlin Wall went up, East German citizens could not escape as easily and the SED no longer had to view West Germany as competition. SED party leaders now saw an opportunity to implement an even more radical, more socialist, and less bourgeois version of the Family Code in 1965. Furthermore, the regime now realized that it would have to find ways to overcome the opposition from churches. As a result, despite seemingly similar circumstances as in 1954, the SED had a much easier time passing the law in 1965.

Even with the 1955 and 1956 decrees on the books, the Family Code did not disappear from the ministry's agenda.[2] The decrees covered many of the major issues the SED hoped to address (such as divorce regulations), but the party still aimed to overturn and rewrite the Civil Code as a sign of its radical social restructuring. At the request of Walter Ulbricht at the Fifth Party Congress in 1958, the Ministry of Justice officials produced several new drafts of the Family Code, circulated them among the various other ministries, and prepared to send them to the parliament.[3] The East German media reported on the internal reviews of the law, keeping the public in the loop on important ministry decisions about parental custody, adoption rights, declaration of paternity, and property rights.[4]

Internal discussions reflected that government officials were contending with the problem of West Germany. The Bundestag committee debates in 1955–56 and the subsequent approval of the Equal Rights Act in the FRG in 1957 (see the previous chapter) presented a new set of problems for Hilde Benjamin and the Ministry of Justice. At this point, with the division of family law realized, and not by their own doing, the SED and the Ministry of Justice had to reconsider their position and language. For instance, Benjamin noted in a letter to Karl Maron, the Minister of the Interior, on 30 April 1958, that the "existence of two sovereign states in the territory of Germany" posed "the question of [if] the applicability of West German law must be regulated the same way as the relationship of laws to other states."[5] She further asserted that the laws were incompatible, as the GDR did not uphold discrimination based on race, sex, or religion, like "capitalist societies."[6]

Image 5.1. Staff member holding a copy of the legal code (1957). The staff worker pictured, Elfriede Gross, held a number of jobs before she was nominated as a DFD representative in her district. She became the point person for "women's matters." The photograph was taken by Erich Zühlsdorf. Image courtesy of Bundesarchiv Berlin-Lichterfelde.

In response, by 1959 the Ministry of Justice had made further attempts to prioritize the Family Code. The Politbüro, for its part, issued a formal resolution to pass the Family Code, and this occupied much of Benjamin's attention.[7] The introduction of a new Seven-Year Plan in 1959 accelerated agricultural collectivization and the nationalization of key industries, which led to a spike in defections.[8] The rising numbers of East Germans heading west forced Benjamin and the Ministry of Justice to confront a brutal reality: their citizens and their families were divided. They now had to revisit their earlier stance that West German family law was illegitimate and incompatible. They needed to provide "clear boundaries of the responsibility of the courts of the GDR and the West German courts."[9] They determined that East German courts could adjudicate all matters related to the family, even if the other party resided in West Germany or West Berlin. For example, there was the matter of support for children and "easing the execution of requirements against the party liable for alimony in the Western zone or West Berlin."[10] This decree was one step towards addressing a fundamental quandary facing the Ministry of Justice and East German judges.

The dilemma of adjudication across borders was short-lived, though contemporaries could not have foreseen the possibility that East Germany would close off its borders entirely. In 1952, East Germany had formally closed the German–German border, making it more difficult, though not impossible, for its citizens to flee. The special status of Berlin, however, meant that East Germans could still escape to the West there. By 1956, defections to the West had risen significantly. On 12 August 1961, Walter Ulbricht signed the order to close off East Berlin from the West by erecting the Berlin Wall. This move divided families, prevented East Berliners from going to work in the West, and stopped the refugee drainage to the West. With very limited numbers of East Germans crossing the border after 1961, judges' and ministry officials' concerns about how to implement any procedures concerning marriage or families diminished.

In 1963, the SED again raised the issue of the long-abandoned Family Code. Most contemporaries later credited the renewed interest in the Family Code to Walter Ulbricht's speech at the Sixth Party Congress, held between 15 and 21 January 1963. This Party Congress was especially significant because it was there that Ulbricht introduced the New Economic System (NES) to the GDR. The NES set aside the Five-Year Plans and "de-emphasized central planning and placed more power in the associations (VVB) of socialized industries (VEB)."[11] In addition to calling for economic reforms, Ulbricht insisted that it was "urgent to improve the legal standards, which rule the economic-organizational and cultural-educational activity of the state and economic organs … New legal codes for civil, criminal, and family law will be developed."[12] The Ministers' Council followed up on Ulbricht's proposal in April 1963 with a resolution; in October of that year, it formed a commission to draft a new family law.[13]

The new commission, headed by Benjamin, began its work in January 1964.[14] In a concerted effort to demonstrate equality, the Ministers' Council insisted that the committee include equal numbers of men and women. The Ministers' Council reported in May 1964 that the commission was proceeding apace with discussions.[15] Its progress ended in October 1964, however, when the Ministry of Justice's Women's Working Group and its Department of State and Law intervened, issuing an opinion piece that asked the SED not to pass the new law yet. That piece stated that the law did not go far enough in "delivering and stabilizing marital and familial relationships and the further development of socialist conduct and lifestyle."[16] The working group wanted the draft to explain in more detail what the family meant for socialism and especially for raising the next generation under socialism. Accordingly, the working group argued that the draft focused too much on equality of women and not enough on the family. In an even more drastic turn, the working group alleged that the draft did not "overcome the reflecting commercialization of family relations characteristic of bourgeois families and in bourgeois family law," especially when it came to property law.[17] Finally, it attacked the language of the law, explaining that it was too juridical and difficult for average citizens to understand.[18]

In response, the SED postponed the original plan to conduct a public discussion between October 1964 and January 1965. Also, the legislative drafts changed drastically between September and December 1964.[19] On 18 March 1965, the steering committee of the Ministers' Council of the GDR approved and published the "final" draft of the new FGB. Led by the National Front (the compendium of political parties in the GDR), the trade unions (FDGB), the DFD, the Union of Democratic Jurists of Germany, and the Society for the Dissemination of Scientific Knowledge, with help from social welfare organizations, judges, and attorneys, the discussions would educate the masses on the role of marriage and the family for all citizens (not only women) in their socialist society.[20] The second purpose of the discussions was to inform the public about the status of marriage and family law in West Germany. The SED's propaganda department sent out special documents (the Ministers' Council resolutions and a report on the family from the German Academy of Sciences) on the FGB to the editors in chief of all the media organs and to all lawyers.[21] This time, the SED intended to keep tighter control over the forums.

A month later, on 14 April 1965, the SED held an international press conference in which it formally introduced the new FGB to the public. In her opening address, Benjamin observed that the struggle for a new family law had its roots in the antifascist sentiments of the immediate post-war period, especially given that the Nazis had set out to destroy families with their racist rhetoric

Image 5.2. Hilde Benjamin delivers a speech at the Women's Congress of the GDR (27 June 1964). This photograph, taken by Friedrich Gahlbeck, shows Hilde Benjamin speaking to women in the midst of leading her work on the new family law commission. Image courtesy of Bundesarchiv Berlin-Lichterfelde.

and policies.[22] According to Benjamin, the new FGB, in concert with the labour laws, the youth laws, and collectivized agriculture, would complete the "unified socialist system."[23] She then outlined the importance of the law for women's economic independence, stressing that unlike the capitalist laws that preceded the FGB, this law would provide job and educational opportunities without presuming conflicts between personal and public life.[24] Finally, she emphasized the moral basis of the new law for raising children.[25]

Beyond the SED's goals for the family in its socialist republic, Benjamin acknowledged the significance of the competition with West Germany with regard to a new family law. According to her, "such a law as we have here in this draft is neither imaginable under the circumstances in West Germany, nor under the present circumstances could a genuine discussion among the people be conducted."[26] She attacked the FRG's recent policies towards women, asserting, for example, that West Germany's conscription of women into the civil service would endanger the family and that despite CDU member Elisabeth Schwarzhaupt's appointment as head of a federal ministry and the founding of the European Economic Community, West Germany was full of "empty promises."[27] Finally, she credited the pronouncement of women's rights as a social democratic goal at the 1964 SPD Party Conference as a reaffirmation that the GDR was "an entire historical epoch ahead of the West in the area [of equality]."[28]

After Benjamin's address, the SED opened the floor to questions from the press, notably non-German and non-communist journalists. They asked: how progressive were East Germans compared to West Germans when it came to women's rights? What do Christians have to say about the new law? Was it true what the West German press said – that families would forfeit raising their children to the socialist state?[29] Civil law expert Anita Grandke fielded their questions. Born in 1932, Grandke had spent her formative years in the Soviet zone and the GDR. She studied law at Humboldt University in Berlin (HU) in the early 1950s and then wrote her thesis on property law in a socialist state under the direction of Hans Nathan, the same professor who had been instrumental in family law reforms in the early 1950s. She later became professor of civil and family law at HU herself. Grandke elucidated to the press the ways the GDR had outpaced the FRG in terms of sex equality. She declared that the GDR's law "took seriously the complete development of a woman's personality," allowed women to work, and gave men and women equal childrearing duties.[30] In contrast, West German women by law could only seek employment if it was reconcilable with their duties as mothers and wives. Regarding whether the state would take childrearing duties away, Grandke and her colleague assured the press that the law was meant to "increase and further develop the parental influence in the development of spouses and before all the children."[31]

The following day, 15 April 1965, the East German press exploded with news about the new Family Code. *Berliner Zeitung*, *Neue Zeit*, and *Neues Deutschland* all printed articles and/or drafts of the new law.[32] While the GDR's Family Code may have outpaced the FRG in certain respects, such as divorce reform, the new legislation very clearly placed the heteronormative, dual-parent family model, childrearing, and mothers' reproductive capabilities at its core. The law emphasized the "recognition and appreciation of the accomplishments associated with the birth, upbringing, and care of children." Additionally, it proclaimed that the equality of men and women was vital to "the character of the family and the socialist society," setting down in law that spouses must support each other. Parents also had the right and duty to work closely with society to ensure a healthy upbringing for the children. The state, in turn, was obligated to help families.[33]

If anything, compared to earlier versions of the family law, the new Family Code put even more emphasis on establishing stable and long-lasting partnerships that would produce an abundance of children. The new provisions dictated that upon marriage, men and women over the age of eighteen "establish a closed community for life, based on mutual love, attention, fidelity, understanding, trust, and selfless help." The partners' ability to do so was supposed to be assessed before marriage. It was expected that children would come out of the marriage. All marriage ceremonies would be conducted at the magistrate's office. Couples were free to take either spouse's last name or keep their own, but the child must have one or both parents' names – a stark change from earlier drafts, which allowed couples to hyphenate or keep their own names. Bigamy and incest were expressly prohibited, as was marriage to a disabled person. Spouses were encouraged to live together and run a household together – another key change from the 1950 and 1954 versions, which allowed spouses to live separately. Spouses had equal rights to legal representation. Both parents had equal obligations to raise the children and contribute to the household. If one partner got a new job or decided to pursue further training, the other was expected to support him or her. Unemployed spouses' domestic work was considered equal. The property of children and family members living outside the home could be contributed to the support of the household. Property or income earned during the marriage became common property; property acquired beforehand was personal.[34]

The new law plainly promoted marital harmony, but the end of a marriage had to be addressed as well. Marriages were considered over in four circumstances: death, divorce, annulment, or if one spouse was declared dead. No-fault divorces were now permitted, and the law did not designate a separation period for the couple. At the same time, divorce was still considered a grave matter and could only be completed "for serious reasons ... when the marriage has lost its meaning for the spouses, children, and society."[35] Divorce would be decided by a court, which would rule with the child's best interests in mind. The court would decide which spouse would care for the children, after consultation with youth welfare services. Parents were obligated to not allow their personal disputes to interfere with their parental childrearing duties. After the divorce, spouses could revert to their former names. If one spouse fell ill, the other could take over parental responsibilities and support for an interim period. Marriages could be annulled in a court of law if conducted under a forbidden circumstance (such as bigamy).[36] Couples were clearly encouraged to stay together, and the new law mandated state intervention to assess post-marital life for both spouses and their children.

The new Family Code also highlighted that raising children, especially in the name of socialism, was a paramount goal of the SED-led government. State-run bureaux would help families provide for, raise, and educate their children. Youth welfare services could step in to help make important decisions if parents lived separately. Parents were obligated to make all decisions regarding children mutually unless one fell ill and was unable to contribute. If the parents were not married at the time of birth, mothers were given sole responsibility for the child, though men were obligated to provide support. In the case of unwed parents, the father could either declare himself or be named the father by a court. Fathers were considered whoever had lain with the woman during the conception period, defined as 181 days. Children could be adopted if there was official approval.[37] Finally, the new law defined who a relative or an in-law was in terms of the degree of their relation to the family, the place of youth welfare services, and the statute of limitations for alimony claims.[38]

The preamble to the 1965 Family Code explained the multiple reasons for its provisions. First, the SED viewed the family as the "smallest cell of society" whence the building of socialism came. Socialism, the preamble reminded citizens, would free them from the "falsifications" of bourgeois society. The new Family Code would ensure "free creative work, comradely relations among people, the equal place of women in all areas of life and educational opportunities for all citizens." The SED believed that "harmonious relationships in marriage and the family have a huge influence on the character building of the next generation and on the personal luck and life- and work happiness of the people." The law's emphasis on social organization with the family at the centre would help the SED achieve these goals.[39]

As in 1954, the SED spent the next several months conducting public forums to discuss the law. Stasi documentation indicates that the SED kept a closer eye this time on the development and running of these discussions.[40] Corroborating reports, recorded biweekly, confirm that the SED took careful notes about the participants. By July 1965, more than 400,000 East Germans had attended the public forums – more than the entire total for the discussions a decade earlier.[41] The SED tracked which issues concerned Germans the most and found that most of their questions were about contracting marriages, marital property, divorce, the basic principles of the law, and miscellaneous issues (such as procedural law).[42]

Also during this time, other members of the National Front in the GDR offered their official endorsements of the law.[43] Some party leaders utilized the language of combating Western influence to appeal to SED leadership. According to Heinrich Homann, the Deputy Chairman of the National Democratic Party of Germany, the 24,000-plus party members who gathered to discuss the law supported it as a form of resistance against the "antinational and anti-humanitarian crisis dictatorship of West Germany."[44] LDPD member Gerhard

Lindner contended that the East German FGB would help fight the "state mo-nopolistic capitalist-dictated living conditions."[45] Lindner also selected quota-tions from the 1957 West German law, such as the right of women to work only if it was reconcilable with household duties, as evidence of the regressive nature of the FRG.[46] Finally, the East-CDU asserted, the FGB proved "the superiority of our socialist social order over the imperial West Germany."[47]

Notwithstanding their general affinity for the law's goals, especially its an-ticapitalist and anti-Western bent, different parties in the National Front held certain reservations about the law.[48] The East-CDU relayed a few critical points that had been raised in public forums but still formally approved the law.[49] The East-CDU's official endorsement of the FGB did not necessarily reflect the views of all the Christians it represented. As they had in 1954, church leaders revolted against the FGB. In April 1965, Alfred Bengsch, the Archbishop of Berlin, wrote on behalf of the Catholic bishops to express their reluctance to support the new law.[50] As the Catholic Church leadership had done in 1954, Bengsch argued that the new law replaced the "intimate space of the family" with atheistic state intervention.[51] Bengsch's letter focused largely on the goals of Christians to raise their children a particular way, indicating that other po-tential arguments (such as reunification) no longer carried the same weight as they had in 1954.

Protestant leaders took a different tack than their Catholic counterparts. They formed committees and printed handouts for their members to use. One that caused the SED particular consternation was the "10 Questions" handout, which the church leadership encouraged its members to use as guidance for provoking public discussions.[52] On 22 April 1965, Hans-Jürgen Behm, head of the Protestant chancellery in East Berlin, sent out a list of ten provocative ques-tions to the leaders of the member churches of the EKD. Some of the questions were direct critiques of the FGB, such as, "Can it be the 'utmost task' of Chris-tian parents to raise their children for the building of socialism?" Other ques-tions were less polemical and pointed out confusing provisions. For example, who would make a decision if the spouses could not agree? And what would be the role of the youth welfare services, which did not yet exist? The handouts clearly had an impact on lower-tier church leaders. A letter from a pastor from Schwarzenberg to the members of the Volkskammer echoed the language of the first question, asking them "to explain the term 'socialist'" and why the law had to be understood as "materialist and atheist."[53]

The handouts alarmed the SED and especially the Stasi. By June 1965, the Stasi was keeping close watch on church leaders. Stasi informants reported that on 16 June 1965, the leaders of the eight regional churches planned to draft a letter to the government (as it turned out, they did not do so). One member, Friedrich-Wilhelm Krummacher, the Bishop of Pomerania, opposed such a step because it would weaken the churches' positive assessment of the law.[54] He also argued that under the constitution, the churches had no right to demand religious education – they could only provide opportunities for worship – so their potential to intervene was weak. The only member of the meeting who appeared sympathetic to the SED was Moritz Minderheim, the Bishop of Thüringia. According to the Stasi, Minderheim opposed passing out handouts or writing a formal petition because "in far-reaching Christian circles the Family Code will be affirmed" – in other words, he recognized that many churchgoers would not contest the law.[55]

The SED conducted public discussions until 30 September 1965. According to the SED's estimates, 752,671 citizens convened in 33,973 locations to discuss the law; these gatherings, and readers' and radio listeners' letters, together generated to 23,737 proposals for the new law.[56] Meanwhile, the mass media and the women's press in the GDR promoted the new legislation. The May 1965 issue of the women's magazine *Für Dich* featured an article on "intact marriages," which explored the inner happiness of one Berlin couple, the Karls.[57] Their family was happy, and Gisela Karl maintained that she could pursue her career because her daughter, husband, and mother all pitched in around the home. In June 1965, *Für Dich* published an article by Inge Lange, then the chairwoman of the Women's Commission of the SED Central Committee, who told readers that if the GDR wanted to achieve full equality, then the onus was on men to change their expectations of marital life, fatherhood, and women's employment.[58] Finally, in July 1965, the same magazine printed a round-table discussion with leading legal experts in the GDR, who focused on the parallel West German reforms as means to foster support for their own legislation. They called the West German Equal Rights Act "a farce" and stated that it reinforced the "three big K's" and the regulations of the old Civil Code.[59] Each of these publications delivered the same general message to readers: the GDR's reforms were nonpareil and the best step towards addressing social and economic disparities.

On 11 November 1965, the Ministers' Council of the GDR issued its approval and sent the legislative draft to the Volkskammer, where, in early December, various subcommittees met to finalize the draft of the Family Code. In support of the legislation, the Committee for Labor and Social Policy suggested supplementing the new Family Code with housing policies to encourage "child-abundant families," better childcare facilities, better promotion opportunities for working women, and further aid for single parents.[60] The committee also reiterated the SED's desire to outdo the West. The chairman stated: "The sense is not – as in bourgeois family law – to establish an abundance of complicated juridical formulations for marriage, in which a conflict may occur … but rather a way of behaviour for the people with the disposition for marriage, a responsibility that springs from a high moral position that the marriage has in a socialist society."[61] With this statement, the chairman was making a subtle critique of the West while lauding the new morality of the East. The committee acknowledged, however, the ongoing conflict between the GDR and FRG, asking Benjamin to reiterate "how much bigger the interest must be, if West German women had such a law … The national meaning may not be abstract, but rather must be concretely defined."[62]

The idea of a unified legal system arose in discussions held by the Constitutional and Legal Committee of the Volkskammer a few days later. At one point, Benjamin called the new law an example to follow, unlike the West German version, which she argued "failed to regulate existing daily problems of the family" and deserved "to replace the BGB in museums."[63] When Benjamin spoke to her fellow parliamentarians, she emphasized that family law was akin to the Legal Code of Labor, the Law for LPGs, and education law. It was a "deciding cornerstone" in "state development."[64] She was declaring, in effect, that the new Family Code was progressive while the Western law was archaic.

In December 1965, the Volkskammer met to approve the new Family Code. Several themes characterized the session. Benjamin reiterated the historic importance of the Family Code to the SED's agenda for "economic and social development, [and] the unified socialist legal system."[65] Sharing these sentiments, Roberta Gropper, a DFD/FDGB member representing the Committee for Work and Social Policy, stated that the new Family Code was important because it would expand women's equality in the workplace to their families and had potential "for the development of a new, socialist morality."[66] Both comments made it clear that the SED saw the GDR's economic changes as a triumph and that it could now turn its attention to social, legal, and moral transformations, using the family as its vessel.

The transformation of the GDR's family law into one with the aim of "building socialism" came about with a constant eye towards the West. Benjamin pointed out that the West German family law (passed in 1957) perpetuated the old capitalist and patriarchal structures of the BGB.[67] Her colleague Inge Lange took this point a step further, condemning the "men of the bourgeois monopoly in the Bonn cabinet, the ideologues of the CDU/CSU and their employees in the editorial and radio stations beyond the Elbe" for spreading false information about the new Family Code in the GDR.[68] She added that the Family Code attracted "huge attention in the West German public sphere," causing "West German families to compare our law with the West German reality and [they] can recognize, which state efforts exist for a healthy, stable family."[69] Finally, resorting again to the language of unification, Lange asserted that the "reactionary forces in West Germany … already destroy the unity of Germany."[70] The members of the Volkskammer were relying on comparison with the West to garner support for the new Family Code, insisting that it was the West, not the East, that had divided family law and thereby weakened women's status in society.

The law went into effect on 1 April 1966. The approval of the new Family Code amounted to a revolution. In stark contrast to the old Civil Code, which divested married women and mothers of equal rights and power vis-à-vis their husbands, the new socialist Family Code prescribed a more egalitarian family model. Earlier legislation such as the 1950 Law for the Protection of Motherhood had removed controversial provisions such as the right of men to make all decisions for their wives and children. Now, the Family Code designated both spouses as equal partners in marriage, childrearing, and household maintenance. All property earned or bought during the marriage was common property. The law now allowed no-fault divorce. It offered other concrete changes besides, such as permitting married couples to take either spouse's surname. Except for some minor revisions in 1975, the Family Code would remain valid in the GDR until August 1990.

In the meantime, the GDR continued to undergo major changes. After initial successes, by the mid-1960s, Ulbricht's NES was encountering growing criticism. Moreover, Ulbricht was on the outs with the new Soviet leader, Leonid Brezhnev. By 1967, Ulbricht was eager to regain control over the party-led government. He forced Benjamin to step down from the Ministry of Justice that year. That same year, at the Party Congress, he rebranded the NES as the Economic System of Socialism and declared that a new constitution was needed that would accurately reflect the historical progression of the GDR since 1949. On 9 April 1968, after weeks of public discussion and a plebiscite, the new constitution went into effect. The 1968 constitution abandoned the façade of democratic pluralism. It formally designated the GDR "as simply 'a socialist state of workers and farmers.'"[71] It explicitly forbade democratic structures such as political parties (besides the SED and those in the National Front) and was far more Stalinist than its 1949 predecessor.[72]

The 1968 constitution marked another turning point for the equal rights of men and women in the GDR. Most significantly, for the purposes of this book, it introduced a new equal rights clause. The old constitution guaranteed men and women equal rights and promised marriage and the family special state protection. The new constitution elevated these earlier stipulations with this guarantee: "Men and women are equal and have the same legal status in all areas of social, public [staatlich], and personal life. The promotion of women, especially in professional qualification, is a social and state goal." The new text also qualified that it was the socialist state that protected mothers and children, promising that "pregnancy leave, special medical care, and material and financial support will be granted through birth and child allowances."[73]

These expanded forms of state support would not go into effect until the 1970s, under new leadership in the GDR. In 1971, Erich Honecker took over as First Secretary of the SED. Walter Ulbricht – viewed as a relic of the Stalinist era – had faced humiliating economic failures and political missteps vis-à-vis the new Soviet leadership. Brezhnev, in office since 1964, had been pursuing détente with the United States, a policy with which Ulbricht disagreed. With the support of Soviet leaders, Ulbricht was ousted and Honecker installed as First Secretary. Honecker now placed the GDR on a different course. Until this point, the dictatorship's focus had been on providing basic needs, not fulfilling consumers' desires.[74] Under Honecker, the GDR became a "welfare dictatorship," meaning that he aimed to raise the living standards of East Germans.[75] For married women and mothers especially, Honecker's reforms represented a significant change. Since its inception, the GDR had rhetorically supported women's equality and had permitted women to work full-time. Now, under Honecker's government, paid maternity leave was lengthened, the workweek was shortened, wages were increased, family tax credits rewarded larger families, and guaranteed housework days were extended to all women, regardless of marital status. New construction projects ensured larger apartments equipped for appliances that would make housework easier.[76] These reforms set the GDR on a new path regarding women's rights.

It was not until after the collapse of the GDR that academics pursued serious study of what women's roles in the family and workplace had looked like under Honecker. Unlike in West Germany, sociology had not been well developed as an academic discipline in East Germany. As with other levels of education in the GDR, SED party loyalists had taken over higher education, imbuing it with a Marxist-Leninist, materialist agenda. In the 1950s, universities such as Humboldt University of Berlin did not incorporate any study of fields, such as sociology, that were deemed too "Western" or "bourgeois." As a result, the types of surveys of family life that could be taken in the FRG were not conducted in the Soviet zone or the nascent GDR in the 1950s. In the mid- to late 1950s, the SED changed course. Nikita Khrushchev's rise to power in the Soviet Union after Joseph Stalin's death in March 1953 had prompted a "thaw." His famous "Secret Speech," delivered to the Communist Party of the Soviet Union in February 1956, hastened a bloc-wide defrosting of higher education. SED cadres were now expected to provide more of an empirical basis for their materialist interpretations. Sociologists, once largely shunned, began finding their way into East German research institutes and universities. It would be a few decades, however, before East German academics began addressing issues such as women's roles, marriage, and the family.

Thus, reflections on marriage, the family, and women's rights in decades past did not come until after German reunification. For academics like Sibylle Meyer and Eva Schulze, the early 1960s were a "breaking point," a time when the SED regime began to take women's full employment more seriously.[77] Unlike earlier studies conducted in West Germany, which zeroed in almost exclusively on examining male authority, Meyer and Schulze's focused on different generations of women's experiences under state socialism. Their study ultimately suggested that the GDR had successfully changed its denizens' mindsets through social policy. One prominent theme was the triangulation between women's work, childrearing, and generational status. The juxtaposed statements of Frau

J. (born 1936) and Frau Z. (born 1970) offer some insights into the perceived changes within the GDR. Frau J. noted that hallmarks of the GDR social welfare net, such as preschools (*Kinderkrippen*) and childcare subsidies, did not yet exist when she was younger and raising her children.[78] In contrast, Frau Z. stated that she always knew she would have children and a career; unlike Frau J., she had no doubt she would be able to juggle it all.[79]

A second theme at the heart of their study was equality between partners. Younger interviewees implied that the gendered division of labour was dissipating. Frau S. (born 1955), for instance, stated that she would drop off and pick up their child while her husband did the grocery shopping for the family.[80] Similarly, Frau K. (born 1958) spoke of alternating childcare and grocery shopping with her husband, because it was too difficult to shop with a small child.[81] In each case, the men seemed to be stepping up as more equal partners in the 1970s. Though by the time of Meyer and Schulze's survey, the matter was irrelevant – reunification policies had eliminated the East German welfare state – the women's responses spoke to major shifts in the GDR over the course of its existence.

At the same time, other studies demonstrated that a deep-seated cultural conservatism continued to exist in the GDR.[82] Petra P., for instance, experienced pressure to marry. Born in 1953, she became pregnant while she was attending university in the early 1970s. Though the 1949 constitution and the 1965 Family Code did not require her to marry, her parents urged her to do so. She eventually divorced her alcoholic husband and remarried. Her case demonstrates two key points about the relationship between legal changes and women's lives. On the one hand, Petra witnessed the power of cultural conservatism still present in the GDR by the late 1960s and early 1970s. Despite all the changes under the GDR, her parents still adhered to old notions of marriage and family structures, which ended up pushing Petra into an early and unsuccessful marriage. On the other hand, the relaxation of divorce law meant that Petra could easily exit that marriage, a right that would have been denied to her before 1965. Similarly, Eva S. got pregnant out of wedlock in her early twenties. Her parents, embarrassed by the prospect of an illegitimate grandchild and unmarried daughter, kicked her out of the house.[83] While she did eventually marry the father, she nearly lost custody of their child in divorce proceedings because her husband argued that she spent too much time at work and did not spend enough time at home with the child.[84] Both cases demonstrate that cultural conservatism was still quite strong in the GDR, even when the legal system offered a path to more equal rights.

While the law promised complete equality, practice in many areas was often different. Another common theme among the women interviewed was the sense of "false emancipation" in the GDR, especially when it came to the imbalance between work life and domestic duties.[85] Despite total equality under the law, women still did the bulk of household work. This trend was true regardless of age or generation. Katharina S. (b. 1942), for instance, had her children prior to the Family Code's approval and the installation of the welfare state in the GDR. At the time, she could only stay home for two months with her newborn, although the SED-led government later increased this time to one year. She had to keep working, so she placed her child in a *Kinderkrippe*, or a day care centre.[86] Similarly, Gitta N. remarked that in her line of work (filmmaking), women were rare because "women always had other responsibilities and couldn't devote themselves 150 percent to their careers. It's women who bear children, not men. It's women who take care of children, not men. Those are the classic images with which we lived."[87] For these women in the GDR, childrearing remained primarily a woman's domain.

Several women stressed that while the GDR's legal system supported equality, the reality was much different. Several interviewees mentioned that after the *Wende*, their state-sponsored social support systems were cut. Many suggested, however, that the state system had not been particularly effective under the GDR. Maria C., for instance, pointed out that work schedules made it difficult for mothers to do laundry, cook, or conduct bureaucratic businesses.[88] Tina F. similarly cited the long work hours, though she praised the GDR's state-subsidized daycare system and school system.[89] According to Tina F., childcare and housework prevented women in the GDR from attaining the higher education and training they needed to progress in their careers.[90] The state provided women a paid "housework day," but several women alluded to problems with this. Maria C. pointed out that it was not enough time off to accomplish much; furthermore, it was not initially given to single women without children.[91] Still, compared to West Germany, where no state-subsidized daycare existed and women had been actively discouraged from working full-time until the 1960s, the GDR seemed to be working for women.

Although the GDR had introduced no-fault divorce and expanded women's rights in other critical ways far beyond what West Germany had done in the 1950s and 1960s, East German women still struggled for complete equality with men in their daily lives. In the GDR, this societal consensus manifested itself in the discussions surrounding the new 1968 constitution, which included a much stronger equality clause. For older generations of East Germans – some born prior to the division of Germany, some born early in the GDR's existence – it was difficult to shake long-held social and cultural beliefs and practices as they related to gender roles, particularly the gendered division of labour and the stigma of illegitimacy. It was only after Honecker's reforms in the 1970s that these old notions and behaviours started to change widely. Furthermore, in 1975, the SED initiated reforms to the 1965 Family Code in the GDR. The 1975 Introductory Act to the Civil Code of the German Democratic Republic altered some key passages in the 1965 legislation, namely concerning inheritance and parental authority. In addition, Eric Honecker, the new SED General Secretary and chairman of the Ministers' Council of the GDR, began to introduce welfare measures. He did so in response to both women's demands within the GDR and pressure from the Soviet Union to change course and help workers.[92] By this point, under Honecker's "welfare dictatorship," many East Germans' notions of the ideal family and partnership had begun to change as they embraced single motherhood and more state aid for childrearing and reproduction. Honecker and the SED were ready to enact pro-natalist policies to restore the declining birth rate and add momentum to the shift away from heavy industry towards consumerism.[93]

West Germany after Equality, 1957–1970s

In June 1957, while the GDR was struggling to pass its own law, the West German Bundestag finally approved the Equal Rights Act. When the CDU/CSU won an overwhelming majority in the September 1957 elections, however, the party did so with the knowledge that it had not won over every segment of West German society. Nor had it been able to push through the patriarchal law the party had championed since the early 1950s. The ruling party was finally forced to compromise. For women's associations, members of the SPD and the FDP, and other social organizations, the new law was a triumph, but only in certain areas of marital and family relations. The new law still reinforced the male-breadwinner/female-homemaker family model, ensuring that married women still attended to their domestic obligations above all. Throughout the 1960s and early 1970s, then, marriage and family law remained controversial. The FRG was aware almost immediately that the Equal Rights Act was incomplete. West Germans would be unable to change it, however, until after 1968, when the political situation became more favourable to progressive reforms.

The lingering limitations of the 1957 law were not lost on contemporaries. Almost immediately, the West German media had offered a range of commentary on its most controversial stipulations. Some newspapers were congratulatory, calling the law a "significant step" towards marital equality.[94] Others were more critical. *Die Zeit*, for example, declared that the Bundestag had "allowed the fallacy to resurface … about the legal anchoring of the equality of women and mothers."[95] Similarly, *Der Spiegel* explored the frenzy of the final weeks before the law went into effect on 1 July 1958. According to the anonymous author, "ten thousand married men and in fewer numbers married women hurried in the last weeks to their notaries" as they anticipated the arrival of the forthcoming law.[96] Under the new marital property scheme, couples could manage each other's property only if they had express permission. Presumably, West Germans rushed to notaries to formally establish that one spouse could manage the other's property. The author praised the new, equitable property scheme but disparaged the law's treatment of parental rights, for it continued to invest all final authority in the father. "The inequality of men and women," the author asserted, "has been fully accomplished here."[97]

As *Der Spiegel* identified, unequal parental rights remained a point of contention in the Federal Republic. In July 1959, a year after the law went into effect, the Federal Constitutional Court ruled that men no longer had complete parental authority. That court's decision can be attributed in part to the intervention of Erna Scheffler, the only female judge on the high court. Scheffler had earned a law degree in 1914, working first as a lawyer and then as a judge before the Nazis expelled her from her position because of her "non-Aryan" heritage.[98] Scheffler's earlier correspondence with liberal feminists like Marie-Elisabeth Lüders had attuned her to the main problems with family law reforms.

The 1957 law and subsequent 1959 ruling were important strides for women's rights in marriage and the family, but several issues, such as divorce and illegitimacy, were left unresolved by the end of the 1950s. An expansion of divorce rights – specifically, replacing the guilt clause with no-fault divorce – was an issue the Bundestag had skirted in the 1950s. Also, the 1957 law still reified the sexual division of labour. It had loosened regulations so that married women had more leeway to work part-time, but they were still only supposed to do so if it was reconcilable with their household obligations. Family law also continued to reinforce hierarchies among women. The debates of the 1950s had barely touched on illegitimacy law and the rights of unwed mothers; at their core, these had been discussions of married women's rights. These issues were left for the politicians of the 1960s to tackle.

Dramatic changes came on 11 August 1961, when the Bundestag passed the Law to Reform Family Law. The new law expanded the rights of children born after the dissolution of a marriage (a subject that had been ignored in the earlier debates).[99] It provided further avenues for men and children to dispute legitimacy.[100] The new law also overturned several measures in the 1946 Allied Control Council law. For instance, those who had committed adultery in the past were no longer barred from marrying again.[101] Also, women no longer had to wait ten months to remarry.[102] The law also granted greater authority to the custody court. For example, the court now had the authority to permit special dispensations for men and women to marry before the age of majority, or to marry people related by marriage or "sexual relations."[103] Foreigners could seek the court's dispensation to marry without a witness from their home.[104] Despite all these changes, the 1961 law left other matters as they were. For example, women were still nominally in charge of the household, and illegitimacy would remain a legal disadvantage until 1970.[105] Divorce also remained unaddressed. The CDU/CSU had proposed adding no-fault divorce to the legislation, but the SPD and FDP rejected the measure in favour of broader reforms.[106]

Since the 1961 law did not address illegitimacy or make full-scale divorce reforms, Social Democrats and some Free Democrats continued pressuring their Christian conservative compatriots throughout the early 1960s to change family law and societal perceptions of marriage and the family more broadly. For instance, an SPD-led Bundestag committee determined in its 1963 "Survey of the Situation of Women in Professions, Family, and Society" that housewives' contributions were increasingly being viewed as equal to men's work outside the home and that there was a "new understanding of marriage as partnership."[107] The same report noted that "the development process is still in flux" and that legal changes to the status of women had not yet upended lingering social practices.[108] The SPD vowed in 1964 at its Party Congress to work towards women's equality, noting that this area had yet to be fully addressed.

The SPD and some FDP members had drafted these reports, the impact of which would largely depend on the waning power of the CDU/CSU and their ability to accumulate electoral power. The 17 September 1961 election saw the CDU/CSU lose its absolute majority in the Bundestag as the SPD and the FDP made electoral gains of 4.4 and 5.1 per cent respectively.[109] The final tallies put the CDU/CSU at 45.3 per cent, the SPD at 36.2, and the FDP at 12.8. The SPD's marked shift towards the centre with the 1959 Godesberg Program had boosted its electoral prospects. Sensing that the CDU/CSU's support among women within the party was crumbling, in November 1961, Konrad Adenauer appointed Elisabeth Schwarzhaupt as the first female member of his cabinet; she would lead the newly created Federal Ministry of Health. Adenauer, who had always been reticent about women's equality, found his hand forced when CDU women conducted a sit-in to convince him to appoint a female cabinet minister.[110]

In October 1963, Christian conservative rule weakened still more when Adenauer resigned as chancellor following a year of scandals such as the *Der Spiegel* affair.[111] The Minister of Economics, Ludwig Erhard, was appointed his successor and held on to power through the 1965 election thanks to a coalition with the FDP. At times, Erhard's administration gave in to the demands of the parliamentary opposition. In 1965, while still chancellor, he agreed to commission a two-year study on the status of the family in West Germany, intended to "assess the material and spiritual situation of the family" in order to "instruct a rapidly changing society."[112]

Erhard did not stay in power long enough to see the results of that report. In fact, he held on for only one more year, until November 1966. By then, the economy had begun tanking, and the FDP withdrew from the CDU/CSU–FDP coalition for the first time in nearly two decades. Kurt-Georg Kiesinger, a Christian Democrat from Baden-Württemberg whose earlier membership in the Nazi Party had drawn scrutiny throughout his time in post-war politics, served as chancellor from 1966 to 1969. Kiesinger formed a grand coalition with the FDP and the SPD. For the first time ever in West German politics, the Social Democrats enjoyed a modicum of power in the Bundestag. At this point, the FRG entered "a second foundational era for West German social policy" and the welfare state, a decision largely shaped by changing family structures.[113]

Under Kiesinger's leadership, two important things happened. First, the report commissioned by Erhard was presented to the Bundestag in January 1968. Those who drafted it made it clear that it was a "situational analysis rather than a performance report" on the status of the family.[114] In addition to exploring the condition of the family in the FRG, the report homed in on another familiar theme: the status of family law and families in the GDR. Most of the report was simply informative, offering commentary on the different sections of the Family Code and comparing data from the GDR and FRG. It was generally apparent that the Bundestag had accepted the status quo with East Germany, for the data analysis seemed largely devoid of politicized commentary. Some parts of the report, however, highlighted the lingering tensions between the two sides.[115] For instance, the report's authors contended that "the situation of the family in the other part of Germany was decidedly influenced by the political and economic developments after the war."[116] Bundestag members remained reluctant to acknowledge that family law in West Germany had been influenced by the same trends. Furthermore, the authors continued to blame the SED in the GDR for dividing Germany along cultural and legal lines. They maintained that the passage of the Family Code in 1965 had "removed an important part of the legal unity of Germany."[117] They did not acknowledge, however, that West Germany had passed its own legislation in 1957 and had contributed to legal division nearly a decade before the GDR. Even by 1968, the earlier Cold War tensions present in family law debates had not disappeared, and they still factored into West German politicians' deliberations over the status of women and the family in the FRG.

The changes in marital and familial constellations continued to occupy the attention of West German policy-makers on both sides of the aisle. In 1968, the West German Ministry of Justice established a Marriage Law Commission. By this point, SPD member and Protestant leader Gustav Heinemann headed the Ministry of Justice, which had long been under the control of the FDP or the CDU/CSU, and he pushed through his party's reforms. Heinemann, incidentally, had been instrumental in 1954 in opposing the GDR's Family Code, using his position as a Protestant leader to place pressure on the SED. Throughout 1970 and again in 1972 – this time under SPD member Gerhard Jahn's leadership – this commission assembled a list of proposals for divorce law and other regulations.

The Social Democrats had long spearheaded reforms from within the Bundestag. Further momentum now came from outside the parliament, in the form of the 1968 New Women's Movement.[118] In January 1968, women in the Socialist German Student League (SDS) formed the Action Council on Women's Liberation, with the goal of addressing childcare. To that end, they founded the Kinderläden movement. Months later, in September 1968, the women involved in this movement gained infamy at the SDS convention in Frankfurt am Main. When movement leader Helke Sander addressed the male members of the convention, pleading for their support, they ignored her. Frustrated, Sigrid

Damm-Rüger threw a tomato at male SDS leaders. The moment is often hailed as the start of the New Women's Movement in West Germany.

Like its predecessors – the various women's associations active in the 1940s and 1950s – the New Women's Movement wanted to ameliorate the uneven burden women faced in society, particularly the demands of juggling paid work and motherhood. For the prior generation, this issue had two facets. First, a consensus had to be achieved regarding the complementary "equal but different" roles that men and women played in society. Even the SPD in the 1950s agreed that married women, if possible, should be afforded the opportunity to stay home. The difference was that the SPD recognized that circumstances would not allow many women to be full-time homemakers and mothers. The SPD wanted to harness state power to give women and couples flexibility as required. The CDU/ CSU wanted to use the power of the state to reify more rigid gender roles. Second, the prior generation's efforts required working within the system. For them, the key to change had been working within official channels – circulating petitions, for example – to send a collective message to the Adenauer government.

The New Women's Movement diverged from the earlier movement in two ways. For one thing, it no longer bought the idea that men and women were "equal but different." Instead, it promoted autonomy and self-determination for women as well as solidarity among women.[119] For 1968ers, self-determination meant the right to choose, whether that referred to bodily autonomy or to the workplace. Moreover, their take on gender roles went beyond recognizing and responding to circumstantial change. For 1968ers, the next logical step was liberation and the reconfiguration of society. Instead of embracing laws or policies that protected reproductive and domestic labour – and thus reinforced women's place as homemakers and mothers – 1968ers rebelled against them. The shift was not just ideological – the introduction of birth control in the FRG in 1961 helped convince women that autonomy was possible.[120] Moreover, unlike their forebears, the women of the 1968 New Women's Movement no longer sought to work within the spaces men had assigned to them – not in their homes, their partnerships, or the public sphere. Rather than seeking state support for mothers, the 1968ers went outside the system, creating their own childcare options via the Kinderläden movement. Similarly, they opted for extraparliamentary political protests instead of trying to negotiate with unsympathetic politicians in the Bundestag.

The New Women's Movement soon had little to worry about, for it had gained a sympathetic ally in the federal government in 1969 with the rise of Willy Brandt, the FRG's first chancellor from the SPD. In the September 1969 elections, the SPD gained considerable strength. While it did not gain enough votes to earn a majority in the Bundestag, it had enough support to form a coalition government with the FDP and appoint Brandt as the new chancellor. Brandt had been gaining name recognition in West German households. Born just before the First World War broke out, Brandt had joined the Socialist Youth at a young age and eventually escaped Nazi Germany in 1933, fearing political persecution. He went to Norway, where he participated in the antifascist resistance. He returned to Berlin in 1946 to work as a journalist. He entered politics in 1949 as a Bundestag representative from West Berlin and later became the mayor of West Berlin, serving from 1957 to 1966. He made his first bid for chancellor in 1961, losing to Adenauer. His second bid in 1965 similarly failed. The waning popularity of the CDU/CSU and the backing of the SDS and the Extraparliamentary Opposition (APO) helped Brandt secure the post in 1969.

The SPD/FDP coalition now had enough clout to push through reforms in lingering problem areas, such as marriage and family law. One FDP representative later called those reforms the "centrepiece" of the SPD/FDP agenda.[121] The other central pillar of Brandt's agenda was *Ostpolitik*, or the "new Eastern policy," which had important consequences for marital and familial relations as well. *Ostpolitik* was intended to restore relations between the GDR and the FRG. It was a recalibration of the Hallstein Doctrine, which was predicated on the belief that the FRG should not formally recognize the GDR. On 26 May 1972, for instance, the Transit Agreement between the two Germanys permitted West Germans to travel to East Berlin and East Germany; in return, East Germans could visit the FRG on an emergency basis to see family members. On 11 May 1973, the Bundestag finally approved the Basic Treaty, which established formal relations between the two Germanys. As noted earlier, West German politicians, especially those in the CDU/CSU, had relied heavily on the Hallstein Doctrine as a justification for avoiding any critical discourse with East Germany regarding family law reforms. Furthermore, the strong anticommunist sentiments of the early Adenauer years had served to eliminate communist opposition in West Germany, which helped tilt discussions of family law reforms in conservatives' favour. Now, the two Germanys recognized each other and travel across borders was much simpler than before.

However, these new relations affected the two Germanys unevenly. While West Germans and West Berliners could travel to East Germany with few consequences, East Germans were not afforded the same privileges and faced harsh punishment if they violated travel regulations. In some cases, more open travel had detrimental effects on families. The case of Verona Chambers, an East German woman, illustrates this problem. Her husband received permission to visit his aunt in West Berlin in 1988 and never returned. Verona now encountered discrimination from East German state officials, who encouraged her to pursue a divorce. By the time her request to immigrate was granted, the Berlin Wall was falling.[122] In Chambers's case, she did not opt to divorce her husband. But it is telling that the SED regime offered divorce as an option in this context. Though the 1965 Family Code had legalized no-fault divorce, the SED was set on encouraging the heteronormative nuclear family. In this case, it preferred pursuing divorce and family separation over family unity to prevent further defections to West Germany.

Image 5.3. A West Berlin woman visits her son's family in East Berlin at Christmas (26 December 1964). A photograph, taken by Erwin Schneider, depicting a West Berlin resident who was able to travel to East Berlin to see her son and his family. Starting in 1963, West Berliners could travel to the East at Christmas time if they applied for visas and passed inspection at the border. Image courtesy of Bundesarchiv Berlin-Lichterfelde.

Rapidly changing social conditions and the ongoing problems facing couples and families finally led West German politicians to revisit the issue of equal rights in marriage and the family. In 1973, for instance, the West German Bundestag reviewed the initial draft of the First Act for the Reform of Family Law – the successor to the 1957 Equal Rights Act. The legislation, proposed by Brandt government, would strengthen the old law's commitment to "spousal community," allow couples to decide which surname they preferred (as long as it was the same), and make both spouses responsible for the household income. Also, it would no longer restrict married women's right to employment.[123] More significantly, the legislative draft introduced no-fault divorce and new regulations on filing and subsequent judicial procedures.[124] The Minister of Justice,

Gerhard Jahn, introduced the new legislative draft to the Bundestag on 8 June 1973. Jahn himself had spent his early life witnessing injustice. He was born in 1927, the eldest son of a mixed Protestant–Jewish couple. His parents divorced in 1942, supposedly so that his father could escape his marriage to a Jew and marry his mistress, who was expecting a child. His Jewish mother, Lilli Jahn, was a well-known physician who opposed the Nazis, which led to her incarceration at Breitenau and murder at Auschwitz. Jahn, spared because of his "mixed race" status in Nazi Germany, was eventually pressed into Wehrmacht service. After the war, he earned his Abitur, studied law, and entered the SPD. It is not a far reach to assume that these early experiences with marriage inequality and familial strife left a deep impression on him and contributed to his personal desire to see through reforms of the law.

Jahn's opening comments pointed to long-standing problems with the law dating back to its inception in 1900. He noted poignantly that even as some legal regulations changed, "to this day, a unilateral primacy of the husband remains sustained."[125] The original law enforced a gendered division of labour, and women and children still had to bear their husbands' and fathers' names, among other measures.[126] By the early 1970s, however, circumstances had changed. Jahn now called for a strengthening of legal equality between partners, a loosening of divorce regulations, an easing of the social and economic burdens of partners after divorce, aid to elderly divorcees with pension schemes (particularly housewives, who had been excluded from the workforce for years), and assorted procedural changes.[127]

In addressing each of these points, Bundestag members proposed different solutions. The SPD and FDP agreed that the law could not impose a separation of roles on men and women, or as Jahn called it, "an obsolete legal definition of marriage as a housewife marriage."[128] The only role of the law, according to the SPD and FDP, was to ensure that men and women were equal in the realm of family law.[129] Meanwhile, the CDU/CSU, though it did not stress the importance of equality, more or less agreed with the SPD and FDP that the end goal was to strengthen partnerships. The CDU/CSU focused instead on "quality of life" for marital partners.[130]

Another point on which all sides tacitly agreed was that divorce regulations needed to be loosened. They did not agree, however, on how to handle the social and economic consequences, especially alimony. Under the old Civil Code, one party had to be declared the guilty party, and the guilty party was not entitled to alimony. The alimony provision was closely linked to the problem of pensions. These provisions adversely affected married, unemployed women, who, if declared the guilty party, would have no financial support after years away from the workforce. Pensions were especially tricky for couples who divorced late in life. For retired women who had spent decades out of the labour force, their husband's pension was their only potential source of income. While all parties could agree that the guilt principle could be removed, they could not agree on how alimony and pensions should be allocated. The SPD called for alimony to be allocated to either partner, but contingent on four factors: age, illness, child-care responsibilities, or an inability to find employment in their field. In these cases, the SPD argued, the ex-spouse should be entitled to alimony from the other. Pensions, then, would be divided between the two spouses.[131]

The CDU/CSU, however, called for clarity on several issues related to alimony and pensions. It demanded to know whether the law would differentiate between the "separation period" and thereafter.[132] According to the CDU/CSU, claims to alimony ought only to be made in exceptional cases and should not be the rule. Erhard used the example of a woman who leaves her husband to rendezvous with ex-boyfriends. In this kind of case, he asserted, "the sense of justice is not reasonable."[133] The CDU/CSU lawmakers also opposed the new pension scheme, arguing that it took away from those truly in need in West German society.[134]

In the end, the legislative draft went off for review by the Bundestag Legal Committee and several subcommittees.[135] In the meantime, West German poli-tics underwent a shake-up when the West German intelligence service discovered that one of Brandt's personal assistants, Günter Guillaume, was an East German spy. Brandt resigned in May 1974, handing the West German government over to his successor, Helmut Schmidt, a less inflammatory SPD centrist. Even with this change of command, the Bundestag's constellation would not change until the September 1976 elections, which was after the 1976 legislation was passed. The SPD was still the largest party in the Bundestag and still formally in a coalition with the FDP in 1975, when the legislation went up for review.

The First Bill for the Reform of the Marriage and Family Law finally returned to the Bundestag in December 1975; it passed in 1976. In many ways, the draft and the main points of discussion had not changed much from 1973. The Bun-destag was still trying to "solve" alimony, pensions, the dissolution of marriage, and the fundamental inequalities embedded in marital relations, among other assorted matters. What the Bundestag eventually settled on was quite like the 1973 proposal. The new law addressed two key components of the previous divorce legislation. First, it addressed the causes of divorce. The guilt principle was replaced with the concept of irreconcilable differences, with some precon-ditions attached. Couples separated for a year could easily obtain a divorce; those who had been separated for three years or longer were automatically con-sidered candidates for irretrievable breakdown. Also, a hardship clause pro-vided for exceptional circumstances within the three-year separation period. Furthermore, the new law included a "kiss and make up" clause, with the goal of encouraging reconciliation, thus allowing couples to try living together again without restarting the clock on the formal separation period.

Second, the new law addressed the consequences of divorce. Perhaps most significantly, alimony payments were no longer linked to the cause of divorce.

Under the old regulations, either the guilty party or the spouse who had petitioned for divorce and obtained one with no fault (a rare circumstance) had
to pay alimony. Under the new law, alimony was only required in cases where
one spouse could not financially support himself or herself. The idea here was
to rectify economic inequality rather than harp on conduct during the marriage. Alimony could also cover educational costs, in cases where a partner had
paused his or her training during marriage. It also allowed divorced spouses to
continue to claim alimony even after remarriage. The new law also provided a
new pension scheme, which ultimately became a pension-splitting scheme. In
short: spouses who had not worked during a marriage were not entitled to their
spouse's pension if they pursued a divorce. If they had spent the entirety of the
marriage with the understanding that they would be supported in old age by
their spouse's pension, a divorce would result in a rude awakening. Therefore,
the new law proposed transferring some of the pension benefits into a social
security account for the affected spouse.

After 1 July 1977, in both Germanys, no-fault divorce, the freedom to reject
the paternal surname, and the unconditional right of women to work outside the
home were written into law. Still, West Germany faced myriad structural issues
that prevented women from experiencing more liberation. The changed law had
little effect on labour force mobilization. Compared to the GDR, women in the
FRG tended to work full-time in lower numbers. Part of this gap can be attributed to other structural problems. In the FRG, half-day schooling remained the
norm after reunification, and no state-sponsored daycare existed. Women were
forced to choose between a career and staying at home. These types of policies
and practices meant that the FRG was still primarily following a male-breadwin-
ner/female-homemaker/female part-time worker model by 1990.

Major political and economic changes within each state, as well as the recent
relaxation of tensions between the two Germanys – the crowning achievement
of Willy Brandt – facilitated these new reforms in the 1970s. Throughout the
late 1960s, Brandt had pursued his policy of *Ostpolitik*, aimed at easing tensions
between East and West.[136] By 1975, when the "First Law" was under scrutiny by
the Bundestag and the new law was approved in the GDR, the Cold War struggle that had for so long marked the discourse and decisions regarding marriage
and family law in both Germanys was beginning to thaw.

By the end of 1957, neither East Germany nor West Germany had a comprehensive law on the books. The FRG had managed to pass a law, the Equal Rights Act,
that was ultimately very limited in its scope. This law still constrained women's
rights in marriage and the family in certain ways. Court cases, pressure from

the SPD and the FDP, and the 1968 New Women's Movement provided impetus for the new law in the 1970s. Meanwhile, the GDR, for all its trumpeting of a new law in 1954, had passed no new legislation at all. At the time, opposition from society had prevented radical reform. By 1965, the SED had learned crucial lessons from its last go-around. Also, the GDR was by then enclosed. This time, the ruling party was prepared to suppress opposition and push through wider-ranging reforms than it had been capable of in 1954. Twenty years later, both German states had more extensive laws on the books. The GDR had finally enacted the radical reforms in 1965 that it had promised its citizens a decade earlier. Moreover, the two German states had inched closer to each other's views on gender roles, women's rights, and the place of the family.

The 1950s had seen most of Western and Eastern Europe in a holding pattern in terms of changing gender roles; the 1960s and 1970s marked an era of change for many European states. In 1965, France changed its Civil Code to give married women full control over their personal property, although men still controlled joint marital property.[137] Italian men and women gained the right to a divorce and equal parental rights in the 1970s.[138] In addition, the 1968 social movements across Western Europe called into question long-held assumptions about gender roles. While the Soviet Union and the Eastern Bloc had ostensibly abolished patriarchal laws in the 1940s and 1950s, their governments did not follow up with more extensive state support for couples and families until the 1960s and 1970s. Many families continued to suffer because of the shortage of consumer goods (particularly appliances) that would have offset the "double burden" faced especially by employed mothers.[139]

The German–German cases continued to stand out, even in the wider context in which the winds of change were growing stronger. A few unique factors played a role here. One was the construction of the Berlin Wall. Prior to 1961, Germans could cross borders fairly frequently, at least in Berlin.[140] Divorced or separated couples could still see their children, even if they were living in different sectors. After 1961, the sealed borders cut off these contacts. This situation differed from the rest of Eastern Europe, where cross-border marriages were less frequent. Another was the 1972 treaty between the two sides. For two decades, the two Germanys had not formally recognized each other. While the borders remained closed and militarized, there were more opportunities for families to correspond and reunite. Finally, even as the two Germanys moved closer to each other in terms of marriage and family laws, patterns in everyday life in each state were diverging. By 1990, when German reunification finally took place, expectations of gender roles in the two states had become quite different. More than thirty years later, the legacies of these different laws – in terms of policies, attitudes, and nostalgia – remain evident among those of the older generation.

Conclusion

Reconstructing the Family in Comparison across Post-War Europe

Stunning pronouncements about gender and the family in Europe have rocked the media in the past decade. In Hungary and Poland, far-right, populist-run governments have invested in family subsidies and offered tax breaks in support of "traditional families."[1] In Germany, the far-right political party Alternative for Germany (AfD) has garnered attention for declaring that "the traditional family will save the German people."[2] In its 2017 official program, the party professed support for pro-natalist family policies, but only for "heterosexual nuclear families of German origin."[3] The AfD also called for tightening divorce laws, strengthening the roles of men and fathers, and outlawing "gender ideology [, which] marginalizes natural differences between the sexes."[4] Feminist organizations such as the Gunda Werner Institute have countered such claims, arguing that "democracy depends on diversity" and that it is undemocratic to "re-strengthen patriarchal thought- and behavioral patterns."[5]

The AfD's alarming rhetoric is hardly new in Germany. As this book has shown, since German unification in 1871, conservative and far-right parties have clashed with liberals and leftists over gender roles in marriage and the family, which both sides have viewed as the basis of German society and culture. This struggle intensified in 1896, when German legislators passed the Civil Code, a controversial law that designated women as second-class citizens in marriage, parental rights, and marital property. Throughout all the upheavals in early twentieth-century Germany, the Civil Code remained intact. The law stayed valid well into the post-war period, when the burgeoning Cold War split Germany into the liberal democratic, capitalist Federal Republic of Germany (FRG) in the West and the communist German Democratic Republic (GDR) in the East. On both sides of the German–German border, politicians, the media, leaders of social organizations, and average Germans debated how to adapt the old Civil Code to fit the agendas of their newly divided and competing states. Finally, legislators in both states replaced the old law with the 1957 Equal Rights Act in the West and the 1965 Family Code in the East. The tensions generated by the Cold War conflict drove forward, but at times halted, the parallel reforms of marriage and family law in the 1950s and early 1960s. This book has also outlined the paradoxical relationship between law and daily life for East and West Germans.

Unexpectedly, despite all the efforts of politicians in both Germanys, family laws in the two states came closer to resembling each other in the 1970s than they had in the first two decades after the Second World War. In 1975, the SED initiated reforms to the 1965 Family Code in the GDR. The Introductory Act to the Civil Code of the German Democratic Republic, which came into force on 19 June 1975, altered some key passages of the 1965 law, namely those concerning inheritance and parental authority. Meanwhile, the Bundestag put the finishing touches on the First Law for the Reform of the Marriage and Family Law, approved by the Bundestag on 14 June 1976 and enacted on 1 July 1977. By 1977, in both states, no-fault divorce, the freedom to reject the paternal surname, and the unconditional right of women to work outside the home were written into law. Yet by the late 1970s, with the Cold War beginning to thaw, East and West German politicians continued to accept the existence of two different models of marital and family life in the two Germanys.

That moment of acceptance was a long time coming. In May 1945, when the Second World War ended, it was unclear which paths Europeans, and especially Germans, would choose to rebuild their societies.[6] Leaders of women's organizations across occupied Germany had one vision: using the post-war moment as a tabula rasa for women's rights, especially in marital and familial relations. They urged their respective parties and occupiers to consider changing the old Civil Code, but with only fleeting success. Everything changed with the formal separation of East and West Germany in 1949. Now gender, women's rights, and the family were no longer simply part of the post-war reconstruction process. All three had been transformed into battlegrounds in the Cold War struggle for hegemony between the two Germanys.

The special relationship between the two Germanys left its mark on the parallel family law reforms in numerous ways. Changing international relations between the two Germanys in the early Cold War fundamentally shaped the final forms of the new Equal Rights Act in the FRG and the Family Code in the GDR. The separation, the possibility of reunification, further division with the Berlin Wall, and the thawing of tensions between the two Germanys in the 1970s signified points where Cold War competition intervened, thus redirecting the parallel family law reforms in the 1950s and 1960s. The rapidly changing domestic situations in the two countries set in motion by the Cold War drove forward these reforms. In the GDR, the SED-led dictatorship, intent on "building socialism" in the early 1950s, began to crush its political opposition,

installed a centralized planned economy, and set out to foment a social revolution by radically restructuring marital and familial models. Meanwhile, West
Germany fell under the rule of the Christian conservative chancellor, Konrad
Adenauer. Despite the CDU/CSU's clear majority and Adenauer's authoritarian
style of governing, resistance in society and the Bundestag was strong enough
to force the ruling party to compromise on certain key provisions in the Equal
Rights Act, such as the one that would have removed the husband's right to
decide. In both states, the ruling parties were neither all-powerful nor invulner-
able to criticism in the 1950s. When they had to, the governing parties bowed
to society's demands.

Alongside political changes, economic reconstruction and new economic
policies drove the new marriage and family laws. In the East, early on, even
before the two sides formally divided, the Soviets and the SED set out to establish a planned, production-based economy in the Soviet zone (later, the GDR).
For both pragmatic and ideological purposes, the SED sought out female labour, initially from single women and later from married women, to support
its Five-Year Plans for its socialist "workers' and peasants' state." As a result, the
male-breadwinner/female-homemaker family model became the norm in the
GDR. Across the border in West Germany, the Christian conservative government created a social market economy that privileged male labour outside the
home and valued female labour only in the home. The Adenauer government's
own economic policies led to an economic boom so strong that policy-makers
had no choice but to permit female part-time labour. In part this was to address
the labour shortage, but mostly it was to promote consumerism by boosting
German families' spending capacity. Reluctant to abandon its idealized image
of the family, legislators settled on a "temporary" solution that allowed married
women to work part-time. This resulted in a new family model: a male breadwinner and female homemaker/part-time worker. The increasing prevalence
of this model in the FRG in the 1960s forced legislators to reconsider marriage
and divorce law in the early 1970s.

In West Germany, social and cultural expectations changed over the course
of the 1950s and 1960s until policy-makers had no choice but to seriously
reassess the law. The wartime destruction had pushed many Germans in the
Western zones of occupation towards the male-breadwinner family model as a
source of stability. Adenauer and his Christian conservative government were
more than happy to oblige those groups in society – especially Protestants and
Catholics – who demanded policies that would foster this type of family. Over
time, however, the CDU/CSU's vision of the ideal family – male breadwinner,
female homemaker – had to be "modernized" in the face of profound economic
changes, political forces within and outside the FRG, and societal opposition
from women's organizations, trade unions, independent professional associations, and some media outlets. Policy-makers decided to use part-time work

for mothers to keep the breadwinner family intact; this would allow women to earn the surplus income many families desired in order to consume more goods. Meanwhile, by the end of the 1960s, a new generation of women who had been raised in West Germany began to challenge the gendered norms under which they had been socialized. By 1968, their new expectations no longer fit the economic and political circumstances they were encountering as young adults. Their frustrations became the cornerstones of the rising New Women's Movement.

The political, social, and economic changes spurred by the Cold War competition were the most immediate driving forces behind the two Germanys' family law reforms, but there were other, less obvious factors besides that accounted for their diverging paths. For instance, the remnants of old legal structures and institutions mattered immensely in the GDR and the FRG. The two states inherited the same 1900 law, but they dealt with its legacies quite differently. For political and economic reasons tied to the Cold War, the SED abandoned early on the Weimar template for equal rights in the constitution. At the same time, the SED never objected to state protection of the family as a fundamental constitutional right, meaning that certain continuities from the Weimar Republic existed in the GDR. When it came to reforming the Civil Code, the SED attempted to balance its commitments to the family and to women's equality with men. In certain ways, the new Family Code's emphasis on egalitarian marriage was a radical departure from the 1900 Civil Code. Still, the new Family Code of 1965 emphasized long-term partnerships with abundant children as the key to building a socialist, antifascist post-war state. The SED was more willing to break with legal tradition because it claimed to be forging a new, post-fascist, socialist, post-war German state with few ties to pre-1945 Germany.

By contrast, the FRG staked its claims to legitimacy on the notion that it was a liberal democracy – albeit new and improved – in line with German tradition and that the preceding twelve years had been an aberration in the German *Rechtsstaat*. From the beginning, Christian conservative politicians and legal experts in the West wanted to keep the old Civil Code's regulations on marriage and the family, believing that sexual differences justified differences in civil rights. Later, they remained reluctant to change the Civil Code, arguing that its prescriptions for a patriarchal family structure would help the social and cultural reconstruction of (West) Germany. Finally, though, under immense pressure from Social Democrats, Free Democrats, Communists (until 1956), trade unions, women's associations, and professional organizations, they were forced to agree to compromises that reformed the constitutional and legal tradition.

In both Germanys throughout the 1950s and 1960s, the parallel reforms of marriage and family law, at their core, were about expanding the legal rights of married women and mothers and contracting the rights of married men and fathers. The 1957 Equal Rights Act, though not as far-reaching as the Free and Social Democrats had hoped, reified the traditional male-breadwinner/ female-homemaker family model by "modernizing" and reforming it. The law finally gave married women some autonomy in decision-making within their marriages and families while continuing to limit their ability to work outside the home. The Equal Rights Act thus took away rights from men on some level while still allowing them the position of authority in the home and in their partnerships. The 1965 Family Code in the GDR pursued a more radical over-haul of the old law, making partners completely equal in every regard. Still, the law did not challenge conceptions of the heteronormative, nuclear family. In daily life in the GDR, married women continued to be burdened with most domestic labour as they took on full-time jobs outside the home in the planned economy. In the 1970s, the parallel reforms of the marriage and family laws in the 1960s and 1970s in the GDR and the FRG catalysed further discussions about altering the gendered division of labour and rethinking marriage and family models. Those discussions continue to this day.

Just as important as the more tangible social, economic, and political fac-tors was the role of language in advancing these debates. As these overarch-ing changes took place, various actors in politics, social organizations, and the media in both Germanys employed conflicting discourses to both defend and disparage legal reforms. For one thing, discourses about gender images and gender relations as the foundation of social order resonated throughout West and East Germany. In the West, Christian conservatives, echoing earlier pre-1945 arguments, lauded the patriarchal family model as set out in the Civil Code as a vessel for stabilizing calamitous post-war conditions and restoring (West) Germany to its "natural" social and gender order. Their Social Dem-ocratic, Free Democratic, and, in the first half of the 1950s, Communist op-position argued that family law needed to change with the times and adapt to a wholly different demographic reality and economic structure. The SED in the East, meanwhile, emphasized stability in its own way, focusing on how bourgeois, capitalist social and economic orders had contributed to Germa-ny's destruction. Marriages and families that were more egalitarian, their logic followed, would prevent such instability from ever infecting German territory again. Their opponents in the major churches, however, stressed that the Fam-ily Code disrupted the natural order and interfered with Christians' rights to raise their families as they pleased.

These same actors relied on rhetoric about historic memory as well. At times, they reached deep into the historic vault to the late nineteenth and early twen-tieth centuries. Some Christian conservative and Free Democratic politicians, for example, extolled previous governments' interpretations of women's status and roles in the family. Meanwhile, some Social Democratic, Free Democratic, Communist, and independent female activists in both Germanys proclaimed that past regimes had not done enough to ensure equal rights for men and women. Additionally, just about all policy-makers of all political persuasions in both Germanys agreed that the Third Reich offered a negative example of state intervention in marriage and the family.

Above all, on both sides of the German–German border, the Cold War loomed large in political discourse, albeit in different ways and to different degrees. In the East, a constant theme from the late 1940s well into the mid-1950s was the problem of legal unity. The SED desperately wanted to beat the FRG to reforms, but party leaders hesitated at times because they feared being accused of dividing Germany (though they simultaneously argued that their version of the law would unite all Germans). Once West Germany passed its 1957 law and the Berlin Wall went up, the SED was no longer concerned about unity. West Germans spoke of legal unity as well, but *how* they discussed it changed over time. In the early 1950s, the SPD tried to keep legal unity in mind. By the late 1950s, none of the major parties were mentioning possible reunification. In both states, politicians stressed how family law reforms on the other side of the Iron Curtain were detrimental to all Germans, though again, these discourses tended to be employed more heavily by the SED in the GDR.

In the end, the 1957 Equal Rights Act in the FRG and the Family Code in the GDR created similar patterns in both states. Neither law challenged the idea that the heteronormative family was the cornerstone of German society, though they imagined the relations within the family quite differently. Moreover, in practice, similar gendered divisions of labour existed on both sides of the German–German border, meaning that women typically bore the brunt of domestic labour even when the law promised them equal partnership. Still, the differences between the two sides were critical and obvious. By the mid-1970s, different responses to economic circumstances, political systems, imbalanced gender ratios, and diverging social and cultural norms had set the two states on separate paths regarding family law and gender roles.

These debates in East and West Germany took place in the context of wider, pan-European discussions about women's rights, family, and gender role transformations. To some extent, the German debates looked familiar to other Europeans. In Western Europe, contemporaries had much the same mixed reactions as West Germans. Women's rights activists wanted full equality, while policy-makers desired a "return" to the "traditional" family. Throughout the 1950s, several Western European countries pursued a series of laws and policies designed to reconstitute the traditional family and limit female emancipation. In West Germany and the Netherlands, for instance, politicians set stores' closing times at 5 p.m., a roundabout measure intended to prevent women from working full-time jobs.[7] Regulations like this had the desired effect; in 1947, 98 per cent of married Dutch women were not working outside the home.[8] Furthermore, Dutch men – much like in West Germany – remained the legal heads of their households until 1970.[9] In Great Britain, family allowances were paid to the husband as the paternal head of the family.[10] Female suffrage had been either restored or granted for the first time, yet women's formal political participation did not increase dramatically. These laws and policies were meant to severely limit women's emancipation in the name of restoring society to its old order.

Meanwhile, on the other side of the Iron Curtain, communist leaders were also talking about female emancipation and protecting families, upholding the Soviet Bloc as a "utopia of perfect sexual harmony."[11] This claim had its limits: Soviet "sexual harmony" meant reforging the traditional family and raising the birth rate, not sexual liberation.[12] Unlike in the West, the Eastern Bloc promoted female emancipation through job training and full-time paid labour.[13] Furthermore, Communist parties encouraged women's political activity through party-led women's organizations. But even though women were being integrated into the workforce, political sphere, and educational institutions in higher numbers than in the West, they never fully escaped the societal expectations of domesticity or the lower status of women. Women's wages, for instance, tended to be lower, and they often took lower-paying jobs near their homes to ensure that they could continue to carry out their household work.[14] Socialist governments promised a broad swath of social services and consumer goods to alleviate domestic burdens for women, but they rarely delivered. Differing levels of infrastructure and development across Eastern Europe, as well as consumer goods shortages, added to the weight women carried, for they were spending even more time than their Western counterparts washing laundry or searching for necessary items, such as tampons or pads, in the grocery stores.[15] Eastern European states really only offered subsidies for childbearing and childcare, which did not totally ease the "triple burden" of full-time employment, housework, and political activity for women.[16] Men did not take on the same triple burden because they did not contribute to day-to-day household upkeep in the same way.

To some degree, the two Germanys typified the trends in each sphere of influence. Women's civil equality in marriage and family law in West Germany lagged relative to British and Scandinavian laws. At the same time, West German law's treatment of women was on par with legislation in France, Italy, Spain, Portugal, and the Netherlands.[17] Sometimes, West Germany went to greater extremes than the others. As one example, family allowances were distributed to men as wage supplements, whereas in countries like France, it went to the mothers as a direct subsidy.[18] Overall, however, the FRG did not deviate dramatically from the trends in other secular liberal democracies in Western Europe. Meanwhile, the GDR closely followed trends in the Eastern Bloc regarding women's employment, maternity benefits, and so on. In some areas, such as female employment, the GDR led the Eastern Bloc and the industrialized world. By 1966, 49.1 per cent of the workforce was female.[19] In a few areas, such as the decriminalization of abortion, the SED dictatorship was slower than in most of the Soviet Bloc – it waited until 1972 to take that step.[20] Thus, gender policies in the German states, to some degree, were not radically different from those of their counterparts in the Western and Eastern spheres of influence.

Still, the two Germanys were exceptional in that they were the only states in post-war Europe that shared a common legal tradition and history, especially of the Nazi past. Furthermore, Germany was the only state divided in half by the forces of the Cold War. Other countries, like the Netherlands and Hungary, may have cited the Cold War as a reason to construct their own laws regarding gender and the family in certain ways. Countries like Austria and Czechoslovakia even shared borders with the Soviet and Western blocs. But their citizens still did not experience the social, legal, and logistical challenges wrought by the Cold War in the same ways that East and West Germans did daily. Eastern and Western Europeans outside of Germany did not have to consider the effects of dividing family law on future reunification, alimony payments, divorce, or any number of other decisions related to partnerships and parenthood. Only Germans faced that unique situation.

These differences remained evident even after German reunification in 1990. The fall of the Berlin Wall in 1989 quickly led to the reunification of Germany in 1990, with East Germany being absorbed into the Federal Republic. Virtually overnight, all the laws and policies in East Germany that had shaped women's lives – state-subsidized daycare, abortion rights, and the Family Code, among others – disappeared. In the 1990s and early 2000s, by law, all German women, regardless of their origins, were the same. This fact was not lost on women in the former East Germany, who lamented the impact of reunification on gender roles, economic opportunities, and family structures even while they welcomed other aspects of their new capitalist, democratic state. It was not until 2002 that the Civil Code saw major reforms once again. Meanwhile, the welfare state and certain subsidies, such as *Kindergeld*, has been extended to cover children from heterosexual marriages for both German and immigrant families (provided they are employed and pay into the tax system). In 2017, the Civil Code's provisions were altered to include same-sex couples.

While these are encouraging developments, Germany still faces the same tough question that first arose in the 1949 constitutional debates: what role should the state play in reconciling gender equality with the protection of families? In 2017, over 70 per cent of German women were working part- or full-time, and they tended to earn less than men. According to the Organisation for Economic Co-operation and Development (OECD), closing these gaps requires "encouraging a greater role of fathers in caregiving, strengthening childcare supports for pre-school children and developing out-of-school-hours care supports."[21] Out of the three solutions, the second – strengthening childcare support for preschoolers – remains the most elusive. More and more Germans want to send their children to daycare at an earlier age, but they cannot get placed because there are too few caretakers and not enough facilities. In 2013, the Bundestag passed a compromise solution, a law that both guaranteed parents spots for children one and older in a daycare facility and promised subsidies to stay-at-home parents if they opted out of the state-run *Kitas*. This part of the law has since been struck down by the Federal Constitutional Court.

As a result, Germans still have not found a solution that works for all parties. Germans remain hindered by childcare shortages. According to one 2022 report, German *Kitas* will be 384,000 spots short by 2023, leaving parents high and dry.[22] Often, when facing no childcare and smaller salaries than their male partners, women end up leaving the workforce. This decision can have long-term effects, including personal dissatisfaction and a stunted career trajectory that ultimately reinforces old gender hierarchies. It also affects the German (and by extension, European) economy by forcing talented workers out of the pool. Far-right parties, like the AfD, are pushing the reseparation of gender roles by proposing that stay-at-home parents be recognized as equal to state facilities, which would mean that the state would have to fund the care they provide. Hungarian, Polish, and French far-right politicians, among others, are calling for the same. But their proposals still do not resolve the core problem: structural sexism. Germans thus stand at a crossroads: they must decide what role the state should play in their daily lives. Is the role of the state to preserve the gains towards gender equality that men, women, and families have made, or is it to revert to the inequitable family model that long prevented women from achieving any kind of economic independence? Only when these inequities are eliminated will European families experience true stability and will partners see complete equality before the law.

Notes

Introduction

1 See Basic Law of the Federal Republic of Germany, 1949, http://www. documentarchiv.de/brd/1949/grundgesetz.html; "Die Verfassung der Deutschen Demokratischen Republik vom 7. Oktober 1949," http://www.documentarchiv.de /ddr/verfddr1949.html#b1.

2 Heineman, *What Difference Does a Husband Make?*, 3.

3 See Fishman, *From Vichy to the Sexual Revolution*, for the French case. Similarly, Malgorzata Fidelis's monograph *Women, Communism, and Industrialization in Postwar Poland* (Cambridge, 2010) covers the significance of gender hierarchies, traditional families, and women's work for the Polish case.

4 Moeller, *Protecting Motherhood*, 2.

5 Christoph Klessmann, "Abgrenzung und Verflechtung."

6 Oertzen, *Teilzeitarbeit und die Lust am Zuverdienen*, 12, 359.

7 Gerhard, *Frauen in der Geschichte des Rechts*, 811.

8 Oertzen and Rietzschel, "Das 'Kuckucksei' Teilzeitarbeit."

9 Hagemann, "Between Ideology and Economy"; Hagemann, "A West-German '*Sonderweg*'?"; Mattes, "Economy and Politics."

10 Hagemann, "A West-German '*Sonderweg*'?"; Mattes, "Economy and Politics"; Gerhard, "Family Law and Gender Equality," 81.

11 Moeller, *Protecting Motherhood*, 7.

12 Christoph Klessmann, "Introduction," in *The Divided Past*, 2.

13 Shortly after German reunification, historians such as Christoph Klessmann and Konrad H. Jarausch began calling for histories that foreground the special "entangled and demarcated" relationship between the two Germanys. See Klessmann, "Abgrenzung und Verflechtung"; Jarausch, "'Die Teile als Ganze erkennen," 15; Konrad H. Jarausch and Michael Geyer, *Shattered Past: Reconstructing German Histories* (Princeton: Princeton University Press, 2003), 1–33; Sabrow, "Historisierung der Zweistaatlichkeit"; Anderson, *A Dramatic*

Reinvention; Balbier, *Kalter Krieg auf der Aschenbahn*; Castillo, *Cold War on the Home Front*; Herf, *Divided Memory*; Poiger, *Jazz, Rock, and Rebels*; Schreiter, *Designing One Nation*; and Sheffer, *Burned Bridge*. While Astrid M. Eckert's monograph *West Germany and the Iron Curtain: Environment, Economy, and Culture in the Borderlands* (Oxford: Oxford University Press, 2019) does not explicitly cover both Germanys, it serves as an important study of the interactions between the two sides and references similar themes as this study.

14 Haupt and Kocka, "Comparative History," 31; Werner and Zimmermann, "Beyond Comparison," 35; Haupt and Kocka, *Comparative and Transnational History*; Kaelble, *Der Historische Vergleich*.

15 As one example, see Frank Bösch, ed. *A History Shared and Divided: East and West Germany since the 1970s* (New York: Berghahn, 2018), which barely addresses gender.

16 Merkel, "Sex and Gender in the Divided Germany." Moeller, *Protecting Motherhood*, and Harsch, *Revenge of the Domestic*, are the two classic examples of full-length studies that have laid important groundwork for understanding the politics of gender and the family in each German state, but largely excluded comparative aspects.

17 See, as examples of East–West comparisons: Heineman, *What Difference Does a Husband Make?*; Budde, *Frauen Arbeiten*; Poiger, *Jazz, Rock, and Rebels*; Sachse, *Der Hausarbeitstag*; Hagemann, "Between Ideology and Economy"; Treber, *Mythos Trümmerfrauen*; and Freeland, "Behind Closed Doors."

18 Pedersen, "Comparative History and Women's History." Pedersen observes that comparative women's and gender history can "offer meaningful explanations for particular outcomes" (99).

19 As mentioned above, recent works such as Fishman, *From Vichy to the Sexual Revolution*, and Fidelis, *Women, Communism, and Industrialization*, offer important comparative reference points.

20 For the American discussion of families in the Cold War era, see May, *Homeward Bound*; and Joanna Meyerowitz, ed., *Not June Cleaver: Women and Gender in Postwar America, 1945–1960* (Philadelphia: Temple University Press, 1994). For the Russian/Soviet case, see Utrata, *Women without Men*.

21 Ferree, *Varieties of Feminism*; Frevert, "Frauen auf dem Weg zur Gleichberechtigung." For an overview, see Davis, "The Personal Is Political."

22 For a similar comparative argument, see Jacquelyn Dowd Hall, "The Long Civil Rights Movement and the Political Uses of the Past," *Journal of American History* 91, no. 4 (2005): 1233–63.

23 In this book, I do not argue that the GDR had a developed "civil society" in the 1950s and 1960s. Still, to paraphrase historian Jürgen Kocka, I seek out the "residuals of civil society [that] survived the dictatorships." Kocka, *Civil Society and Dictatorship*, 29.

24 Harsch's *Revenge of the Domestic* most clearly lays out this narrative.

25 The following, while similar, do not explore the networks connecting these groups: Reich-Hilweg, *Männer und Frauen sind gleichberechtigt*; Notz, *Frauen*

in der Mannschaft; Notz, *Mehr als bunte Tupfen im Bonner Männerclub*; Holz, *Zwischen Tradition und Emanzipation*; and S. Heinemann, *Frauenfragen sind Menschheitsfragen*.

26 See, as one example, Chappel, "Nuclear Families in a Nuclear Age," 85.

27 Kocka, *Civil Society and Dictatorship*, 39.

28 See, as an example of a study that pinpoints the beginning of civil society in the GDR in the 1980s, Olivo, *Creating a Democratic Civil Society in Eastern Germany*.

29 Even in the Soviet Union, this was the case. In the 1930s, Stalin reoriented the Soviet Union away from libertine gender roles and back toward the traditional family. Goldman, *Women, the State and Revolution*.

30 Gerhard, "Family Law and Gender Equality," 81.

31 Gerhard, "Family Law and Gender Equality," 77.

32 Werner and Zimmermann, "Beyond Comparison," 35.

33 Kocka, *Comparison and History*, 30.

34 Klessmann, "Introduction," 3; see also Werner and Zimmermann, "Beyond Comparison," 30–50; and Christoph Klessmann et al., eds., *Deutsche Vergangenheiten –eine gemeinsame Herausforderung: Der schwierige Umgang mit der doppelten Nachkriegsgeschichte*, 9–13, 12, and 30 (Berlin, 1999).

35 Hagemann, Harsch, and Brühöfener, "Introduction," in *Gendering Post-1945 German History*, 2.

36 Hunt, *The New Cultural History*; Chartier, *On the Edge of the Cliff*; for media and history, see Führer et al., "Öffentlichkeit – Medien – Geschichte."

37 Pierson, "Increasing Returns," 252; Ute Frevert and Heinz-Gerhard Haupt, eds., *Neue Politikgeschichte. Perspektiven einer Historischen Politikforschung* (Frankfurt am Main: Campus, 2005); and Karen Hagemann and Sonya Michel, eds., *Civil Society and Gender Justice: Historical and Comparative Perspectives* (New York: Berghahn, 2011).

1 Reimagining Post-War German Families, 1945–1947

1 I borrow this term from Mazower, *Dark Continent*, 229.

2 Blackbourn, *The Long Nineteenth Century*, 243, 259.

3 Crosby, *The Making of a German Constitution*, traces the entire process of drafting the Civil Code, with some special attention to women, gender, and the family. See also John, *Politics and the Law in Late Nineteenth-Century Germany*.

4 Kommission zur Ausarbeitung des Entwurfs eines Bürgerlichen Gesetzbuches, 3.

5 Gross, *The War against Catholicism*, 185.

6 Verhandlungen des Deutschen Reichstags, 31. Sitzung, 4. February 1896, 740.

7 "Die historischen Wurzeln des Deutschen Frauenrats," accessed 14 December 2021, https://www.frauenrat.de/verband/geschichte; see Schaser, *Frauenbewegung in Deutschland 1848–1933*, 33, 54, 63.

8 Die Verfassung des Deutschen Reichs ("Weimarer Reichsverfassung") vom 11. August 1919.

9 Die Verfassung des Deutschen Reichs ("Weimarer Reichsverfassung") vom 11. August 1919.

10 Schwab, "Gleichberechtigung und Familienrecht in 20. Jahrhundert," 796–801.

11 Sneeringer, *Winning Women's Votes*, 12; Boak, *Women in the Weimar Republic*, 200–1.

12 Blasius, *Ehescheidung in Deutschland 1794–1945*, 157–8.

13 Usborne, *The Politics of the Body in Weimar Germany*, 82.

14 Mouton, *From Nurturing the Nation to Purifying the Volk*, 198–9.

15 Schwab, "Gleichberechtigung und Familienrecht," 796–801.

16 Koonz, *Mothers in the Fatherland*, 143.

17 For more on Nazi family policy, see Pine, *Nazi Family Policy*, 8, 16; and Bock, *Zwangssterilisation im Nationalsozialismus*, 380.

18 Heineman, *What Difference Does a Husband Make?*, 21–3; Koonz, *Mothers in the Fatherland*, 372.

19 Fraenkel, *The Dual State*, xiii–xiv; Steinweis and Rachlin, *The Law in Nazi Germany*, 2.

20 Hedemann, Lehmann, and Siebert, *Volksgesetzbuch*, vol. 22, 11; Schubert, "Die Stellung der Frau im Familienrecht," 828–50.

21 Moeller, *Protecting Motherhood*, 21; Weinberg, *A World at Arms*, 838.

22 Niehuss, *Familie, Frau und Gesellschaft*, 28.

23 Berghahn, *Modern Germany*, 177.

24 Dollard, *The Surplus Woman*, 200.

25 Rüdiger Overmans placed the number at 5.3 million. See Overmans, *Deutsche Militärische Verluste im zweiten Weltkrieg*, 16–17, 228; Elizabeth Heineman places the number of casualties between 3 and 4 million. See Heineman, *What Difference Does a Husband Make?*, 48. Frank Biess offers a more conservative estimate at 1.5 million. Biess, *Homecomings*, 19.

26 Heineman, *What Difference Does a Husband Make?*, 3.

27 Heineman, *What Difference Does a Husband Make?*, 210; Donna Harsch uses a more conservative estimate of 5 million. See Harsch, *Revenge of the Domestic*, 20.

28 Heineman, *What Difference Does a Husband Make?*, 210.

29 "Bevölkerungsentwicklung," last modified 2012, Statistisches Bundesamt: Statistisches Jahrbuch 2011.

30 Moeller, *Protecting Motherhood*, 27.

31 Volker Berghahn mentions that official Allied governance began on 5 June 1945. See Berghahn, *Modern Germany*, 177.

32 Jarausch, *After Hitler*, 28.

33 Biess, *Homecomings*, 45; Biess, "Men of Reconstruction," 335.

34 Fehrenbach, "Rehabilitating Fatherland"; Biess, *Homecomings*, 12–13; Jeffords, "The 'Remasculinization' of Germany in the 1950s"; Moeller, "The 'Remasculinization' of Germany in the 1950s"; Rahden, "Fatherhood, Rechristianization, and the Quest for Democracy"; Poiger, "A New, 'Western' Hero?"

35 Biess, "Men of Reconstruction," 342.
36 Heineman, *What Difference Does a Husband Make?*, 112.
37 Klessmann, *Die doppelte Staatsgründung*, 45; Berend, *Case Studies on Modern European Economy*, 187.
38 Rouette, *Sozialpolitik als Geschlechterpolitik*, 17.
39 Biess, *Homecomings*, 117.
40 F. Maier, "Zwischen Arbeitsmarkt und Familie," 258.
41 Heineman, *What Difference Does a Husband Make?*, 90.
42 This was SMAD Order 253. Obertreis, *Familienpolitik in der DDR*, 44; Harsch, *Revenge of the Domestic*, 50–1.
43 Heineman, *What Difference Does a Husband Make?*, 92.
44 Heineman, *What Difference Does a Husband Make?*, 44, 80.
45 For more on women's service in the military in Nazi Germany, see Hagemann, "Mobilizing Women for War." To be sure, not all women worked. Women who had married and lived with their spouses before the war could collect a family allowance and work to support their children, but the family allowance was docked according to a percentage of a woman's income. Consequently, many wives found it more financially rewarding to stay home. See Heineman, *What Difference Does a Husband Make?*, 61–4; and Hachtmann, *Industriearbeit im "Dritten Reich."*
46 Treber, *Mythos Trümmerfrauen*, 202.
47 Harsch, *Revenge of the Domestic*, 20.
48 Moeller, *Protecting Motherhood*, 29; Herzog, *Sex after Fascism*, 67.
49 Moeller, *Protecting Motherhood*, 30.
50 Moeller, *Protecting Motherhood*, 32; Buske, *Fräulein Mutter und Ihr Bastard*, 196.
51 Heineman, *What Difference Does a Husband Make?*, 251.
52 Moeller, *Protecting Motherhood*, 24, 30–31; Heineman, *What Difference*, 83.
53 Heineman, *What Difference Does a Husband Make?*, 118, discusses the case of one woman whose husband blamed her for his physical ailments when she refused to have sex with him. Moeller, *Protecting Motherhood*, 10, discusses a similar case.
54 Frau S., Kempowski-Biografien 0025/1–3, 45, Archiv der Akademie der Künste, Berlin. Names have been changed to protect author's identity.
55 Frau R., Kempowski-Biografien 2373. "Eine Mutter erinnert sich …" 29, 49. Archiv der Akademie der Künste, Berlin.
56 Frau A., Kempowski-Biografien 2163, 55. Archiv der Akademie der Künste, Berlin.
57 Frau A., Kempowski-Biografien 2163, Archiv der Akademie der Künste, Berlin.
58 Frau A., Kempowski-Biografien 2163, Archiv der Akademie der Künste, Berlin.
59 Frau A., Kempowski-Biografien 2163, Archiv der Akademie der Künste, Berlin.
60 Moeller, *Protecting Motherhood*, 32.
61 Herzog, *Sex after Fascism*, 67–68.
62 Heineman, *What Difference Does a Husband Make?*, 126.
63 Fait, "Supervised Democratization," 57–8; Klessmann, *Die doppelte Staatsgründung*, 28.
64 Kontrollratsgesetz Nr. 1 (20 September 1945).

65   Kontrollratsgesetz Nr. 16 (Ehegesetz) (20 February 1946).

66   Kontrollratsgesetz Nr. 16 (20 February 1946).

67   "Gesetz über die Änderung und Ergänzung familienrechtlicher Vorschriften und
      über die Rechtstellung der Staatslosen (12 April 1938); Gesetz gegen Missbräuche
      bei der Eheschließung und der Annahme an Kindes statt (23 November 1933).
      The 1946 law, for instance, upheld sections of the 1938 "Law on the Change and
      Addition of Family Law Regulations and the Legal Status of Stateless Persons,"
      which had overturned the BGB's regulations on entering and nullifying marriages,
      divorce, custody, the legal status of children born to annulled marriages, and
      marriage among persons already related by marriage. Furthermore, the 1946
      law kept parts of the 1933 "Law against Abuses of Marriage and the Adoption of
      Children." Apart from minor revisions set by the Kontrollratsgesetz Nr. 52, passed
      on 21 April 1947, the Ehegesetz remained on the books until 1955 in the East and
      1957 in the West.

68   Kontrollratsgesetz, §1 (20 February 1946).

69   BGB §1365–70.

70   BGB §1354.

71   BGB §1628.

72   BGB §1355.

73   BGB §1357.

74   BGB §1356.

75   Mai, "The United States in the Allied Control Council," 50.

76   Mai, "The United States in the Allied Control Council," 55.

77   Dr. Kuhnt an Herrn Präsidenten des Zentral-Justizamtes, 30 November 1946,
      Z21/566, BArch Koblenz; Lacherbauer an das Generalkonsulat der türkischen
      Republik, 2 June 1948, Z21/569, BArch Koblenz; An den Herrn Präsidenten des
      Zentraljustizamtes, 14 October 1948, Z21/569, BArch Koblenz.

78   Dr. Kuhnt an Herrn Präsidenten des Zentral-Justizamtes, 30 November 1946,
      Z21/566, BArch Koblenz.

79   An den Herrn Präsidenten des Zentraljustizamtes, 14 October 1948, Z21/569,
      BArch Koblenz.

80   Annedore Z. an Die Frau von heute, Nr. 14, September 1946.

81   G.K. an Die Frau von heute, Nr. 6, March 1947.

82   Harsch, Revenge of the Domestic, 28–9.

83   Goldman, Women, the State and Revolution, 2–4, 338. Since 1918, the Soviets, in
      particular female activists like Alexandra Kollontai, had grappled with the "woman
      question" in Russia with varying degrees of success. The Communist Party had
      a Women's Department (Zhenotdel) that had called for an end to the bourgeois
      family order in 1918. In other words, capitalism forced women to choose between
      their families and work; socialism provided a solution to this double burden.
      Although the Zhenotdel's influence faded in the 1930s, especially as Stalin called
      for a strengthening of the role of the family, the idea of women's emancipation
      remained a core tenet of the Soviet platform.

84 Naimark, *The Russians in Germany*, 129; Harsch, *Revenge of the Domestic*, 29.

85 Naimark, *The Russians in Germany*, 132.

86 Harsch, *Revenge of the Domestic*, 30–1; Ingeborg Nödinger, "'Mitwissen, mitverantworten und mitbestimmen,'" 122.

87 Demokratischer Frauenbund Deutschlands, *Geschichte des DFD* (Leipzig: Verl. für d. Frau, 1989), 46. See also Genth, *Frauenpolitik und Politisches Wirken von Frauen*, 49, 56–7; Harsch, *Revenge of the Domestic*, 31; Heineman, *What Difference Does a Husband Make?*, 181–3.

88 Obertreis, *Familienpolitik*, 34.

89 Opelt, *DDR-Erwachsenenbildung*, 56; Demokratischer Frauenbund Deutschlands, *Geschichte des DFD*, 65; see also Moeller, *West Germany under Construction*, 43, for information on Durand-Wever's aid work in the immediate post-war years. She had opposed the Nazis but soon found there was little political space for her in the Soviet zone as well. Harsch, *Revenge of the Domestic*, 41–2. In December 1946, the ZFA – led by the physician Anne-Marie Durand-Wever, an unaffiliated female activist who later defected to the West – suggested an "independent, unified, democratic" and allegedly non-partisan women's organization to Soviet military leaders. Initial resistance from male SED leaders gave way after female activists such as Käthe Kern and Elli Schmidt convinced them that an SED-controlled mass organization could divert women's attention from bourgeois parties like the Christian Democrats.

90 Heineman, *What Difference Does a Husband Make?*, 183; Nödinger, "'Mitwissen,'" 125.

91 The ZFA had other commissions as well, such as the Arbeitskommission für Arbeit und Sozialfürsorge; Kommission für Gesundheitsfragen; Arbeitskommission Hauswirtschaft/Volkswirtschaft; and the Arbeitskommission für Kultur und Erziehung. It was not uncommon for women to serve on multiple commissions at once. See Protokoll, November 1946, DY 34/21619, BArch Berlin.

92 Irmgard Zündorf, "Biografie Hilde Benjamin."

93 Übersicht: Herausgegeben von der Arbeitskommission für Rechtsfragen beim Zentralen Frauenausschuß, 7 August 1946, DY 34/21619, Bl. 1, BArch Berlin. The document does not indicate which meeting this was; however, the text notes how important their task is and what they aim to do – often hallmarks of first meetings.

94 Übersicht, DY 34/21619, Bl. 1–2, BArch Berlin.

95 Käthe Kern, "Menschenrechte – nicht Männerrechte," *Die Frau von heute* 1, 16, December 1, 1946, 2.

96 "Entscheidend – ist Dein Mann! Sagt heute noch das BGB, das vor 50 Jahren fertiggestellt wurde," *Für Dich*, May 1947, 5. The Soviet zone produced a magazine by the same name of the later *Für Dich*. In 1950 *Für Dich* and *Die Frau von heute* merged. See Barck, Langermann, and Lokatis, *Zwischen "Mosaik" und "Einheit."*

97 Hilde Benjamin, "Gleichberechtigung, Ja – Aber Auch Gleiche Rechte," *Für Dich*, April–May 1948, vols. 17, 19, 20, 21, 22.

98   Elli Schmidt, "Zur wahren Gleichberechtigung der Frau," *Die Frau von heute*, October 1946, 8.

99   "Schmidt, Elli," last accessed February 11, 2017, https://www.bundesstiftung -aufarbeitung.de/wer-war-wer-in-der-ddr-%2363%3B-1424.html?ID=3074. Schmidt was born in 1908 and trained as a seamstress before joining the KPD. She went to Moscow during the war and returned with the Red Army in June 1945. She became an important figure in the women's committees in the Soviet zone.

100 "Der Staat schützt die Ehe," *Die Frau von heute*, 2 September 1948, 15.

101 "Mein Mann wünscht eine unpolitische Frau," *Die Frau von heute*, 8 April 1947, 18.

102 "Um die mitarbeitende Ehefrau," *Die Frau von heute*, 12 June 1947, 18.

103 "Hat mein Mann das Recht zur Scheidung?" *Die Frau von heute*, 6 March 1947, 18.

104 Protokoll über die Sitzung des Unterausschusses "Familie" der Frauenarbeitsgemeinschaft am 28.10.1947, Ost-CDU VII-010-1713, Archiv für Christlich-Demokratische Politik-Sankt Augustin (ACDP).

105 Protokoll über die Sitzung des Unterausschusses "Familie" der Frauenarbeitsgemeinschaft am 28.10.1947, Ost-CDU VII-010-1713, Archiv für Christlich-Demokratische Politik-Sankt Augustin (ACDP).

106 Henicz and Hirschfeld, "Die erste Frauenzusammenschlüsse"; Holz, *Zwischen Tradition und Emanzipation*, 52.

107 S. Heinemann, *"Frauenfragen sind Menschheitsfragen,"* 163; Hauser, "Alle Frauen unter einem Hut?"; Möller, "Der Frauenausschuss in Hamburg-Harburg"; Nödinger, "'Mitwissen, mitverantworten und mitbestimmen'"; Henicz and Hirschfeld, "Der Club Deutscher Frauen in Hannover"; idem, " 'Wenn die Frauen wüßten"; Tscharntke, *Re-Educating German Women*, 119.

108 Tscharntke, *Re-Educating German Women*, 19. The British Military Government, for instance, assigned women's affairs to its Civic Development Section in the summer of 1946. A year later it renamed the division the Women's Affairs Section. The Office of Military Government, United States (OMGUS) established its own Women's Affairs Section of the Education and Cultural Affairs Branch nearly two years later, in March 1948, after pressure from American women's rights activists to address the "women's problem" in post-war Germany. See Zepp, *Redefining Germany,* 247–8; and Boehling, "Gender Roles in Ruins," 54, 56. The French never formally set up a bureau for women. See Stark, "The Overlooked Majority," iii.

109 Boehling, "Gender Roles in Ruins," 56–7; Tscharntke, *Re-educating German Women,* 72. Tscharntke points out that this point of view was not entirely confined to British women, but rather came from some prominent German women as well, such as Agnes von Zahn-Harnack. See also Zepp, *Redefining Germany*, 81.

110 Tscharntke, *Re-Educating German Women,* 72–3.

111 Boehling, "Gender Roles in Ruins," 56.

112 For instance, the German Female Citizens' Union (Deutscher
Staatsbürgerinnenverband, DSV) – founded in 1865 as the ADF and renamed in the
1920s – picked up its work again in 1947 and formally re-established itself in 1949.
"Geschichte des Verbands," accessed 26 October 2016, http://www.staatsbuergerinnen.
org/philosophie/geschichte.html; see also Stoehr, "Cold War Communities," 318.

113 "Herta Gotthelf 1902–1963." The women's office was headed by Herta Gotthelf,
a female activist who had edited the Social Democratic women's newsletter
Genossin in the pre-war years and then spent the war in exile.

114 FDP women started gathering at the *überregional* level in 1947 but did not start a
federal group until 1949. See Heinemann, *"Frauenfragen sind Menschheitsfragen,"*
126. CDU women started meeting at the regional level in the late 1940s and
launched a federal committee in the 1950s. See Holz, *Zwischen Tradition und
Emanzipation*, 60–5, 72–3, 299–300. At the helm of these groups were women
like Helene Weber, a former Center Party representative in the Reichstag, and
Elisabeth Schwarzhaupt, a leader in the Evangelische Frauenarbeit.

115 Icken, *Der Deutsche Frauenrat*, 51.

116 Holz, *Zwischen Tradition und Emanzipation*, 96–7. Women like Theanolte
Bähnisch, a lawyer and Social Democrat from Hannover, who founded the Club
deutscher Frauen, and Elisabeth Schwarzhaupt, who founded the Frankfurter
Frauenausschuss, established groups at the local and regional levels with the aim
of achieving the pre-1933 bourgeois women's movement's "non-confessional" and
"non-party" goals.

117 After 1945, organizations like the Catholic German Women's Association
(Katholischer Deutscher Frauenbund, KDFB) and German Protestant Women's
Work (Evangelische Frauenarbeit Deutschlands, EFD) continued their work
under the umbrella of the major churches. See "Geschichte des KDFB," accessed
26 October 2016, http://www.frauenbund.de/wir-ueber-uns/bundesverband/
geschichte-des-kdfb; and Dagmar Biegler, *Frauenverbände in Deutschland*, 72–5.
Other organizations, such as Protestant Women's Aid (Evangelische Frauenhilfe,
EF) and the German Protestant Women's Association (Deutsch-Evangelischer
Frauenbund, DEF), were also part of these debates.

118 Gotthelf an Esser, April 30, 1947, 2/KSAA000178, Archiv der sozialen
Demokratie; see also Notz, *Frauen in der Mannschaft*, 43.

119 Holz, *Zwischen Tradition und Emanzipation*, 99.

120 Henicz and Hirschfeld, "Die erste Frauenzusammenschlüsse," 94, 96.

121 Schissler, "German and American Women," 564. See also Boehling, "Gender
Roles in Ruins," 66.

122 Although smaller than the other organizations, it still boasted 5,700 members in
North Rhine–Westphalia alone in 1950, and its growing numbers caused enough
consternation that the Adenauer regime banned its members from serving in
public office. See Icken, *Der Deutsche Frauenrat*, 51.

123 Tscharntke, *Re-Educating German Women*, 163.
124 Icken, *Der Deutsche Frauenrat*, 57. When HICOG ceased funding German organizations, it instead bought subscriptions to the newsletter *Informationen für die Frau*. See Informationsdienst fuer Frauenfragen e.V., 15 November 1954, B106/48585, BArch Koblenz.
125 Icken, *Der Deutsche Frauenrat*, 52.
126 Zepp, *Redefining Germany*, 157–8. Donna Harsch documents the process in her article "Public Continuity and Private Change?" Genth's 1996 edited volume *Frauenpolitik* examines the special case of Berlin women's groups. Henicz and Hirschfeld, "Die erste Frauenzusammenschlüsse," 97.
127 Boehling, "Gender Roles in Ruins," 55.
128 As one example, see "Founding Program of the Frankfurter Frauenausschuss," accessed 25 October 2016, http://digam.net/dokumente/911/1.jpg; Genth, *Frauenpolitik*, 150, also mentions this.
129 Founding Program of the Frankfurter Frauenausschuss. The FFA would become the Frankfurter Frauenverband in 1947; see Harsch, "Public Continuity and Private Change?," 43; Heinemann, *"Frauenfragen sind Menschheitsfragen,"* 160.
130 "Q47 Vorschlag eines Arbeitsprogramm für den Frauenausschuss der Stadt Dortmund," in *Frauen in der deutschen Nachkriegszeit*, 210–211; see also " 'Club Deutscher Frauen' in Hannover," in Henicz and Hirschfeld, *Frauen in der deutschen Nachkriegszeit*, 224.
131 Many women's associations did not develop national umbrella organizations until 1948 or the early 1950s; as a result, their records from the earlier period remain spotty.
132 On 28 December 1947, for instance, a local SPD women's committee leader from Regensburg sent a list of proposals regarding illegitimacy and paternity to the SPD Women's Office. See Schlichtinger an Gotthelf, 28 December 1947, 181 (2/KSAA000181), Archiv der sozialen Demokratie.
133 "Siebzehnte Sitzung des Hauptausschusses 3. Dezember 1948," in Wernicke, Booms, and Vogel, *Der Parlamentarische Rat*), 511. For internal Western SPD discussions, see "SPD-Frauentagung in Wuppertal," *Neuer Vorwärts*, 11 September 1948, 6; and "Wuppertal," *Genossin*, October 1948, 117.
134 Roeger an Frauenarbeitsgemeinschaft der CDU/CSU Deutschlands, 14 July 1948, Frauenvereinigung/Frauen-Union/EFU, 04-003-001/1, Archiv für Christlich-Demokratische Politik-Sankt Augustin.
135 Heineman, *What Difference Does a Husband Make?*, 127–8.
136 "Wuppertal," *Genossin*, October 1948, 117.
137 "Sie und das Recht," *Sie*, 23 March 1947, 11.
138 "Sie und das Recht," *Sie*, 6 April 1947, 11; "Sie und das Recht," *Sie*, 20 July 1947, 11.
139 "Sie und das Recht," *Sie*, 15 June 1947, 11; "Sie und das Recht," *Sie*, 3 August 1947, 11.
140 "Sie und das Recht," *Sie*, 10 August 1947.
141 "Briefe an die Herausgeber," *Sie*, 27 July 1947, 5.

142 "Briefe an die Herausgeber," *Sie*, 13 July 1947, 4.

143 "Briefe an die Herausgeber," *Sie*, 3 August 1947, 4.

144 Reports Women's Affairs, box 51, file 5, Women's Affairs Branch, Semi-Annual Report, 1 July–31 December 1949. National Archives, College Park, Maryland (accessed July 2008). According to this OMGUS report: "The Women's Affairs unit ... is based on the recognition of the fact that German women are in a decisive position either to promote or retard the development of Germany as a democratic state."

145 Grazia, *How Fascism Ruled Women*; Rossi-Duria, "Italian Women Enter Politics," 92–93.

146 Fishman, *From Vichy to the Sexual Revolution*, 3.

147 Fishman, *From Vichy to the Sexual Revolution*, 8.

148 Penny Summerfield, "'It Did Me Good In Lots of Ways,'" 17.

149 Fidelis, *Women, Communism, and Industrialization*, 2.

150 Ashwin, *Gender, State, and Society*, 85.

151 Aaron O'Neill, "Gender ratios in select countries after the Second World War 1950," 7 September 2021, Statista.com/statistics/1261433/ post-wwii-gender-ratios-in-select-countries.

2 Gender Equality and the Family in the Two German Constitutions, 1948–1949

1 For Käthe Kern's biography, see Amos, *Die Entstehung der Verfassung*, 59; and "Käthe Kern," last modified October 2009, https://www.bundesstiftung-aufarbeitung.de/de/recherche/kataloge-datenbanken/biographische-datenbanken /kaethe-katharina-kern. Kern was born in 1900 and joined the SPD in 1920, eventually becoming leader of the SPD Greater Berlin women's committee. She joined the SED in 1946 and became, alongside Elli Schmidt, a chairwoman of the SED Central Committee women's department.

2 Käthe Kern, "Bonn gegen Frauenrechte," *Die Frau von heute*, January 1949, 10.

3 Kern, "Bonn gegen Frauenrechte," 10.

4 Scholars who have written on gender and the family in the two provisional constitutions have not fully explained how and why East and West German politicians adopted matching equality clauses. Moeller, *Protecting Motherhood*, 40. Moeller has argued that the West German Basic Law was "an explicit response to the past of National Socialism, to the social dislocation of the immediate postwar period, and to the present global conflict between east and west," but he does not cite even earlier legal or constitutional precedents, nor does he go into detail about the Cold War competition, since his study focuses on the West. Amos, *Entstehung*, 37. Regarding the East German case, historian Heike Amos has outlined constitutional debates in general as a product of Soviet and Western disagreements and paid scant attention to gender in the People's Council. Donna Harsch's monograph *Revenge of the Domestic: Women, the Family, and Communism*

in the German Democratic Republic (Princeton: Princeton University Press, 2007) inexplicably skips the constitutional debates.

5 Moeller, *Protecting Motherhood*, 40, briefly mentions the role of the Cold War but does not conduct a systematic comparison.

6 Contemporaries used the word *Reichsverfassung*. The word "Reich" transliterates to "empire" or "realm" and in other contexts, referred to the German Empire. In this context, given that World War II put an end to German imperial aims, I translate it as "national."

7 Patrick Major, *The Death of the KPD: Communism and Anti-Communism in West Germany, 1945–1956* (Oxford: Clarendon Press, 1997), 37; Harsch, *Revenge*, 38; Monika Kaiser, "Change and Continuity in the Development of the Socialist Unity Party of Germany," *Journal of Contemporary History* 30, no. 4 (1995): 687.

8 Konrad H. Jarausch, *After Hitler: Recivilizing Germans, 1945–1995* (Oxford: Oxford University Press, 2006), 130–131. Historian Konrad H. Jarausch argues that part of the problem stemmed from different conceptions of democracy in the Soviet and Western sectors, namely democratic centralism versus federalism.

9 Amos, *Entstehung*, 38.

10 Amos, *Entstehung*, 37. Translation: "Verfassung der demokratischen deutschen Republik." The SED also presented a draft outlining the *Parteivorstand* of their party.

11 Pieck and Ulbricht, both Communists before 1933, spent the Second World War in exile in Moscow before returning to Germany with the Red Army in April 1945. Grotewohl and Fechner, former Social Democrats, were imprisoned during the war for their SPD membership and resistance to the Nazis. Weber, "Pieck, Wilhelm," https://www.deutsche-biographie.de/gnd118594273.html#ndbcontent; Husemann, "Walter Ulbricht"; Dorlis Blume and Irmgard Zündorf, "Otto Grotewohl," last modified 19 February 2016; Markus Würz, "Max Fechner," last modified 19 February 2016, https://www.hdg.de/lemo/biografie/max-fechner.html.

12 For Karl Polak's biography, see Amos, *Entstehung*, 37–50.

13 Amos, *Entstehung*, 53, 358–405. Historian Heike Amos's comprehensive study on the subject does not explain why, apart from mentioning that Soviet authorities disagreed on it. Two authorities within SMAD did not agree on the matter and sent it to Moscow, where higher-ups, likely because of increasing tensions among the Allies in Germany, also tabled the problem. The reasons are not clearly stated in Amos's study of the issue. Amos, however, also did not focus on gender and may have glossed over the issue in an otherwise comprehensive study. One possibility is that the Soviets wanted to see how local elections in their zone would go before broaching the topic. Another likely reason was that the draft, which closely resembled the old Weimar constitution, was too moderate in nature. Although Polak made some key changes, the text still replicated much of the liberal, bourgeois language of the constitution of the failed Weimar Republic and did not offer a radically transformed template for a future German socialist state under the thumb of the Soviet Union.

14 For further information on Walter Ulbricht's rise to power in the Communist Party of Germany, see Weitz, *Creating German Communism*, 293–303, 318–22.

15 Amos, *Entstehung*, 54.

16 The committee was comprised of sixteen representatives from each of the five *Länder* in the Soviet zone, as well as delegates from the different groups within the SED. Amos, *Entstehung*, 58–9.

17 Harsch, *Revenge of the Domestic*, 35–40; Amos, *Entstehung*, 59.

18 Die Verfassung des Deutschen Reichs ("Weimarer Reichsverfassung") vom 11. August 1919.

19 Amos, *Entstehung*, 64.

20 "1936 Constitution of the USSR," December 1936, http://www.departments. bucknell.edu/russian/const/36cons04.html#chap10. Käthe Kern petitioned the SMAD authorities on 11 November 1946. Five days later, the draft was published in *Neues Deutschland* with the equal rights clause in it. Given Otto Grotewohl's outright dismissal of Kern's suggestion and the quick turnaround of the SED's draft, I suggest that the SMAD intervened and ordered the SED to include the clause, although there is no documentation in materials I have examined that gives a definitive answer either way. Since the Soviets' own constitution included an equal rights clause in Article 122, it is possible that they saw this as a prime opportunity to "Sovietize" the SED and the Soviet zone, using the equal rights clause in the constitution as another vessel.

21 See also "Entwurf einer Verfassung für die deutsche demokratische Republik vom 14. November 1946," in Amos, *Entstehung*, 358–405.

22 Majabert Foerstner, "Die Frau in der Verfassung," *Neues Deutschland*, 28 November 1946, 4; Käthe Kern, "Die Frau und der Verfassungsentwurf," *Neues Deutschland*, 26 November 1946, 4; Friedrich Möglich, "Das Frauenproblem im Verfassungsentwurf," *Neues Deutschland*, 15 December 1946, 4.

23 The Americans had started to draft *Land*-level constitutions in June 1946 in Württemberg-Baden, Bayern, and Hessen. Britain soon followed suit, though its states (Schleswig-Holstein and Nordrhein–Westfalen) did not ratify their constitutions until 1949 and 1950, respectively.

24 "Stimmen aus dem Westen," *Neues Deutschland*, 19 December 1946, 4. The article cited an excerpt of a Rhenish women's group's discussion, originally printed in the "West German People's Echo," a newspaper published by the KPD in Dortmund for the Western sectors. Joesten, *The German Press in 1947*, http://hdl.handle.net/2027/ mdp.39015049425583. *The People's Echo* had a general circulation of about 147,000.

25 "Stimmen aus dem Westen," *Neues Deutschlands*, 19 December 1946.

26 Walpole, *Area Handbook for Germany*, 589.

27 Walpole, *Area Handbook for Germany*, 589.

28 "Zum Verfassungsentwurf der CDU," *Neues Deutschlands*, 28 December 1946.

29 Otto Grotewohl, "Nationale Selbsthilfe," *Neues Deutschland*, 22 February 1948, 1. He used the term "Vorparlament"; a few weeks later, Liberal Democratic Party chairman Wilhelm Külz also called for the People's Congress to be changed into a

parliament, suggesting the name German People's Council (Deutscher Volksrat); Amos, *Entstehung*, 135.

30 The *Volksrat* had 300 delegates total: 85 from the SED, 42 CDU, 43 LDP, 10 from the Vereinigung der gegenseitigen Bauernhilfe, 70 from the DFD, FDGB, DBD, FDJ, Kulturbund, and VVN, and 50 "unaffiliated." See Amos, *Entstehung*, 139. The six committees of the People's Council were: Friedensvertrag (Peace Treaty); Verfassungsausschuss (Constitutional Committee), Wirtschaftsausschuss (Economic Committee), Justizausschuss (Justice Committee), Kulturausschuss (Cultural Committee), and Ausschuss für Sozialpolitik (Committee for Social Policy). Although the apparent purpose of the People's Council was to form a government and constitution for all of Germany, the balance of power was always tilted largely in favour of the SED, given that most of the committees were run by SED members and the SMAD approved all final decisions. The Verfassungsausschuss had thirty members, twelve of whom belonged to the SED. The CDU had three members; the LDPD had six; mass organizations had five; and there was one "non-party" delegate. Grotewohl, the former chairman of the SED constitutional committee, oversaw the group. Amos, *Entstehung*, 140–1, 144.

31 Verfassungsausschuss, 9. Sitzung, Deutscher Volksrat, 13 July 1948, DA 1/154, Bl. 9, BArch Berlin.

32 Verfassungsausschuss, 9. Sitzung, Deutscher Volksrat, 13 July 1948, DA 1/154, Bl. 9, BArch Berlin.

33 Verfassungsausschuss, 9. Sitzung, Deutscher Volksrat, 13 July 1948, DA 1/154, Bl. 7, BArch Berlin.

34 Kern was also a member of the DFD, which had formed its own constitutional committee, whence Kern's proposals came. Verfassungsauschuss, 9. Sitzung, Deutscher Volksrat, 13 July 1948, DA 1/154, Bl. 18, BArch Berlin.

35 4. Tagung des Deutschen Volksrats, 3 August 1948, DA 1/5, Bl. 53–54, BArch Berlin.

36 Verfassungsauschuss, 9. Sitzung, Deutscher Volksrat, 13 July 1948, DA 1/154, Bl. 54, BArch Berlin. Interestingly, Benjamin did not cite the earlier SED draft, but rather the unpublished North Rhine–Westphalia state constitution, which also stated: "Männer und Frauen sind gleichberechtigt."

37 For biography on Hildegard Heinze, see "Hildegard Heinze," accessed 28 November 2016, https://www.bundesstiftung-aufarbeitung.de/de/recherche/kataloge-datenbanken/biographische-datenbanken/hildegard-damerius-heinze.

38 Verfassungsauschuss, 9. Sitzung, 13 July 1948, DA 1/154, Bl. 23, BArch Berlin.

39 Verfassungsauschuss, 9. Sitzung, 13 July 1948, DA 1/154, Bl. 23. Emphasis mine.

40 4. Tagung des Deutschen Volksrats, 3 August 1948, DA 1/5, Bl. 53, BArch Berlin.

41 Verfassungsauschuss, 9. Sitzung, 13 July 1948, DA 1/154, Bl. 18, BArch Berlin.

42 4. Tagung des Deutschen Volksrats, 3 August 1948, DA 1/5, Bl. 53, BArch Berlin.

43 5. Tagung des Deutschen Volksrats, 22–4 October 1948, DA 1/6, Bl. 122, BArch Berlin.

44 Garner, "Public Service Personnel," 140–1.

45 The Americans had started to draft *Land*-level constitutions in June 1946 in Württemberg-Baden, Bayern, and Hessen. Britain soon followed suit, though its states (Schleswig-Holstein and Nordrhein-Westfalen) did not ratify their constitutions until 1949 and 1950, respectively. For Soviet zone constitutions, see Braas, *Die Entstehung der Länderverfassungen*, 480–525.

46 Major, *The Death of the KPD*, 107.

47 Markovits, "Constitution Making after National Catastrophes," 1308–9. Eleven male delegates convened at Herrenchiemsee in Bavaria to draft the guidelines for the future constitution. According to Markovits, the delegates chose "Basic Law [Grundgesetz]" instead of "constitution [Verfassung]" to emphasize providing a structure for the new German society (1309–10). Konrad H. Jarausch has also asserted that the new Basic Law would represent a combination of German tradition and Allied influence. See Jarausch, *After Hitler*, 114.

48 Jarausch, *After Hitler*, 20.

49 Gimbel, *The American Occupation of Germany*, 224. See also Moeller, *Protecting Motherhood*, 2.

50 Wernicke, Booms, and Vogel, "Vorgeschichte," in *Der Parlamentarische Rat*, 25–52.

51 For biography of Ludwig Bergsträsser, see: "Ludwig Bergsträsser," last modified 1 September 2008, http://www.bpb.de/geschichte/deutsche-geschichte/grundgesetz-und-parlamentarischer-rat/39049/ludwig-bergstraesser-spd. Bergsträsser came to the council having helped draft the Hessian provincial constitution, which included wage equality for men and women.

52 Wernicke, Booms, and Vogel, "Katalog der Grundrechte 21. September 1948," in *Der Parlamentarische Rat*, 16.

53 Die Verfassung des Deutschen Reichs ("Weimarer Reichsverfassung") vom 11. August 1919.

54 Katholikenausschuss Dekanat Eschweiler an den Parlamentarischen Rat in Bonn, 17 November 1948, Z5/109, Parlamentsarchiv Berlin; Katholikenausschuss des Dekanates Erkelenz an den Parlamentarischen Rat, 14 November 1948, Z5/108, Parlamentsarchiv Berlin; Arbeitsgemeinschaft Katholischer Frauen, Eingabe an den Parlamentarischen Rat, 26 November 1948, Z5/110, Parlamentsarchiv Berlin; Diozesankommitee der Katholikenausschüsse in der Erzdiozese Köln an Herrn Presidenten des Parlamentarischen Rates Bonn, 15 November 1948, Z5/110, Parlamentsarchiv Berlin.

55 United Nations, "Universal Declaration of Human Rights," 10 December 1948, https://www.un.org/en/about-us/universal-declaration-of-human-rights; Wernicke, Booms, and Vogel, "Vierundzwanzigste Sitzung 23. November 1948," in *Der Parlamentarische Rat*, 643.

56 May, *Homeward Bound*, 8.

57 Goldman, *Women, the State, and Revolution*, 338.

58 Goldman, *Women, the State, and Revolution*, 340.

59 "Vierundzwanzigste Sitzung 23. November 1948," 643.
60 Wernicke, Booms, and Vogel, "Sechste Sitzung 5. Oktober 1948," in *Der Parlamentarische Rat*, 135. Public office, as committee chairman and law professor Hermann von Mangoldt defined it, included civil servants (Beamten) and honorary civil service appointees (Ehrenbeamten). For a biography of Hermann von Mangoldt, see "Hermann von Mangoldt," last modified 1 September 2008, http://www.bpb.de/geschichte/deutsche-geschichte/grundgesetz-und-parlamentarischer-rat/39105/hermann-von-mangoldt-cdu. He had been a member of the Nazi lawyers' union and maintained his teaching position throughout the Third Reich. In 1948 he was elected to the Landtag of Schleswig-Holstein.
61 Wernicke, Booms, and Vogel, "Sechsundzwanzigste Sitzung 30. November 1948," in *Der Parlamentarische Rat*, 752.
62 Wernicke, Booms, and Vogel, "Sechsundzwanzigste Sitzung 30. November 1948," 752.
63 Wernicke, Booms, and Vogel, "Sechsundzwanzigste Sitzung 30. November 1948," 738–9.
64 Wernicke, Booms, and Vogel, "Sechsundzwanzigste Sitzung 30. November 1948," 747–8.
65 Wernicke, Booms, and Vogel, "Sechsundzwanzigste Sitzung 30. November 1948," 749.
66 Wernicke, Booms, and Vogel, "Sechsundzwanzigste Sitzung 30. November 1948," 748. For biography of Thomas Dehler, see Wengst, *Thomas Dehler*.
67 Franzius, *Bonner Grundgesetz und Familienrecht*, 26, 47, 52, 78. They based their own understanding of equal rights on the official opinion of liberal jurist and fellow council delegate Richard Thoma, outlined in a published critique of the Catalog of Basic Rights.
68 Wernicke, Booms, and Vogel, "Sechsundzwanzigste Sitzung 30. November 1948," 739.
69 Wernicke, Booms, and Vogel, "Sechsundzwanzigste Sitzung 30. November 1948," 741.
70 Wernicke, Booms, and Vogel, "Sechsundzwanzigste Sitzung 30. November 1948," 741.
71 Wernicke, Booms, and Vogel, "Sechsundzwanzigste Sitzung 30. November 1948," 741.
72 Wernicke, Booms, and Vogel, "Sechsundzwanzigste Sitzung 30. November 1948," 742.
73 Wernicke, Booms, and Vogel, "Siebzehnte Sitzung des Hauptausschusses 3. Dezember 1948," in *Der Parlamentarische Rat*, 510.
74 Wernicke, Booms, and Vogel, "Siebzehnte Sitzung des Hauptausschusses 3. Dezember 1948," 510.
75 Böttger, *Das Recht auf Gleichheit und Differenz*, 123; Die Hessische Landesregierung, "Ein Glücksfall für die Demokratie," 39–40.
76 Wernicke, Booms, and Vogel, "Siebzehnte Sitzung des Hauptausschusses 3. Dezember 1948," 510–11.
77 Wernicke, Booms, and Vogel, "Siebzehnte Sitzung des Hauptausschusses 3. Dezember 1948," 513.
78 Wernicke, Booms, and Vogel, "Siebzehnte Sitzung des Hauptausschusses 3. Dezember 1948," 513. Max Becker had been a member of the German People's

Party (DVP) during Weimar. For Becker's biography, see "Max Becker,"
last modified 1 September 2008, http://www.bpb.de/geschichte/
deutsche-geschichte/grundgesetz-und-parlamentarischer-rat/39047/
max-becker-fdp.

79 Wernicke, Booms, and Vogel, "Siebzehnte Sitzung des Hauptausschusses 3.
Dezember 1948," 512.

80 Wernicke, Booms, and Vogel, "Siebzehnte Sitzung des Hauptausschusses 3.
Dezember 1948," 514.

81 Wernicke, Booms, and Vogel, "Siebzehnte Sitzung des Hauptausschusses 3.
Dezember 1948," 511.

82 Wernicke, Booms, and Vogel, "Siebzehnte Sitzung des Hauptausschusses 3.
Dezember 1948," 515.

83 Wernicke, Booms, and Vogel, "Siebzehnte Sitzung des Hauptausschusses 3.
Dezember 1948," 515.

84 Wernicke, Booms, and Vogel, "Siebzehnte Sitzung des Hauptausschusses 3.
Dezember 1948," 511.

85 Wernicke, Booms, and Vogel, "Siebzehnte Sitzung des Hauptausschusses 3.
Dezember 1948," 511.

86 The transcript was reprinted in the Social Democratic women's newspaper
Genossin, January 1949, 12: 1, 15. I have not been able to find any specific
secondary sources on the Munich Rundfunk.

87 "Bonn und das Konkordat," *Die Zeit*, 23 December 1948.

88 "Volksrat gegen Spalterverfassung," *Neues Deutschland*, 21 December 1948, 2.

89 Heineman, *What Difference Does a Husband Make?*, 143; Moeller, *Protecting
Motherhood*, 41. Ines Reich-Hilweg mentions the public outcry as well in her
analysis of Article 3's impact in West Germany, but she never goes into detail
about how it was conducted. Reich-Hilweg, *Männer und Frauen sind
gleichberechtigt*, 21–2.

90 Die Beamtinnen und weiblichen Angestellten im Arbeitsamt Frankfurt a/M an den
Parlamentarischen Rat, 8 January 1949, Z5/112, Parlamentsarchiv Berlin.

91 Freier Gewerkschaftsbund Hessen an den Vorsitzenden des Parlamentarischen
Rates Herrn Dr. Adenauer, 15 December 1948, Z5/95, Parlamentsarchiv Berlin.

92 Industriegewerkschaft Metall für die Britische Zone und Bremen an Herrn Dr.
Adenauer, 30 December 1948, Z5/110, Parlamentsarchiv Berlin, Z5/110.

93 Arbeitsgemeinschaft Frauenringe der französischen Zone, 9 January 1949, Z5/112,
Parlamentsarchiv Berlin; Frauenring Siegerland an den Hauptausschuss des
Parlamentarischen Rates, 10 December 1948, Z5/95, Parlamentsarchiv Berlin;
Frauenring der britischen Zone, 14 December 1948, Z5/97, Parlamentsarchiv
Berlin; Weiblichen Abgeordneten des Niedersächsischen Landtages an den
Parlamentarischen Rat in Bonn, 29 December 1948, Z5/96, Parlamentsarchiv
Berlin; Frauenring der britischen Zone, 31 December 1948, Z5/111,
Parlamentsarchiv Berlin.

94 Heidelberger Frauenverein an den Parlamentarischen Rat, Z5/110,
    Parlamentsarchiv Berlin. Little is known about von Falkenberg. Gustav Radbruch
    and Günter Spendel mention her stint at the University of Heidelberg. See
    Radbruch and Spendel, *Biographische Schriften*, 462. See also "NL Falkenberg,
    Erdmuthe, 1910–2003," last accessed 11 February 2017, https://findstar
    .scopearchiv.ch/detail.aspx?ID=68374. For similar petition, see Frauengruppe
    Karlsruhe, 3 January 1949, Z5/110, Parlamentsarchiv Berlin.

95 The original text stated: "Männer und Frauen haben die gleichen staatsrechtlichen
    und privatrechtlichen Rechte und Pflichten."

96 Süddeutsche Frauenarbeitskreis Nürnberg an den Parlamentarischen Rat, 21
    December 1948, Z5/111, Parlamentsarchiv Berlin.

97 Deutsche Dunlop Gummi Compagnie an den Parlamentarischen Rat, 28 January
    1949, Z5/113, Parlamentsarchiv Berlin; Heraeus an den Parlamentarischen Rat,
    2 February 1949, Z5/114, Parlamentsarchiv Berlin. For more on the Deutsche
    Dunlop Gummi Compagnie, one of Germany's leading rubber companies, see
    Forbes, *Doing Business with the Nazis*, 142. For more on Heraeus, see Schrank,
    Heraeus.

98 Frauenring Wuppertal an den Hauptausschuss des Parlamentarischen Rates, 1
    January 1949, Z5/111, Parlamentsarchiv Berlin; Frauenausschuss Hamburg an
    den Parlamentarischen Rat, 6 January 1949, Z5/111, Parlamentsarchiv Berlin.

99 For a biography of Ilk, see Vierhaus and Herbst, *Biographisches Handbuch*, 375.

100 Herta Ilk an Informationsdienst Nr. 62, A5–50, Archiv der
    Liberalismus-Gummersbach.

101 Wernicke, Booms, and Vogel, "Zweiundvierzigste Sitzung des Hauptausschusses
    18. Januar 1949," 1315–17.

102 Wernicke, Booms, and Vogel, "Zweiundvierzigste Sitzung des Hauptausschusses
    18. Januar 1949," 1310.

103 Wernicke, Booms, and Vogel, "Zweiundvierzigste Sitzung des Hauptausschusses
    18. Januar 1949," 1311.

104 Wernicke, Booms, and Vogel, "Zweiundvierzigste Sitzung des Hauptausschusses
    18. Januar 1949," 1311.

105 Wernicke, Booms, and Vogel, "Zweiundvierzigste Sitzung des Hauptausschusses
    18. Januar 1949," 1312–14.

106 Markovits, "Constitution Making after National Catastrophes," 1316–17.

107 Käthe Kern, "Deutscher Verfassungsplan oder 'Auftrag aus fremder Hand'?," *Die
    Frau von heute*, 1 September 1948, 10; Kern, "Grundrechte: der Bürger und der
    Frauen," *Die Frau von heute*, October 1948; Kern, "Bonn gegen Frauenrechte," *Die
    Frau von heute*, January 1949.

108 Grundgesetzentwurf, 10 February 1949, DA 1/157, Bl. 70–129, BArch Berlin.

109 Verfassungsausschuss, 13. Sitzung, February 18, 1949, DA 1/157, Bl. 37, BArch
    Berlin.

110 Sitzungsschlussbericht der 13. Sitzung, February 18, 1949, DA 1/157, Bl. 25,
    BArch Berlin. They selected Käthe Kern, Helene Beer, and Dr. Hildegard Heinze.

111 Hans Nathan later published the "Theses" in *Neue Justiz*, the organ of the German Justice Administration (the precursor to the Ministry of Justice). Hans Nathan, "Zur Neugestaltung des Familienrechts," *Neue Justiz*, Nr. 5, May 1949, 104.

112 Nathan, "Zur Neugestaltung des Familienrechts," 104.

113 Nathan, "Zur Neugestaltung des Familienrechts," 103.

114 Breithaupt, "Nathan, Hans," https://www.deutsche-biographie.de/gnd13867647X. html#ndbcontent.

115 Fulbrook, *Anatomy of a Dictatorship*, 93.

116 Benjamin an Volksrat, 4. Tagung, 3 August 1948, DA 1/5, BArch Berlin.

117 Nathan, "Zur Neugestaltung des Familienrechts," 102–3.

118 Nathan, "Zur Neugestaltung des Familienrechts," 103.

119 Benjamin an Volksrat, 4. Tagung, 3 August 1948, DA 1/5, BArch Berlin; Nathan, "Zur Neugestaltung des Familienrechts," 102–3. See also "Wirkungen der Ehe im allgemeinen," 1949, DA 1/110, BArch Berlin.

120 Fulbrook, *Anatomy of a Dictatorship*, 24–5.

121 Chaperon, "'Feminism Is Dead,'" 156.

122 "Constitution of the People's Republic of Hungary," 20 August 1949; "Constitution of the Polish People's Republic," 1952.

3 The Failed Reforms of Family Law in East and West Germany, 1949–1953

1 Carnott an Adenauer, 9 March 1950, B141/2018/11, BArch Koblenz.

2 Lück an MdJ, 14 August 1950, DP 1/7198, Bl. 29, BArch Berlin.

3 Harsch, *Revenge of the Domestic*, 61.

4 Grünbaum, *Deutsche Einheit*, 13.

5 For biographies of Otto Grotewohl and Wilhelm Pieck, see Hoffmann, *Otto Grotewohl*; and Weber, "Pieck, Wilhelm," https://www.deutsche-biographie.de /gnd118594273.html#ndbcontent. See also Frank, *Walter Ulbricht*.

6 "Gleichberechtigung vor dem Gesetz," *Die Frau von heute* 6, 1950, 6; "Otto Grotewohl antwortet den Frauen," *Für Dich* 11, no. 5, 12 March 1950, 3; Socialist Unity Party Program, April 1946, http://www.cvce.eu/de/obj/politisches _programm_der_sed_berlin_21_und_22_april_1946-de-d9c5faf7-5c39-43fa -aa3f-88d5431e3746.html.

7 Benjamin, *Vorschläge zum neuen deutschen Familienrecht*.

8 Gesetz zur Neuordnung des Familienrechts, 1950, DP 1/8028, Bl. 2–3, BArch Berlin. As they noted on page 2 of the document, they did not intend to change provisions regarding engagement (§§1297–302), custody (Vormundschaft, §§1773–921), and the 1946 marital law (Kontrollratsgesetz Nr. 16). They explain that these provisions were not necessarily disruptive to Gleichberechtigung and were practical in everyday life.

9 §1, Gesetz zur Neuordnung des Familienrechts, 1950, DP 1/8028, Bl. 5, BArch Berlin.

10 §2, Gesetz zur Neuordnung des Familienrechts, 1950, DP 1/8028, Bl. 6, BArch Berlin.

11 §3, Gesetz zur Neuordnung des Familienrechts, 1950, DP 1/8028, Bl. 6, BArch Berlin.

12 §4, Gesetz zur Neuordnung des Familienrechts, 1950, DP 1/8028, Bl. 6, BArch Berlin.

13 §6, Gesetz zur Neuordnung des Familienrechts, 1950, DP 1/8028, Bl. 8, BArch Berlin.

14 §7, Gesetz zur Neuordnung des Familienrechts, 1950, DP 1/8028, Bl. 8, BArch Berlin.

15 §10–11, Gesetz zur Neuordnung des Familienrechts, 1950, DP 1/8028, Bl. 10, BArch Berlin. Accruals would not include the spouses' separate property (earned by inheritance), items not included in the marital contract, property acquired after separation, or property acquired (due to an adjustment) before separation.

16 §1, Gesetz zur Neuordnung des Familienrechts, 1950, DP 1/8028, Bl. 5, BArch Berlin. This provision echoes §1353 of the original BGB.

17 §§1297–302, Gesetz zur Neuordnung des Familienrechts, 1950, DP 1/8028, Bl. 2, BArch Berlin.

18 Gesetz zur Neuordnung des Familienrechts, 1950, DP 1/8028, Bl. 2, BArch Berlin.

19 Fiedler and Meyen, *Fiktionen für das Volk*, 7, 9.

20 In early 1950, for instance, the two papers ran series of articles by the jurist Heinrich Löwenthal and Hanna Keusch explaining the proposed changes to the regulations on family name, parental authority, marital property, and age of majority. For a biography of Heinrich Löwenthal, see Wentker, *Justiz in der SBZ/DDR 1945–1953*, 445; for various articles, see "Welchen Namen soll in die Zukunft die Frau führen?" *Berliner Zeitung*, 11 January 1950, 6; "Elterliche Gewalt oder Elterliche Sorge?" *Berliner Zeitung*, 21 February 1950, 6; "Herabsetzung des Volljährigkeitsalters," *Neues Deutschland*, 26 February 1950, 4; "Ein neues eheliches Güterrecht ist nötig," *Berliner Zeitung*, 10 March 1950, 6; and "Gleichberechtigung vor dem Gesetz," *Die Frau von heute* 6, 1950, 6.

21 Hans Nathan, "Um die Neugestaltung," *Neues Deutschland*, 9 April 1950, 5.

22 Wilhelmine Schirmer-Pröscher, "Frauen 'bevorzugt' behandelt," *Berliner Zeitung*, 23 April 1950, 4.

23 Protokoll öffentliche Frauenversammlung des DFD am 30.1.50 Kreisverband Wittenberge, 30 January 1950, DP 1/8038, BArch Berlin.

24 Lieber Rundfunk!, 5 February 1950, DP 1/8038, Bl. 79, BArch Berlin.

25 An den Berliner Rundfunksender, 7 February 1950, DP 1/8038, Bl. 76, BArch Berlin.

26 See for example, An die Landesregierung Sachsen – Justizministerium – in Dresden, 19 February 1950, DP 1/8038, Bl. 41. BArch Berlin. As another letter from Nathan to the Zentralverband landwirtschaftlicher Genossenschaften Deutschlands from 13 March 1950 already indicated, the process had been delayed until the end of the summer. See Nathan an Zentralverband landwirtschaftlicher Genossenschaften Deutschlands, 13 March 1950, DP 1/8038, Bl. 45. BArch Berlin.

27 Gesetz der Arbeit zur Förderung und Pflege der Arbeitskräfte, zur Steigerung der Arbeitsproduktivität und zur weiteren Verbesserung der materiellen und kulturellen Lage der Arbeiter und Angestellten, 1950, https://www.verfassungen.de/ddr/gesetzderarbeit50.htm.

28 See as one example Karin Zachmann's study *Mobilisierung der Frauen*.

29 Gesetz der Arbeit zur Förderung und Pflege der Arbeitskräfte, zur Steigerung der Arbeitsproduktivität und zur weiteren Verbesserung der materiellen und kulturellen Lage der Arbeiter und Angestellten, 1950, http://www.verfassungen.de /de/ddr/gesetzderarbeit50.htm

30 Moeller, *Protecting Motherhood*, 155.

31 Schmalz, "Gesetzlicher Mutterschutz Gestern und heute; Gerhard, *Frauen in der Geschichte des Rechts*, 753. See also Buggeln and Wildt, *Arbeit im Nationalsozialismus*, 155–6.

32 The Americans withdrew their support in August 1945; the British waited until 3 May 1946. Ruhl, ed. *Frauen in der Nachkriegszeit*, 235.

33 "Vorschläge des DFD," 7 March 1950, DY30/IV 2/17/30, 0024, BArch Berlin. See also Käthe Kern, "Die DDR sorgt für Mutter und Kind," *Tägliche Rundschau*, 28 March 1950.

34 "Das Politbüro der SED an die Frauen," *Neues Deutschland*, 19 April 1950.

35 Niederschrift über Besprechung des Entwurfs eines Gesetzes über die gesellschaftliche Stellung der Frau am 8.6.1950, 8 June 1950, DY30/IV 2/17/30, BArch Berlin.

36 Niederschrift über Besprechung des Entwurfs eines Gesetzes über die gesellschaftliche Stellung der Frau am 8.6.1950, 8 June 1950, DY30/IV 2/17/30, BArch Berlin.

37 Goldman, *Women, the State, and Revolution*, 337; see also Stone, "The New Fundamental Principles," 394–5. Stone suggests that divisions in the Soviet hierarchy prevented them from reforming their own 1944 family law until the 1960s.

38 Herzog, *Sex after Fascism*, 193; "Frauenrechte vor der Volkskammer," *Nacht-Express*, 22 September 1950; "Gesetz über neues Familienrecht," *Berliner Zeitung*, 22 September 1950.

39 §12–18, Drucksache Nr. 142, *Protokolle der Provisorische Volkskammer der DDR* (Berlin: Volkskammer, 1950), 232–3.

40 *Protokolle der Provisorische Volkskammer der DDR* (Berlin: Volkskammer, 1950), 524, 525, 526, 538.

41 Obertreis, *Familienpolitik in der DDR*, 114.

42 "Gesetz über den Mutter- und Kinderschutz und die Rechte der Frau," *Berliner Zeitung*, 28 September 1950, 4; see also Käthe Kern, "Gleichberechtigung der Frau wird verwirklicht," *Neues Deutschland*, 27 September 1950, 2; "Gesetz über den Mütter- und Kinderschutz und die Rechte der Frauen," *Bauern-Echo*, 28 September 1950; "Gesetz über die Rechte der Frau," *Neues Deutschland*, 28 September 1950.

43 "Das Recht der Frau wird verwirklicht," *Neues Deutschland*, 14 November 1950.

44 "Gesetz über den Mutter- und Kinderschutz und die Rechte der Frau," *Berliner Zeitung*, 28 September 1950, 4.

45 "Wir wollen diesem Gesetz Ehre machen!" *Berliner Zeitung*, 30 September 1950, 6.

46 "Gesetz der Frau für manche eine harte Nuß," *Berliner Zeitung*, 7 October 1950, 6.

47 "Herr Wegner lernt von seiner Frau," *Neue Zeit*, 29 September 1950, 3.

48 "Nach §15 des Frauengesetzes," *Berliner Zeitung*, 29 September 1950, 2.

49 Mary Fulbrook, *A History of Germany, 1918–2014*, 203.

50 Gesetzgebungskommission, 2 December 1952, DP 1/VA 6483, BArch Berlin.

51 Kos, "Politische Justiz in der DDR," 396.

52 Herf, *Divided Memory*, 108.

53 Bruce, *Resistance with the People*, 159; see also Ostermann, *Uprising in East Germany 1953*, xxxi.

54 Hans Nathan, "Frauengesetz und die Familienrechtsreform," *Tägliche Rundschau*, 6 January 1951; Obertreis, *Familienpolitik*, 130.

55 Gesetzgebungskommission, 2 December 1952, DP 1/VA 6483, BArch Berlin; also in DP 1/7893/2, BArch Berlin.

56 Gesetzgebungskommission, 2 December 1952, DP 1/VA 6483, BArch Berlin.

57 Rudolf Brumme an MdJ, 12 March 1950, DP 1/8038, Bl. 57, BArch Berlin. Others wrote to inquire about adoption and custody rights. Nathan an Thiele, 15 April 1950, Bl. 71, DP 1/8038, BArch Berlin. See also Erich Thiele an MdJ, 5 April 1950, DP 1/8038, Bl. 70, BArch Berlin.

58 Obertreis, *Familienpolitik*, 118.

59 Obertreis, *Familienpolitik*, 119.

60 Harsch, *Revenge of the Domestic*, 51, 210.

61 Gesetzgebungskommission, 2 December 1952, DP 1/VA 6483, BArch Berlin.

62 Gesetzgebungskommission, 2 December 1952, DP 1/VA 6483, BArch Berlin.

63 Schroeder, *Der SED-Staat*, 116, 120–1.

64 Biedermann, *Deutschland in der Nachkriegszeit 1945–1949*, 62.

65 Bark and Gress, *A History of West Germany*, 325; Jarausch, *After Hitler*, 136.

66 Verhandlungen des Deutschen Bundestages [1.] Deutscher Bundestag, 5. Sitzung, 20 September 1949, 22. According to Weitz, as a liberal capitalist, Adenauer was not entirely supportive of the social market economy at first, but the competition with the East pushed the FRG to embrace some welfare provisions. Weitz, "The Ever-Present Other," 219–20.

67 Spicka, *Selling the Economic Miracle*, 27.

68 Spicka, *Selling the Economic Miracle*, 33.

69 Granieri, *The Ambivalent Alliance*, 31–3.

70 Moeller, *Protecting Motherhood*; Niehuss, *Familie, Frau und Gesellschaft*; Weitz, "The Ever-Present Other"; see also Rölli-Alkemper, *Familie im Wiederaufbau*; Rahden, "Fatherhood, Rechristianization"; and Jeffords, "The 'Remasculinization' of Germany."

71 For a study on women's part-time work, see Oertzen, *Teilzeitarbeit und die Lust am Zuverdienen*.

72 Verhandlungen des Deutschen Bundestages [1.] Deutscher Bundestag, 5. Sitzung, 20 September 1949, 26.

73 VDBT, 5. Sitzung, 20 September 1949, 27.

74 VDBT, 5. Sitzung, 20 September 1949, 26.

75 "University Studies," last accessed 28 November 2020, https://noelle-neumann .de/biography/biography-university-studies. The polls were conducted by the Allensbach Institute for Public Opinion Research, an institute with conservative leanings founded by Elisabeth Noelle-Neumann and her spouse, Erich Peter Neumann, in 1947.

76 Noelle-Neumann, *The Germans*, 64.

77 BGB §1564–1567.

78 Noelle-Neumann, *The Germans*, 73.

79 Noelle-Neumann, *The Germans*, 67.

80 Antrag der Fraktion der SPD, Drucksache 176, Verhandlungen des Deutschen Bundestages [1.] Deutscher Bundestag, 3 November 1949; Antrag der Fraktion der SPD, Drucksache 177, Verhandlungen des Deutschen Bundestages [1.] Deutscher Bundestag, 8 November 1949; Antrag der Abgeordneten Renner und Genossen, Drucksache 206, Verhandlungen des Deutschen Bundestages [1.] Deutscher Bundestag, 15 November 1949.

81 Nathanius an die Herren Bundesminister, 26 April 1950, B141/2055/43, BArch Koblenz; Dehler an Ilk, 3 August 1950, B141/2055/48, BArch Koblenz; Ilk an Dehler, 1 September 1950, B141/2055/49, BArch Koblenz. In their correspondence regarding a committee on family law, neither side recommended or mentioned Communist Party members, although the party had more representatives in the Bundestag than the Center Party and numbers comparable to those of other parties such as the DP and the Bayern Party. The ministry's reluctance to engage with communists on the issue reflected its leaders' ambivalence about the party.

82 VDBT, 20./21. Sitzung, 2 December 1949, 626. For biography of Lehr, see Kurt Düwell, "Robert Lehr," last accessed 31 December 2016, http://www.kas.de/wf /de/37.8217.

83 VDBT, 20./21. Sitzung, 1 December 1949, 566.

84 VDBT, 20./21. Sitzung, 2 December 1949, 566.

85 "Wie sieht der Gleichberechtigung der Frau aus?" *Frankfurter Allgemeine Zeitung*, 23 November 1949, 9. The paper was founded in November 1949.

86 Alfred Thoß, "Eherecht und Ehetragik," *Die Zeit*, 19 January 1950, http://www.zeit .de/1950/03/eherecht-und-ehetragik/seite-3.

87 "Gleichberechtigung der Frau," *Frankfurter Allgemeine Zeitung*, 2 March 1950, 3.

88 "Jung und anmutig," *Die Zeit*, 10 July 1987, 1.

89 According to *Der Spiegel*'s obituary, she was so well-known for her work on the *Denkschrift* that she was nicknamed "Gleichberechtigung-Marie." "Gestorben," 9 December 1991, *Der Spiegel* 50 http://www.spiegel.de/spiegel/print/d-13491790. html. Not much is known about her political affiliation. Robert Moeller indicates that she was Catholic, but party association is not clarified. See Moeller, *Protecting Motherhood*, 253.

188 Notes to pages 81-3

90 Maria Hagemeyer, "Denkschrift über die Anpassung des geltenden Familienrechts an den Grundsatz der Gleichberechtigung von Mann und Frau (Art. 3 Abs. 2 GG) erforderliche Gesetzesänderungen," Teil I, 5, B106/43313, BArch Koblenz.

91 Hagemeyer, "Denkschrift," Teil I, 7.

92 Hagemeyer, "Denkschrift," Teil I, 14–15.

93 Hagemeyer, "Denkschrift," Teil I, 9–10.

94 Hagemeyer, "Denkschrift," Teil I, section 10.

95 Hagemeyer, "Denkschrift," Teil I, 26.

96 Moeller's *Protecting Motherhood* outlines this meeting's discussions, 82–6. See also Franzius, *Bonner Grundgesetz und Familienrecht*, 59–60. Franzius explains that the Deutscher Juristentag agreed to remove the *Stichentscheid* and that courts could intervene when disagreements over children arose. The issue of surnames remained unclarified. For a transcript of Erna Scheffler's speech and Ulmer's rebuttal, see Leitsätze zum Referat Landesverwaltungsgerichtsrätin Dr. Scheffler, B411/5, Bl. 30–31, BArch Koblenz.

97 Hagemeyer, "Denkschrift," Teil I, 3.

98 Hagemeyer, "Denkschrift," Teil I, 3.

99 Hagemeyer, "Denkschrift," Teil I, 3.

100 Moeller does not give Hagemeyer's *Denkschrift* much attention, which is rather surprising given how much controversy it sparked in the FRG.

101 Hagemeyer, "Denkschrift," Teil I, 9.

102 Allen, *Women in Twentieth-Century Europe*, 81–3; Sandström and Garðarsdóttir, "Long-Term Perspectives on Divorce," 10.1080/03468755.2017.1384661.

103 Hagemeyer, "Denkschrift," Teil I, 4.

104 Hagemeyer, "Denkschrift," Teil I, 5.

105 Karsten an Frauenorganisationen, March 1951, B106/43313, BArch Koblenz; Woodsmall an Hagemeier, B141/2017, Bl. 11, BArch Koblenz; Einladung zur Tagung des D.A.B. in Nürnberg vom 28.–30. Juli 1951, B141/2017, BArch Koblenz. Many of these organizations and even the Office of the US High Commissioner for Germany invited Hagemeyer to speak on the subject of family law.

106 Stellungnahme des Deutschen Akademikerinnenbundes e.V., 7 April 1952, B141/2029/60, BArch Koblenz; Stellungnahme des Deutscher Anwaltvereins, 13 March 1952, B411/481, BArch Koblenz; Vorschlag zur Neugestaltung des Rechtes im Sinne der Gleichberechtigung von Mann und Frau, Evangelische Kirche im Rheinland, 18 October 1951, B141/2057/8–15, BArch Koblenz; Stellungnahme der Weltorganisation der Mütter aller Nationen, 11 June 1951, B141/2028/69, BArch Koblenz.

107 Rektor Chr. Müller an Dehler, 6 March 1952, B141/2020/10, BArch Koblenz.

108 Aachener Nachrichten, 26 November 1951, B141/2019/73, BArch Koblenz.

109 Gussmann an Hagemeyer, B141/2019/237, BArch Koblenz.

110 Rektor Chr. Müller an Dehler, B141/2020/10, BArch Koblenz.

111 Wieland an Dehler, 17 October 1951, B141/2019, Bl. 26, BArch Koblenz.

112 Tegeler an Hagemeyer, B141/2020/109, BArch Koblenz. She wrote again in May 1952 to plead her case. See Tegeler an Dehler, B141/2020/133, BArch Koblenz.

113 Müller an Dehler, 20 February 1952, B141/2028/151, BArch Koblenz.

114 These percentages have remained unchanged since 1950. "Decline in Religious Observance among Catholics and Protestants (1960–1989)," *Datenreport 1992. Zahlen und Fakten über die Bundesrepublik Deutschland*, ed. Federal Office of Statistics, trans. Allison Brown (Bonn: Statistisches Bundesamt, 1992), 190–1, http://www.germanhistorydocs.ghi-dc.org/sub_document .cfm?document_id=846.

115 "Katholische Bischöfe zur Familienrechtsreform," 21 February 1952, *Frankfurter Rundschau*, 44. B141/2051/003, BArch Koblenz.

116 Der Rat der Evangelischen Kirche in Deutschland an den Bundesminister der Justiz, 22 March 1952, B141/2057/59, BArch Koblenz.

117 See B141/2060, BArch Koblenz for correspondence between the Ministry of the Interior and the Ministry of Justice.

118 Wengst, *Thomas Dehler*.

119 Begründung zu dem Entwurf eines Gesetzes über die Gleichberechtigung von Mann und Frau auf dem Gebiete des bürgerlichen Rechts und über die Wiederherstellung der Rechtseinheit auf dem Gebiete des Familienrechts, 21 April 1952, B106/43313, BArch Koblenz.

120 Begründung zu dem Entwurf eines Gesetzes über die Gleichberechtigung von Mann und Frau auf dem Gebiete des bürgerlichen Rechts und über die Wiederherstellung der Rechtseinheit auf dem Gebiete des Familienrechts, 21 April 1952, B106/43313, BArch Koblenz.

121 §1355, Änderung des Bürgerlichen Gesetzbuches, Bl. 33, B106/43313, BArch Koblenz.

122 §1356, Änderung des Bürgerlichen Gesetzbuches, Bl. 33, B106/43313, BArch Koblenz.

123 §1357, Änderung des Bürgerlichen Gesetzbuches, Bl. 34/35, B106/43313, BArch Koblenz.

124 §4, Änderung des Bürgerlichen Gesetzbuches, Bl. 11, B106/43313, BArch Koblenz.

125 §1303, 1305, Änderung des Bürgerlichen Gesetzbuches, Bl. 16/17, B106/43313, BArch Koblenz.

126 §11, Änderung des Bürgerlichen Gesetzbuches, Bl. 14, B106/43313, BArch Koblenz.

127 §10, Änderung des Bürgerlichen Gesetzbuches, Bl. 13, B106/43313, BArch Koblenz.

128 §1360, Änderung des Bürgerlichen Gesetzbuches, Bl. 37/38, 38/39, B106/43313, BArch Koblenz.

129 Änderung des Bürgerlichen Gesetzbuches, Bl. 49, B106/43313, BArch Koblenz.

130 Änderung des Bürgerlichen Gesetzbuches, Bl. 151–161, B106/43313, BArch Koblenz.

131 Aktenvermerk über eine Besprechung mit Vertretern der evangelischen und der katholischen Kirche, 4 April 1952, B141/2057/97, BArch Koblenz.

132 1. Entwurf eines Gesetzes über die Gleichberechtigung von Mann und Frau auf dem Gebiete des bürgerlichen Rechts und über die Wiederherstellung der Rechtseinheit auf dem Gebiete des Familienrechts (Familienrechtsgesetz), BMJ, 230. Kabinettssitzung am 27. Juni 1952, Die Kabinettsprotokolle der Bundesregierung.

133 On 4 July 1952, Dehler wrote to the Staatssekretär of the Bundeskanzleramts and the other federal ministers to explain again his reasoning for the new law. See Dehler an Staatssekretär, 4 July 1952, B136/540/123–129, BArch Koblenz.

134 Dehler an Adenauer, 10 July 1952, B136/540, BArch Koblenz.

135 Adenauer an die Herren Bundesminister, 2 September 1952, B136/539/288–9, BArch Koblenz.

136 "CND," September 1951, B106/43313, Bl. 94, BArch Koblenz.

137 Dibelius an Dehler, 22 March 1952, B106/43313, BArch Koblenz.

138 Winfried Martini, "Gleichschaltung der Ehe," *Münchner Merkur*, 27 June 1952, B141/2050/007, BArch Koblenz. For the author's biography, see "Winfried Martini," last accessed December 9, 2016, https://www.munzinger.de/search/portrait/Winfried+Martini/0/6581.html.

139 Ernst Wahl, "Gleichberechtigung von Mann und Frau?," *Frankfurter Neue Presse*, 12 July 1952, B141/2050/009, BArch Koblenz.

140 "Das Familienrechtsgesetz und der Bundestag," *Union in Deutschland* 77, 27 September 1952, 2.

141 Änderungsvorschläge des Bundesrates zum Entwurf eines Gesetzes über die Gleichberechtigung von Mann und Frau, 26 September 1952, B136/540/360, BArch Koblenz. The federal government ultimately rejected this proposal, in order to "promote indeed the best for the family." Stellungnahme der Bundesregierung zu den Änderungsvorschlägen des Bundesrates zu dem Entwurf eines Gesetzes über die Gleichberechtigung von Mann und Frau auf dem Gebiete des bürgerlichen Rechts, September 30, 1952, B136/541/28, BArch Koblenz.

142 The Federal Archives in Koblenz and the SPD archives in Bonn contain a dozen such petitions. See, as two examples, Denkschrift des Deutschen Frauenrings zum Kabinettsentwurf eines Gesetzes über die Gleichberechtigung von Mann und Frau auf dem Gebiete des bürgerlichen Rechts und über die Wiederherstellung der Rechtseinheit auf dem Gebiete des Familienrechts, 23 December 1952, DGB-Archiv 2414450102, Archiv der sozialen Demokratie, Bonn; see also Else Ulich-Beil an den Herrn Bundeskanzler, 1 September 1952, B136/540/282, BArch Koblenz.

143 Meinungsverschiedenheiten im Kabinett über die Gleichberechtigung der Frau, *Die Neue Zeitung*, 1 July 1952, B141/2050/005, BArch Koblenz.

144 "Gegen die Vorrangstellung des Mannes," *Frankfurter Allgemeine Zeitung*, 27 September 1952, B141/2050/45, BArch Koblenz.

145 "Die gute Ehe," *Frankfurter Allgemeine Zeitung*, 27 September 1952, B141/2050/52, BArch Koblenz.

146 Arbeitsgemeinschaft der katholischen deutschen Frauen an den Herrn
     Bundeskanzler Dr. Adenauer, 7 July 1952, B136/540/186, BArch Koblenz; Ev.
     Frauenarbeit an Dibelius, 16 July 1952, EZA 99/638, Evangelisches Zentralarchiv,
     Berlin (EZAB).
147 Drucksache 3802, Verhandlungen des Deutschen Bundestages [1.] Deutscher
     Bundestag, 6.
148 The proposed law was much more extensive, but these were the chief provisions
     that came up frequently in political discourse on the topic.
149 VDBT, 239. Sitzung, 27 November 1952, 11052.
150 VDBT, 239. Sitzung, 27 November 1952, 11058. For Rehling's biography, see
     Ulrike Hospes, "Luise Rehling," last accessed 10 December 2016, http://www.kas
     .de/wf/de/37.8289.
151 VDBT, 239. Sitzung, 27 November 1952, 11060.
152 "Helene Wessel," in Vierhaus and Herbst, eds., *Biographisches Handbuch*, 942.
153 VDBT, 239. Sitzung, 27 November 1952, 11058, 11060. For Meyer-Laule's
     biography, see Vierhaus and Herbst, eds., "Emmy Meyer-Laule," 562; see also
     Notz, *Frauen in der Mannschaft*, 374–86.
154 VDBT, 239. Sitzung, 27 November 1952, 11059, 11069.
155 Edith Sheffer, *Burned Bridge: How East and West Germans Made the Iron Curtain*
     (Oxford: Oxford, 2014), 99.
156 Sheffer, *Burned Bridge*, 97.
157 VDBT, 239. Sitzung, 27 November 1952, 11061.
158 VDBT, 239. Sitzung, 27 November 1952, 11070. For Menzel's biography, see
     Vierhaus and Herbst, eds., "Walter Menzel," in *Biographisches Handbuch*, 553.
159 VDBT, 239. Sitzung, 27 November 1952, 11062.
160 VDBT, 239. Sitzung, 27 November 1952, 11056.
161 "Familienrecht zwischen zwei Feuern," *Deutsche Zeitung*, 12 November 1952,
     B141/2050/69, BArch Koblenz.
162 "Wenn Mann und Frau uneinig sind," *Frankfurter Allgemeine Zeitung*, 29
     November 1952, B141/2050/63, BArch Koblenz.
163 "Die dritte Instanz," *General-Anzeiger*, 29–30 November 1952, B141/2050/64,
     BArch Koblenz.
164 "Parlamentsaussprache über die Gleichberechtigung," *Die Neue Zeitung*, 28
     November 1952, B141/2050/66, BArch Koblenz.
165 Their only support came from the Deutscher Familienverband. See Umstaetter an
     den Herrn Bundeskanzler, 13 April 1953, B136/541/107, BArch Koblenz.
166 "Liebe Constanze-Leserin!" *Constanze*, 8 April 1953.
167 Wurzbacher, *Leitbilder*, 114.
168 Rodnick, *Postwar Germans*, 122.
169 Wurzbacher, *Leitbilder*, 120.
170 Wurzbacher, *Leitbilder*, 133.
171 Wurzbacher, *Leitbilder*, 127.

172 Wurzbacher, *Leitbilder*, 145.
173 Wurzbacher, *Leitbilder*, 139–40.
174 Baumert, *Deutsche Familien*, 139–40.
175 Wurzbacher, *Leitbilder*, 90.
176 Baumert, *Deutsche Familien*, 122–3.
177 Baumert, *Deutsche Familien*, 127.
178 Wurzbacher, *Leitbilder*, 101.
179 Thurnwald, *Gegenwarts-Probleme Berliner*, 278.
180 Thurnwald, *Gegenwarts-Probleme Berliner*, 282.
181 Thurnwald, *Gegenwarts-Probleme Berliner*, 272.
182 Thurnwald, *Gegenwarts-Probleme Berliner*, 267.
183 Curt Garner, "Public Service Personnel," 140–41. See also Bark and Gress, *History*, 255–6, for a general description of civil law reforms. They do not mention women or gender. See also Wengst, *Beamtentum zwischen Reform und Tradition*, for a more comprehensive study of all civil service reform in the immediate post-war period.
184 Thurnwald, *Gegenwarts-Probleme Berliner*, 285.
185 Thurnwald, *Gegenwarts-Probleme Berliner*, 299.
186 Thurnwald, *Gegenwarts-Probleme Berliner*, 292.
187 Thurnwald, *Gegenwarts-Probleme Berliner*, 307.
188 Thurnwald, *Gegenwarts-Probleme Berliner*, 320–1.
189 Thurnwald, *Gegenwarts-Probleme Berliner*, 324.
190 Moeller, *Protecting Motherhood*, 188.
191 Moeller, *Protecting Motherhood*, 190.
192 Moeller, *Protecting Motherhood*, 183.
193 Allen, *Women in Twentieth-Century Europe*, 80.
194 Allen, *Women in Twentieth-Century Europe*, 82.
195 Allen, *Women in Twentieth-Century Europe*, 97.
196 Allen, *Women in Twentieth-Century Europe*, 98, 104.
197 Offen, *European Feminisms*, 385.

4 A Series of Stalemates in East and West Germany, 1953–1957

1 Marschall an das Ministerium, 15 December 1954, DP 1/7200, BArch Berlin; Ostmann an Marschall, 11 March 1955, DP 1/7200, BArch Berlin.
2 Oertzen, *Teilzeitarbeit und die Lust*, 12, 14–15, 359.
3 Jarausch, *After Hitler*, 89.
4 Jarausch, *After Hitler*, 115.
5 Jarausch, *After Hitler*, 116.
6 Rölli-Alkemper, *Familie im Wiederaufbau*, 473.
7 Stefan Marx, "Franz-Josef Wuermeling," last accessed 26 December 2016, http://www.kas.de/wf/de/71.9969.

8   For studies on political Catholicism, see Evans, *The German Center Party*, 56; Wehler, *The German Empire 1871–1918*, 76; Gross, *The War against Catholicism*, 10.

9   Rölli-Alkemper, *Familie im Wiederaufbau*, 107, 416–7.

10 Rölli-Alkemper, *Familie im Wiederaufbau*, 415; Pope Pius XI, "On Christian Marriage," 31 December 1930, http://www.papalencyclicals.net/Pius11/P11CASTI.HTM.

11 Icken, *Der Deutsche Frauenrat*, 121.

12 Entwurf Gethmann eines Briefes an den Herrn Bundeskanzler, NL 1151/225, BArch Koblenz.

13 "Die Gleichberechtigung wird vertagt," *Frankfurter Allgemeine Zeitung*, 23 November 1953, 3. The allies included the conservative German Party and the parliamentary newcomers, the All-German Bloc/League of Expellees and Deprived of Rights.

14 The FDP archive in Gummersbach and the Federal Archive in Koblenz contain sixteen or more petitions. See, as examples, Harmuth an alle Bundestagsfraktion, 28 November 1953, B211/25–1, BArch Koblenz; and Blume an Dehler, 28 November 1953, N1–3000, Archiv des Liberalismus-Gummersbach. Blume asked Dehler to oppose the "dictatorial conduct of the CDU" regarding the forthcoming law. Some groups did want to extend the deadline, though there were fewer of them. See Teuffert an Ilk, 2 April 1953, N2–6, Archiv des Liberalismus-Gummersbach.

15 "Verhandlung über die Gleichberechtigung," *Frankfurter Allgemeine Zeitung*, 26 November 1953, 3. This issue was widely reported in the West German media; see B141/2053, BArch Koblenz, which contains clippings from regional and local papers such as *Deutsche Zeitung, Frankfurter Rundschau, Neue Presse, Rheinische Post, Frankfurter Neue Presse, Mannheimes Morgen, Rhein-Neckar-Zeitung, Rhein-Zeitung, Braunschweiger Zeitung, Stuttgarter Zeitung, Heidelberger Tageblatt, Süddeutsche Zeitung*, and *Westdeutsche Allgemeine*.

16 Entwurf eines Gesetzes über die Gleichberechtigung von Mann und Frau auf dem Gebiete des bürgerlichen Rechtes, [2.] Deutscher Bundestag, Drucksache 224, 29 January 1954, 5–6.

17 Entwurf eines Gesetzes über die Gleichberechtigung von Mann und Frau auf dem Gebiete des bürgerlichen Rechtes, [2.] Deutscher Bundestag, Drucksache 224, 29 January 1954, 5–6; Antrag der FDP, [2.] Deutscher Bundestag, Drucksache 112, 2 December 1953, 6.

18 VDBT, [2.] Deutscher Bundestag, 12. February 1954, 486; Antrag der SPD, [2.] Deutscher Bundestag, Drucksache 178, 13 January 1954, 1.

19 Entwurf eines Gesetzes über die Gleichberechtigung von Mann und Frau auf dem Gebiete des bürgerlichen Rechtes, [2.] Deutscher Bundestag, Drucksache 224, 29 January 1954, 5–6; Antrag der FDP, [2.] Deutscher Bundestag, Drucksache 112, 2 December 1953, 1; Antrag der SPD, [2.] Deutscher Bundestag, Drucksache 178, 13 January 1954, 1.

20 Antrag der FDP, [2.] Deutscher Bundestag, Drucksache 112, 2 December 1953, 1;
    Antrag der SPD, [2.] Deutscher Bundestag, Drucksache 178, 13 January 1954, 1;
    Entwurf eines Gesetzes über die Gleichberechtigung von Mann und Frau auf dem
    Gebiete des bürgerlichen Rechtes, [2.] Deutscher Bundestag, Drucksache 224, 29
    January6 1954, 5–6.

21 VDBT, [2.] Deutscher Bundestag, 12. February 1954, 480.

22 VDBT, [2.] Deutscher Bundestag, 12. February 1954, 485.

23 VDBT, [2.] Deutscher Bundestag, 12. February 1954, 486.

24 For biography of Karl Weber, see "Weber, Karl," last accessed 14 January 2017,
    http://www.munzinger.de/document/00000010949. Weber was born in 1898
    and studied law. He joined the CDU after the Second World War and became a
    Bundestag representative for Koblenz, Rhineland Palatinate, in 1949, serving until
    1965, when he became the Minister of Justice.

25 VDBT, [2.] Deutscher Bundestag, 12. February 1954, 474.

26 VDBT, [2.] Deutscher Bundestag, 12. February 1954, 483.

27 "Ludwig Metzger," last modified 16 December 2016, http://www.lagis-hessen.de/
    pnd/118581570. Born in 1902, Metzger, a practising Protestant himself, joined the
    SPD in 1930. He entered the Bundestag in 1953; VDBT, [2.] Deutscher Bundestag,
    12. February 1954, 498.

28 VDBT, [2.] Deutscher Bundestag, 12. February 1954, 499.

29 "Elisabeth Schwarzhaupt," last accessed 26 December 2016, http://www.kas.de/wf/
    de/37.8331.

30 Moeller, *Protecting Motherhood*, 117.

31 Schelsky, *Wandlungen der Deutschen Familie*.

32 VDBT, [2.] Deutscher Bundestag, 12. February 1954, 490.

33 VDBT, [2.] Deutscher Bundestag, 12. February 1954, 500.

34 VDBT, [2.] Deutscher Bundestag, 12. February 1954, 499.

35 VDBT, [2.] Deutscher Bundestag, 12. February 1954, 502.

36 VDBT, [2.] Deutscher Bundestag, 12. February 1954, 493.

37 VDBT, [2.] Deutscher Bundestag, 12. February 1954, 493.

38 VDBT, [2.] Deutscher Bundestag, 12. February 1954, 493.

39 Moeller, "Heimkehr ins Vaterland." Biess, *Homecomings*; Bruehoefener, "Defining
    the West German Soldier."

40 VDBT, [2.] Deutscher Bundestag, 12. February 1954, 488.

41 VDBT, [2.] Deutscher Bundestag, 12. February 1954, 488.

42 Coser, "Some Aspects of Soviet Family Policy."

43 VDBT, [2.] Deutscher Bundestag, 12. February 1954, 493.

44 VDBT, [2.] Deutscher Bundestag, zu Drucksache 3409, 2. The committee formed a
    subcommittee for family law, whose seventeen members met seventy-seven times
    between 1954 and 1956.

45 "Gleichberechtigungsdebatte vor dem Bundestag," *Union in Deutschland* 14, 17
    February 1954, 4; "Gleichberechtigung in parlamentarischer Sicht. Meinungen
    innerhalb der Fraktionen geteilt," *Union in Deutschland*, 5 March 1954, 1–4.

46 "Charaktersache," *Frankfurter Allgemeine Zeitung*, 13 February 1954, 1. See also "Scharfer Kampf um die Rechte der Frau," *Frankfurter Allgemeine Zeitung*, 13 February 1954, 1. "Briefe an die Herausgeber: Gleichberechtigung," *Frankfurter Allgemeine Zeitung*, 22 February 1954, 2.

47 "Gleichberechtigung – ein überfälliger Wechsel," *Neuer Vorwärts*, 19 February 1954, 4; Herta Gotthelf, "Gleichberechtigung – keine 'Gleichmacherei,'" *Neuer Vorwärts*, 5 February 1954, 1; Charlotte Walner-von Deuten, "Der Kampf um die Gleichberechtigung," *Gleichheit*, January 1954, 1.

48 E.W.H. Arnold, "Sorgenkind 'Familienrecht,'" *Die Zeit*, 27 October 1955, 2.

49 VDBT, [2.] Deutscher Bundestag, zu Drucksache 3409, 3. The longer discussions were outlined subsequently by Franz Seidl, a CSU representative from Dorfen, who spoke on marital property; Karl Wittrock, an SPD representative from Hessen (spousal relations); and Elisabeth Schwarzhaupt, a CDU representative from Frankfurt, who spoke on parental–child relationships. They faced more difficulty defining the *Zugewinnausgleich* clause in cases of separation, divorce, or death. See also Frieda Nadig, "Neuordnung des Familienrechts," *Gleichheit*, April 1957, 85.

50 VDBT, [2.] Deutscher Bundestag, zu Drucksache 3409, 3.

51 Deutscher Akademikerinnenbund an das Bundesjustizministerium, 18 January 1957, NL 1151/226, BArch Koblenz; Karlsruher Frauengruppe an die Herren Vorsitzenden der Fraktionen, 1 February 1957, NL Eduard Wahl, 01-237-026/2, Archiv für Christlich-Demokratische Politik-Sankt Augustin; Frauenring Kehl an Eduard Wahl, 26 January 1957, NL Eduard Wahl, 01-237-026/2, Archiv für Christlich-Demokratische Politik-Sankt Augustin; Deutschen Frauenrings-Ortsring Sinsheim/Elsenz an Eduard Wahl, 15 February 1957, NL Eduard Wahl, 01-237-026/2, Archiv für Christlich-Demokratische Politik-Sankt Augustin; Evangelische Frauenhilfe in Deutschland, Zur Frage des Stichentscheids des Mannes in §1628 des Regierungsentwurfs zum Familienrecht, 17 January 1957, NL 1151/226, BArch Koblenz; Frauenverband Hessen an Herrn Prof. Dr. Wahl, 15 January 1957, NL Eduard Wahl, 01-237-026/2, Archiv für Christlich-Demokratische Politik-Sankt Augustin; Frauenring Baden-Baden an Eduard Wahl, 22 February 1957, NL Eduard Wahl, 01-237-026/2, Archiv für Christlich-Demokratische Politik-Sankt Augustin; Hedi Flitz an den Bundestagsabgeordneten, 14 February 1957, N2-10, Archiv des Liberalismus-Gummersbach; Fini Pfannes an den Herrn Bundesminister der Justiz; 9 February 1957, B141/2015/96, BArch Koblenz; Der Vorstand des Deutsch-Evangelischen Frauenbund an Merkatz, 25 January 1957, B141/2025/94, BArch Koblenz.

52 Caroline Carl an Eduard Wahl, 14 January 1957, NL Eduard Wahl, 01-237-026/2, Archiv für Christlich-Demokratische Politik-Sankt Augustin.

53 Caroline Carl an Eduard Wahl, 18 February 1957, NL Eduard Wahl, 01-237-026/2, Archiv für Christlich-Demokratische Politik-Sankt Augustin. See also a similar letter from Lisbeth Kemmer, 13 February 1957, NL Eduard Wahl, 01-237-026/2, Archiv für Christlich-Demokratische Politik-Sankt Augustin.

54 L. Horning an Eduard Wahl, 11 February 1957, NL Eduard Wahl, 01-237-026/2, Archiv für Christlich-Demokratische Politik-Sankt Augustin.

55 Gertrud Carl an Eduard Wahl, 5 February 1957, NL Eduard Wahl, 01-237-026/2, Archiv für Christlich-Demokratische Politik-Sankt Augustin.

56 "Eduard Wahl," last accessed 13 January 2017, http://www.leo-bw.de/web/guest /detail/-/Detail/details/PERSON/wlbblb_personen/118770799/person. Wahl was born in 1903 and served as a jurist and law professor in Heidelberg before becoming a Bundestag member, representing the CDU, in 1949.

57 Frau K. an Eduard Wahl, 12 March 1957, NL Eduard Wahl, 01-237-026/2, Archiv für Christlich-Demokratische Politik-Sankt Augustin.

58 Melchior an Dehler, 1 February 1954, N1–3000, Archiv des Liberalismus-Gummersbach.

59 Diemer-Nicolaus an Lüders, 8 January 1957, A5–51, Archiv des Liberalismus-Gummersbach.

60 Not much is known about Glaser, other than that she was selected by women's association leaders Nora Melle, Theanolte Bähnisch, and Dorothea Karsten over another contender. Icken, *Der Deutsche Frauenrat*, 69–70. See, for example, *Informationen für die Frau*, September 1954, Anlage A; *Informationen für die Frau*, January 1954, Anlage A; *Informationen für die Frau*, February 1954, Anlage A; *Informationen für die Frau*, May 1954, Anlage A; "Zur Reform des Familienrechts/ Stichentscheid," *Informationen für die Frau*, January 1957, 7–11; "Zum Stichentscheid im Familienrecht," *Informationen für die Frau*, February 1957, 4–6; and "Zum Stichentscheid im Familienrecht," *Informationen für die Frau*, March 1957, 4–6.

61 VDBT, [2.] Deutscher Bundestag, 206. Sitzung, 3. Mai 1957, 11768.

62 VDBT, [2.] Deutscher Bundestag, 206. Sitzung, 3. Mai 1957, 11770.

63 Bericht der Bundesregierung über die Situation der Frauen in Beruf, Familie und Gesellschaft, Deutscher Bundestag, Drucksache V/909, 15.

64 Gesetz über die Gleichberechtigung von Mann und Frau auf dem Gebiete des bürgerlichen Rechts, 18 June 1957, *Bundesgesetzblatt*, 21 June 1957, 609–32. If the pair separated under circumstances other than death, they were required to determine which accruals each had made in marriage. If one spouse's accruals were higher than the other's, then half the surplus amount was to be awarded to the less well-off spouse. If one spouse died, one quarter of their inheritance was to go to the remaining spouse.

65 Gesetz über die Gleichberechtigung von Mann und Frau auf dem Gebiete des bürgerlichen Rechts, 609–32.

66 Bruce, *Resistance with the People*, 159; see also Ostermann, *Uprising*, xxxi.

67 Ostermann, *Uprising*, xxxi; Bruce, *Resistance with the People*, 159.

68 Bruce, *Resistance with the People*, 160, 161; Ramet, "Protestantism in East Germany," 171, 172–4. According to historian Gary Bruce, the SED's discrimination against Christians continued until after the announcement of the New Course. For more on the *Jugendweihe*, see Bolz, *Jugendweihen in Deutschland*.

Jugendweihe had existed among socialists since the late nineteenth century and was also practised in West Germany, so while it was not unique to the SED or East Germany, the way the latter used it as a means to drive out church influence was different from past or Western practice.

69 Ostermann, *Uprising in East Germany*; Taborsky, "The 'New Course,'" 160; Schroeder, *Der SED-Staat*, 139.

70 Schroeder, *Der SED-Staat*, 141. See also Arnulf Baring's well-known study, *Uprising in East Germany*.

71 Millington, *State, Society*, 97; Schroeder, *Der SED-Staat*, 142–3.

72 Childs, *The GDR*, 38. Elli Schmidt was a member of the Party Executive Committee of the SED from 1946 to 1953, a member of the town council of East Berlin, and, together with Käthe Kern, leader of the SED Women's Executive Committee (SED-Frauensekretariat) from 1946 to 1949. In 1953 she lost her positions in the SED; she was rehabilitated in 1956. See "Schmidt, Elli," last accessed 13 February 2017, https://www.bundesstiftung-aufarbeitung.de/wer-war-wer-in-der-ddr-%2363%3B-1424.html?ID=3074.

73 "Alle Inhaftieren kommen vor ein ordentliches Gericht," *Neues Deutschland*, 30 June 1953, 150, 5.

74 See Brentzel, "Unruhe und Aufstieg," for a detailed account of Benjamin's rise to power in 1953.

75 *Protokoll der Verhandlungen des IV. Parteitages der Sozialistischen Einheitspartei Deutschlands in der Werner-Seelenbinder-Halle zu Berlin, 30. März bis 6. April 1954* (Berlin: Dietz Verlag, 1954), 37–40.

76 Namely *Neues Deutschland*, *Neue Justiz*, and *Der Schöffe*.

77 Harsch, *Revenge of the Domestic*, 204–5.

78 §1, "Entwurf eines Familiengesetzbuches der Deutschen Demokratischen Republik," *Neue Justiz*, 30 June 1954, 377.

79 §§2–4, "Entwurf eines Familiengesetzbuches der Deutschen Demokratischen Republik," 377.

80 "Über die Eheschliessung und den Familiennamen," *Neues Deutschland*, 8 July 1954, 6; "Über die vermögensrechtlichen Beziehungen der Ehegatten," *Neues Deutschland*, 17 August 1954, 6; "Die rechtliche Stellung des nichtehelichen Kindes," *Neues Deutschland*, 25 August 1954, 6; "Zum Entwurf des neuen Familiengesetzbuches," *Die Frau von heute*, 9 July 1954, 10; "Zum Entwurf des neuen Familiengesetzbuches," *Die Frau von heute*, 16 July 1954, 10; "Zum Entwurf des neuen Familiengesetzbuches," *Die Frau von heute*, 30 July 1954, 6; "Zum Entwurf des neuen Familiengesetzbuches," *Die Frau von heute*, 6 August 1954, 7; "Zum Entwurf des neuen Familiengesetzbuches," *Die Frau von heute*, 13 August 1954, 13; "Zum Entwurf des neuen Familiengesetzbuches," *Die Frau von heute*, 27 August 1954, 10.

81 Hilde Benjamin, "Über den Entwurf eines neuen Familiengesetzbuches," *Neues Deutschland*, 15 June 1954, 3.

82 "Mit 16 Jahren sollte man noch nicht heiraten," *Berliner Zeitung*, 19 August 1954, 4.

83 "Kein 'Schuldig' mehr beim Scheidungsurteil," *Berliner Zeitung*, 2 September 1954, 6.

84 "Aussprache über das neue Familiengesetz begann," *Berliner Zeitung*, 3 August 1954, 6.

85 Bericht über die Ergebnisse der Diskussion zum Entwurf des Familiengesetzbuches auf der Arbeitstagung im Ministerium der Justiz vom 19.10.1954, S. 1, DO 1/14398, BArch Berlin. These estimates are drawn from reports in SAPMO-BArch Berlin, DY30/IV2/14/35, Bl. 61; DO 1/1555, Bl. 110. See also Harsch, *Revenge of the Domestic*, 205. These meetings were also propagated in the women's press. See, for example, "In dieser Woche besuchten wir: Minister Dr. Hilde Benjamin," *Die Frau von heute*, 25 June 1954, 2.

86 Protokoll über eine Justizaussprache, 24.8.54, DY30/IV2/14/35, Bl. 61–62, SAPMO-BArch Berlin.

87 Protokoll über eine Justizaussprache, Bl. 62–3.

88 Protokoll über eine Justizaussprache, Bl. 61.

89 Mary Fulbrook states that "in the 1950s reunification ranked as one of the most important problems for West Germans" and that it represented "constant aspirations for large numbers of East Germans." See Fulbrook, *Anatomy of a Dictatorship*, 136. Konrad H. Jarausch notes that over time, reunification rhetoric failed. See Jarausch, *After Hitler*, 66.

90 "Aussprache über das neue Familiengesetz begann," *Berliner Zeitung*, 3 August 1954, 6; "Berliner diskutieren das neue Familiengesetz," *Berliner Zeitung*, 11 August 1954, 4.

91 Mühlberg, *Bürger, Bitten und Behörden*, 9; see also Stitziel, "Shopping, Sewing," 265; Zatlin, "Ausgaben and Eingaben"; and Merkel and Mühlberg, "Eingaben und Öffentlichkeit," 13.

92 Strobel an das Kreisgericht Zeulenroda, 30 July 1954, DP 1/23655 (2), Bl. 31, BArch Berlin.

93 Fröhlich an das Ministerium der Justiz, 19 August 1954, DP 1/23655, Bl. 12, BArch Berlin; Ostmann an Fröhlich, Oktober 1, 1954, DP 1/23655, Bl. 13, BArch Berlin.

94 Müller an das Ministerium der Justiz, 16 August 1954, DP 1/23655, Bl. 14, BArch Berlin.

95 Buske, *Fräulein Mutter*.

96 Ebert an das Ministerium der Justiz, 10 July 1954, DP 1/23655 (1), Bl. 31, BArch Berlin. A similar letter came from Edith Lange of Freiberg, who wrote Hilde Benjamin on 11 August 1954 to explain that she was raising her two children alone, that her former husband was not paying his child support on time, and that she wished to change the children's names to her maiden name. The husband had remarried, and she "found it dumb" that he should have to support two families and that she should continue to live with his name through her children, which produced bad memories. See Lange an Benjamin, 11 August 1954, DP 1/23655 (2), Bl. 43, BArch Berlin. The ministry's response on Bl. 42 explained that this was not possible, because the other parent had a right to the children as well.

97 Wächtler an Ficker, 9 March 1955, DP 1/7200, BArch Berlin; Wojciehowski an Benjamin, DP 1/23655 (1), Bl. 166, BArch Berlin.
98 Limpert an das Ministerium für Justiz, DP 1/23655 (1), Bl. 41, BArch Berlin. See also Goltz an die Regierung der Deutschen Demokratischen Republik, 10 December 1954, DP 1/7200, BArch Berlin. Goltz defended the patriarchal name as well, but the ministry's response was that they prioritized "the personal right" of choosing one's name.
99 Fritze an die Frau von heute, DP 1/23655 (1), Bl. 43, BArch Berlin. Adultery was a common concern. See Kuhnt an das Ministerium der Justiz, 12 July 1954, DP 1/23655 (1), Bl. 39, BArch Berlin; Neesemann an Deutsche Kulturgemeinschaft, September 1954, DP 1/23655 (1), Bl. 277, BArch Berlin.
100 Elfriede Knöchel an die Redaktion "Die Frau von heute," 28 August 1954, DP 1/23655, Bl. 263, BArch Berlin; Marta Kerl an "Frau von heute," 2 August 1954, DP 1/23655, Bl. 265, BArch Berlin.
101 101 Gerda Radtke an die "Frau von heute" Leserbriefe, 26 August 1954, DP 1/23655, Bl. 264, BArch Berlin.
102 Fritz Lehmann an die Redaktion der "Frau von heute," 28 August 1954, DP 1/23655, Bl. 270, BArch Berlin.
103 Heydemann an die Regierung der Deutschen Demokratischen Republik, DP 1/23655 (1), Bl. 127, BArch Berlin.
104 Limpert an das Ministerium für Justiz, DP 1/23655 (1), Bl. 41, BArch Berlin.
105 Entschließung der Synode der Evangelischen Kirche in Deutschland zu Fragen der Ehe und Familie, 19. März 1954, 99/639, Evangelisches Zentralarchiv Berlin (EZAB); see also Harsch, *Revenge*, 205.
106 Protokoll über eine Justizaussprache, 24 August 1954, DY30/IV2/14/35, Bl. 62, SAPMO-BArch Berlin.
107 Entschließung der Synode der Evangelischen Kirche in Deutschland zu Fragen der Ehe und Familie, 19. März 1954, 99/639, EZAB.
108 Stellungnahme der Kirchlichen Ostkonferenz zu dem Entwurf eines Familiengesetzbuches der Deutschen Demokratischen Republik, 1 September 1954, 99/639, 1, EZAB.
109 Stellungnahme der Kirchlichen Ostkonferenz.
110 "Um Ehe und Familie," *Die Kirche*, 26 September 1954, DY 30/IV2/14/35, Bl. 75, 77, SAPMO-BArch Berlin.
111 DO 4/1555, BArch Berlin, contains petitions from Pritzwalk, Bautzen, Wildberg, Neuruppin, and Falkensee. See, for example, Evangelischen Gemeinden der Ev. Kirche Berlin-Brandenburg an den stellvertr. Ministerpräsidenten, Herrn Otto Nuschke, 24.11.1954. DO 4/1555, BArch Berlin; Entschliessung, 17 January 1955, DO 4/1555, Bl. 114, BArch Berlin; Evangelisch-Lutherische Landeskirche Mecklenburgs, 7 December 1954, DO 4/1555, BArch Berlin.
112 Gemeindekirchenrat Schulzendorf an den Stellvertreter des Ministerpräsidenten Herrn Otto Nuschke, 3 January 1955, DO 4/1555, BArch Berlin.

113 Bericht über die Versammlung der evangelischen Kirchengemeinde Bautzen am
8.11.1954, DY30/IV2/14/35, Bl. 107, SAPMO-BArch Berlin. According to this
document, 450 people attended. Another document on the same meeting from
DO 4/1555 states that 500 people attended. This document also indicates that the
pastor was informed ahead of time that his meeting was not to be held, but he
chose to have it anyway.

114 Bericht über die Versammlung der evangelischen Kirchengemeinde Bautzen am
8.11.1954, DY30/IV2/14/35, Bl. 107, SAPMO-BArch Berlin.

115 For biography of Wilhelm Weskamm, see Schäfer, "Weskamm, Wilhelm."
Weskamm was born in 1891, appointed Bishop of Berlin in 1951, and died in
1956. For biography of Otto Grotewohl, see "Otto Grotewohl," last modified 19
February 2016, https://www.hdg.de/lemo/biografie/otto-grotewohl.html; and
Wilhelm Weskamm an Otto Grotewohl, 28 August 1954, DY30/IV2/14/35, Bl. 1,
SAPMO-BArch Berlin.

116 Jarausch, *After Hitler*, 193; Harsch, *Revenge of the Domestic*, 205–6. See,
for an example of an individual Catholic priest pursuing the unification
argument, Limbach-Frohna an den Stellvertreter des Ministerpräsidenten,
Volkskammerabgeordneten und Vorsitzenden der Christlich-Demokratischen
Union Deutschlands Herrn Otto Nuschke in Berlin, 2 January 1955, DO 4/1555,
BArch Berlin.

117 Schäfer, *The East German State*, 32.

118 Benjamin an Plenikowski, DY30/IV2/14/35, Bl. 46, SAPMO-BArch Berlin.

119 Aufzeichnung, 6 September 1954, DO 4/2095, BArch Berlin.

120 Maria Hagemeyer, *Der Entwurf des Familiengesetzbuches der "Deutschen
Demokratischen Republik"* (Bonn: Bundesministerium für gesamtdeutsche Fragen,
1955); Benjamin an den Bundesminister der Justiz Herrn Neumayer, 26 July 1954,
DP 1/7892, Bl. 230, BArch Berlin; For biography of Hilde Benjamin, see "Hilde
Benjamin 1902–1989," last modified 3 February 2016, https://www.hdg.de/lemo
/biografie/hilde-benjamin.html.

121 "Ein "Nein?, das wackelt," *Berliner Zeitung*, 7 August 1954, 2; "Gedankenaustausch
über Familiengesetz von Bonn abgelehnt," *Neues Deutschland*, 7 August
1954, 2; "Bonn wünscht keine Verständigung," *Neue Zeit*, 7 August 1954, 2.
For responses from the West German side, see Hagemeyer, *Der Entwurf des
Familiengesetzbuches*, 24. The former Minister of Justice, Thomas Dehler, was
more open to the idea. See Resume einer Besprechung mit Dr. Th. Dehler, DP
1/7892, Bl. 332, BArch Berlin.

122 Benjamin an die Justizverwaltungen und die Gerichte der DDR, 14 August 1954,
DP 1/7889, BArch Berlin.

123 Antikommunistischer Volksbund für Frieden und Freiheit e.V. an alle Juristen, 3,
1954 November DP 1/7889, Bl. 447, BArch Berlin.

124 According to a list of participants, only thirteen West German participants had
RSVPed by 16 October 1954, with another five indicating "maybe." See Liste der
westdeutschen Teilnehmer, 16 October 1954, DP 1/7892, Bl. 385, BArch Berlin.

125 Wolle-Egenolf, *Der Gleichheitsgrundsatz*; W. Bergemann an den Herrn Direktor des Deutschen Instituts für Rechtswissenschaft Herrn H. Büttner, 8 October 1954, DP 1/7889, Bl. 5, BArch Berlin; Beitzke an Herr Büttner, 8 October 1954, DP 1/7889, Bl. 8, BArch Berlin; Borger an Büttner, 12 October 1954, Bl. 7, BArch Berlin; Ebel an Büttner, 2 October 1954, DP 1/7889, Bl. 9, BArch Berlin; Erler an das Deutsche Institut für Rechtswissenschaft, 2 October 1954, Bl. 10, BArch Berlin. Bl. 15–43, 46, 49, 51, 53 all express regrets. Kuhn an Toeplitz, 26 September 1954, DP 1/7892, Bl. 335, BArch Berlin; Würdinger an Herr. Dr. Toeplitz, October 18, 1954, DP 1/7889, Bl. 52, BArch Berlin.

126 Ranke an Kracker von Schwarzenfeldt, 23 September 1955, 99/647, Evangelisches Zentralarchiv-Berlin (EZAB); Kracker von Schwarzenfeldt an Ranke, 22 July 1955, 99/647, EZAB; Ranke an Kracker von Schwarzenfeldt, 24 June 1955, 99/647, EZAB; Kracker von Schwarzenfeldt an Ranke, 8 June 1955, 99/647; Kracker von Schwarzenfeldt an Ranke, 12 May 1955, 99/647, EZAB; Ranke an Herr Präsident, 12 April 1955, 99/647, EZAB; Bosch an Ranke, 9 July 1955, 99/648, EZAB; Kracker von Schwarzenfeldt an Ranke, 16 June 1956, 99/648, EZAB.

127 Elisabeth Schwarzhaupt, "Kirchliche Stellungnahmen zur Familienrechtsreform in der Bundesrepublik und in der Sowjetzone," *Evangelische Verantwortung*, February 1956, 4.

128 Neues Familiengesetz, 13 September 1954, SPD Ostbüro 0247, Archiv der sozialen Demokratie-Bonn.

129 Neues Familiengesetz.

130 "Thesen zum Familienrecht," *Der Tag*, 5 September 1954, DO 4/2905, BArch Berlin. See also "Der Tag," last accessed 26 December 2016, http://www.kas.de/wf/de/71.14859. See also Protokoll, 28 November 1951, A45–50, Archiv des Liberalismus-Gummersbach for notes from the FDP Ostbüro.

131 "Ostkonferenz äußert Bedenken," *Spandauer Volksblatt*, 2 October 1954, DO 4/2905, BArch Berlin.

132 "Kritik an der Familienpolitik der Zone," *Frankfurter Allgemeine Zeitung*, 14 September 1954, 3.

133 "Thesen zum Familienrecht," *Der Tag*, 5 September 1954, DO 4/2905, BArch Berlin.

134 "Familiengesetzbuch für die Zone," *Frankfurter Allgemeine Zeitung*, 16 June 1954, 4.

135 "Des Papstes Garde," *Der Spiegel*, 38, 15 September 1954, 10.

136 Benjamin an Plenikowski, 5 October 1954, DY30/IV2/14/35, Bl. 70, SAPMO-BArch Berlin. Either her intel was faulty or the Bundestag's plans changed, because the law did not go up for a vote until 1957. "Karl Wilhelm Gerst," last accessed 23 December 2016, https://www.munzinger.de/search/portrait/Wilhelm+Karl+Gerst/0/4186.html.

137 Benjamin an Plenikowski, 5 October 1954, DY30/IV2/14/35, Bl. 71, SAPMO-BArch Berlin.

138 Benjamin an all Leiter der Justizverwaltungsstellen und Direktoren der Bezirksgerichte der Deutschen Demokratischen Republik, 27 August 1954, DP 1/7889, Bl. 235–236, BArch Berlin.

139 Bericht über die Ergebnisse der Diskussion zum Entwurf des Familiengesetzbuches auf der Arbeitstagung im Ministerium der Justiz vom 19.10.1954, 2–3, 9–11, DO 1/14398, BArch Berlin.

140 See as one example the response to Heinz Jurischke, written by Dr. Ostmann, in DP 1/23655 (2), Bl. 48, BArch Berlin. "Sie sind jedoch im Irrtum, wenn Sie meinen, dass der Entwurf des Familiengesetzbuches (§29) scheidungsfeindlich sei und Scheidungen fast unmöglich mache."

141 Bericht über die Ergebnisse, 3.

142 Bericht über die Ergebnisse, 32.

143 Bericht über die Ergebnisse, 4.

144 Salfemeier an die Regierung der Deutschen Demokratischen Republik, 27 September 1954, DO 1/14398, BArch Berlin; Vogel an die Regierung der Deutschen Demokratischen Republik, 6 September 1954, DO 1/14398, BArch Berlin; Auszugsweise Abschrift aus dem Protokoll der Arbeitsberatung der erforter Standesämter am 29. Juli 1954, 29 July 1954, DO 1/14398, BArch Berlin; Neubert an das Ministerium der Justiz, 20 October 1954, DO 1/14398, BArch Berlin.

145 "Gustav Heinemann," last accessed 23 December 2016, https://www.hdg.de/lemo/biografie/gustav-heinemann.html.

146 Heinemann an Grotewohl, 20 November 1954, DP 1/243, BArch Berlin.

147 Benjamin an Mielke, 15 April 1955; 21 January 1955, DP 1/243, BArch Berlin. For biography of Erich Mielke, see "Erich Mielke," last accessed 23 December 2016, https://www.hdg.de/lemo/biografie/erich-mielke.html.

148 Auskunftsbericht Nr. 3 über die Situation und Tätigkeit der evangelischen Kirchen in Deutschland vom 1.9.1954 bis 1.9.1955, MfS JHS 001 Z 9/56, BStU 0003, Der Bundesbeauftragte für die Unterlagen des Staatssicherheitsdienstes der ehemaligen Deutschen Demokratischen Republik.

149 Kaschka an das Ministerium, 1 February 1955, DP 1/7200, BArch Berlin. See also Meyer an das Ministerium, 7 February 1955, DP 1/7200, BArch Berlin; Schröder an das Justizministerium der Deutschen Demokratischen Republik, 30 April 1955, DP 1/7200, BArch Berlin; Rödiger an das Ministerium für Justiz, 21 June 1955, DP 1/7200, BArch Berlin; Schodlok an das Ministerium der Justiz, 30 July 1955, DP 1/7200, BArch Berlin; Musculus an das Ministerium der Justiz, 18 August 1955, DP 1/7200, BArch Berlin; Deutschbein an das Ministerium, 1 March 1955, DP 1/7200, BArch Berlin.; Kirchenkreis Zeitz an das Ministerium, 7 March 1955, DP 1/7200, BArch Berlin; Schönberg an das Ministerium für Justiz der Deutschen Demokratischen Republik, 6 February 1955, DP 1/7200, BArch Berlin.

150 For studies on West German rearmament, see Bruehoefener, "Defining the West German Soldier"; and Clay, *Germans to the Front*, 234.

151 "Die neue Verordnung über die Eheschließung und –auflösung," *Neues Deutschland*, 8 December 1955, 3.

152 Protokoll über die Beratung einer Kommission über Fragen das Familiengesetzbuches der Deutschen Demokratischen Republik am 25.5.1959, DY 30/IV 2/12/106, Bl. 8, BArch Berlin. The connection between East German sovereignty and the FGB comes up in a Ministers' Council report on the development of family law. See also Konzeption für das Familiengesetzbuch, 24 October 1963, DC 20 /I/4/834, Bl. 65, BArch Berlin.

153 "Verordnung über Eheschließung und Eheauflösung," *Gesetzblatt der Deutschen Demokratischen Republik*, 24 November 1955, Teil I, Nr. 102 (Berlin, 1955), 849ff. The decree established that men and women could marry at the age of eighteen. Bigamy, incest/adoptive relations, and marrying disabled persons were prohibited. Marriages could be dissolved by death. If a spouse declared dead reappeared, the remarried spouse could only honour the earlier vows once the second marriage was divorced. Divorce could also be granted "for serious reasons" and if "the marriage had lost its purpose for the spouses, children, and society." Courts decided who would have custody of the children. Divorced partners could revert to their former names. If one was unable to support him- or her-self, the other was obligated to provide alimony for a limited period.

154 "Anordnung zur Anpassung der Vorschriften über das Verfahren in Ehesachen an die Verordnung über Eheschließung und Eheauflösung – Eheverfahrensordnung (EheVerfO)," *Gesetzblatt der Deutschen Demokratischen Republik*, 7 February 1956, Teil I, Nr. 16 (Berlin, 1956), 145–8; "Verordnung über die Annahme an Kindes Statt. Vom 29. November 1956," *Gesetzblatt der Deutschen Demokratischen Republik*, 29 November 1956, Teil I, Nr. 109, (Berlin, 1956), 1326.

155 It is telling, of course, that even in the title of the document, the federal government refused to use the GDR's proper title, instead referring to it in irredentist terms as the "Soviet Zone."

156 Hagemeyer, *Zum Familienrecht der Sowjetzone*, 11.

157 Hagemeyer, *Zum Familienrecht der Sowjetzone*, 18.

158 Hagemeyer, *Zum Familienrecht der Sowjetzone*, 11.

159 Hagemeyer, *Zum Familienrecht der Sowjetzone*, 29.

160 Familienrecht in der Sowjetzone, Vortrag bei der Mütterdiensttagung Ende Juni 1955 in Stein bei Nürnberg, I-048-013/4, Archiv für Christlich-Demokratische Politik-Sankt Augustin.

161 Gleichberechtigung der Frau als Aufbau- oder Zerstörungsprinzip, 13–16 March 1956, B211/22-2, BArch Koblenz.

162 Schwarz, *Konrad Adenauer*, 657.

163 Allen, *Women in Twentieth-Century Europe*, 82–3.

5 Achieving Equality in East and West Germany, 1957–1976

1   Frau B., "Der dich auf Adelers Fittichen sicher gefuhrt. Mein Leben," Kempowski-Biografien 6492, Archiv der Akademie der Künste, Berlin.

2   Heineman, *What Difference Does a Husband Make?*, 192; Harsch, *Revenge of the Domestic*, 210; Obertreis, *Familienpolitik*, 232.

3   For the 12 May 1955 version of the "Einführungsgesetz zum Familiengesetzbuch der Deutschen Demokratischen Republik," see DP 1/23655, Bl. 234–244, BArch Berlin. For the 11 May 1955 version of the "Durchführungsverordnung zum Familiengesetzbuch der Deutschen Demokratischen Republik," see DP 1/23655, Bl. 246–270, BArch Berlin. For the 5 April 1955 version of the "Entwurf des Familiengesetzbuches der Deutschen Demokratischen Republik," see DP 1/23655. Bl. 271–312, BArch Berlin. For the 10 June 1955 version, see DO 1/14398, BArch Berlin. In DO 1/14398, there are also undated drafts of the FGB and the Einführungsgesetz. For the 17 March 1958 version of the FGB, see DO 1/14397, BArch Berlin. DO 1/14397 also contains undated versions of the Einführungsgesetz. Benjamin an Maron, 22 April 1958, DO 1/14397, BArch Berlin. The new drafts were reviewed and produced by a group of academics under the guidance of Benjamin, who then circulated their recommendations among the other governmental ministries, whose leaders were sometimes critical of the proposals. See also Bergmann an Ministerium der Justiz, 19 May 1958, DO 1/14398, BArch Berlin; Dombrowsky an Ehrhardt, Einführungsgesetz zum Familiengesetzbuch, 30 May 1958, DO 1/14398, BArch Berlin; Dombrowsky an Ehrhardt, Entwurf des Familiengesetzbuches, 20 May 1958, DO 1/14398, BArch Berlin; Sonntag an Jendretzky, 6 December 1958, DO 1/26466, BArch Berlin; See also Markovits, "Civil Law in East Germany."

4   "Neues zum Entwurf des Familiengesetzbuches," *Neues Deutschland*, May 1958, 3.

5   Benjamin an Maron, Anlage Begründung zum Einführungsgesetz des Familiengesetzbuches, 30 April 1958, DO 1/14397, BArch Berlin. For biography of Karl Maron, see "Gestorben: Karl Maron," *Der Spiegel*, 10 February 1975, 132.

6   Benjamin an Maron, Anlage Begründung zum Einführungsgesetz des Familiengesetzbuches, 30 April 1958, DO 1/14397, BArch Berlin.

7   Vorlage für das Politbüro, 7 April 1959, DY 30/IV 2/13/106, Bl. 22, BArch Berlin.

8   Harsch, *Revenge of the Domestic*, 236.

9   Vorlage für das Politbüro, Bl. 22–23.

10 Vorlage für das Politbüro, Bl. 22.

11 C. Maier, *Dissolution*, 87.

12 Protokoll des VI. Parteitages der sozialistischen Einheitspartei Deutschlands, 15. bis 21. Januar 1963 (Berlin: Dietz Verlag Berlin, 1963), 371.

13 Beschluss zur Konzeption und zum Massnahmeplan zur Ausarbeitung eines neuen Familiengesetzbuches, 25 November 1963, DC-20-I/4/834, Bl. 63, BArch Berlin; see also Protokoll über die konstituierende Sitzung der Grundkommission zur

Ausarbeitung eines neuen Familiengesetzbuches vom 25. Januar 1964, 20 February 1964, DY34/2319, BArch Berlin.

14 Massnahmeplan zur Ausarbeitung eines neuen Familiengesetzbuches, 24 October 1963, DC20/I/4/865, Bl. 77, BArch Berlin.

15 Bericht über den Stand der Gesetzgebungsarbeiten am Familiengesetzbuch, 21 May 1964, DC20/I/4/965, Bl. 41–48, BArch Berlin.

16 Stellungnahme der Abteilung Staats- und Rechtsfragen und der Arbeitsgruppe Frauen zur Vorlage des Ministeriums der Justiz – Entwurf des Familiengesetzbuches, 6 October 1964, DA5/487, BArch Berlin.

17 Stellungnahme der Abteilung Staats- und Rechtsfragen.

18 Stellungnahme der Abteilung Staats- und Rechtsfragen.

19 Beschluß-Entwurf über die öffentliche Diskussion des Familiengesetzbuch-Entwurfs, 1964, DA5/487, Barch Berlin; see also "Entwurf Familiengesetzbuch der Deutschen Demokratischen Republik," 2 September 1964 and 21 December 1964, DY34/2316, Barch Berlin.

20 Beschluß über die öffentliche Diskussion des Entwurfs des Familiengesetzbuches, 18, 1965 March DC 20/I/4/1091, Bl. 118–123, BArch Berlin; Plan gemeinsamer Maßnahmen der Rechtspflegeorgane zur Durchführung der öffentlichen Diskussion des Entwurfs des Familiengesetzbuches, March 1965, DP 2/1509/154–157, BArch Berlin. The resolution passed by the steering committee outlined specific guidelines for the content and conduct of the public discussions to come between April and July 1965.

21 Rudi Singer an alle Chefredaktionen, 26 March 1965, DE 1/52952, BArch Berlin.

22 Internationale Pressekonferenz des Presseamtes beim Vorsitzenden des Ministerrates, 14 April 1965, DC 9/373/1, Bl. 4, BArch Berlin.

23 Internationale Pressekonferenz des Presseamtes beim Vorsitzenden des Ministerrates, Bl. 6.

24 Internationale Pressekonferenz des Presseamtes beim Vorsitzenden des Ministerrates, Bl. 9–10.

25 Internationale Pressekonferenz des Presseamtes beim Vorsitzenden des Ministerrates, Bl. 12–13.

26 Internationale Pressekonferenz des Presseamtes beim Vorsitzenden des Ministerrates, Bl. 20.

27 Internationale Pressekonferenz des Presseamtes beim Vorsitzenden des Ministerrates, Bl. 21.

28 Internationale Pressekonferenz des Presseamtes beim Vorsitzenden des Ministerrates, Bl. 22.

29 Internationale Pressekonferenz des Presseamtes beim Vorsitzenden des Ministerrates, Bl. 23, 28.

30 Internationale Pressekonferenz des Presseamtes beim Vorsitzenden des Ministerrates, Bl. 23.

31 Internationale Pressekonferenz des Presseamtes beim Vorsitzenden des Ministerrates, Bl. 24, 26, 28.

32 "Entwurf des Familiengesetzbuches der Deutschen Demokratischen Republik,"
    Neues Deutschland, 15 April 1965, 9; "Ehe und Familie," *Berliner Zeitung*, 15 April
    1965, 3; "Entwurf des Familiengesetzbuches," *Neue Justiz*, 15 April 1965, 259–71.

33 "Entwurf des Familiengesetzbuches der Deutschen Demokratischen Republik," 3–4.

34 "Entwurf des Familiengesetzbuches der Deutschen Demokratischen Republik," 4–5.

35 "Entwurf des Familiengesetzbuches der Deutschen Demokratischen Republik," 6.

36 "Entwurf des Familiengesetzbuches der Deutschen Demokratischen Republik," 6–7.

37 "Entwurf des Familiengesetzbuches der Deutschen Demokratischen Republik," 8–12.

38 "Entwurf des Familiengesetzbuches der Deutschen Demokratischen Republik," 12–14.

39 "Entwurf des Familiengesetzbuches der Deutschen Demokratischen Republik," 13.

40 Beschlussentwurf über die ersten Massnahmen zur Durchführung der
    öffentlichen Diskussion des Entwurfs des Familiengesetzbuches, 2 April 1965,
    MfS HA XX 5244, BstU 000002, Bundesbeauftragte für die Unterlagen des
    Staatssicherheitsdienstes der ehemaligen Deutschen Demokratischen Republik,
    Berlin.

41 Information über den Verlauf der öffentlichen Diskussionen zum Entwurf des
    Familiengesetzbuches, Stand 17.7.1965, 24 July 1965, DP 1/8186, BArch Berlin. See
    also reports from 9 July, 26 June, 19 June, and October 1965 in the same file.

42 Information über den Verlauf der öffentlichen Diskussionen zum Entwurf des
    Familiengesetzbuches, Stand 17.7.1965, 24 July 1965, DP 1/8186, BArch Berlin;
    Information über den Verlauf der öffentlichen Diskussionen zum Entwurf des
    Familiengesetzbuches, 3 August 1965, DY 31/1075, Bl. 42–43, BArch Berlin.

43 Empfehlungen des Präsidiums des Bundesvorstandes des FDGB an die Vorstände
    und Leitungen der Gewerkschaften zur Teilnahme an der Diskussion des
    Entwurfs des Familiengesetzbuches, 15 April 1965, DY 34/2319, BArch Berlin;
    LDPD Zentralvorstand, May 1965, L4–126, Bl. 78, Archiv des Liberalismus-
    Gummersbach; Stellungnahme des Präsidiums des Hauptvorstandes der CDU zum
    Entwurf des Familiengesetzbuches, July 1965, DP 2/1509, Bl. 75, BArch Berlin;
    Stellungnahme des DFD zum Entwurf des Familiengesetzbuches, 2 September
    1965, DY 31/1019, Bl. 32–36, BArch Berlin.

44 Homann an die Vorsitzende der zentralen Kommission, 31 July 1965, DP 1/23791,
    BArch Berlin.

45 Lindner an LDPD Zentralvorstand, May 1965, L4–126, Bl. 81, Archiv des
    Liberalismus-Gummersbach.

46 Lindner an LDPD Zentralvorstand, May 1965, L4–126, Bl. 81, Archiv des
    Liberalismus-Gummersbach, Bl. 83.

47 Stellungnahme des Präsidiums des Hauptvorstandes der CDU zum Entwurf des
    Familiengesetzbuches, July 1965, DP 2/1509, Bl. 79, BArch Berlin.

48 The NDPD, for example, opposed the marrying age and held differing views on
    marital property. Homann an die Vorsitzende der zentralen Kommission, 31 July
    1965, DP 1/23791, BArch Berlin. The LDPD pointed out that "absolute equality"
    of men and women might interfere with other laws on the books, such as the

Hausarbeitstag. Kurz-Information für die Mitglieder des Politischen Ausschusses des Zentralvorstandes, 2 June 1965, L2–120, Bl. 5, Archiv des Liberalismus-Gummersbach. See also Carola Sachse's monograph on the *Hausarbeitstag* in East and West Germany. Sachse, *Der Hausarbeitstag.*

49 Stellungnahme des Präsidiums des Hauptvorstandes der CDU zum Entwurf des Familiengesetzbuches, July 1965, DP 2/1509, Bl. 82, BArch Berlin.

50 For Bengsch's biography, see "Alfred Bengsch," last accessed 14 January 2017, https://www.bundesstiftung-aufarbeitung.de/wer-war-wer-in-der-ddr-%2363%3b-1424.html?ID=200. Bengsch was born in Berlin in 1921 and was briefly in the Wehrmacht before becoming an American prisoner of war. He was ordained in 1950 and chosen as Bishop of Berlin in 1961.

51 Bengsch an Stoph, April 1965, Ost-CDU VII-013–924, Archiv für Christlich-Demokratische Politik, Sankt Augustin.

52 Evangelisches Konsistorium, 28 May 1965, MfS HA XX 465, BstU 000160, Bundesbeauftragte für die Unterlagen des Staatssicherheitsdienstes der ehemaligen Deutschen Demokratischen Republik, Berlin.

53 Ev.-Luth. Pfarramt, 5 July 1965, BStU 000154, MfS HA XX 465, Bundesbeauftragte für die Unterlagen des Staatssicherheitsdienstes der ehemaligen Deutschen Demokratischen Republik, Berlin.

54 For biography of Krummacher, see "Friedrich Wilhelm Krummacher," last accessed 14 January 2017, https://www.bundesstiftung-aufarbeitung.de/wer-war-wer-in-der-ddr-%2363%3b-1424.html?ID=1934. Krummacher was born in 1901 and joined the NSDAP in 1933. He eventually ended up in a Soviet prisoner-of-war camp and helped Walter Ulbricht and the Soviets. He became the Pomeranian bishop in 1955.

55 Die Stellung der Evangelischen Kirche in Deutschland (EKD) zum Wehr- und Wehrersatzdienst und zum Familiengesetz-Entwurf, 30 June 1965, MfS ZAIG N2. 1074, BstU 000006, Bundesbeauftragte für die Unterlagen des Staatssicherheitsdienstes der ehemaligen Deutschen Demokratischen Republik, Berlin.

56 Begründung des Entwurfes des Familiengesetzbuches, 15 November 1965, DA 5/486, BArch Berlin. See also Begründung des Entwurfes des Familiengesetzbuches, 15 November 1965, DC 20/I/4/1220, Bl. 55, BArch Berlin. As before in 1954, the proposals covered a wide range of opinions. As one example, forums in Schleiz, Freital, and Lichtenberg in May 1965 garnered requests to up the legal marrying age to twenty-one and to allow men to press paternity suits in court. See Fragen einer FGB-Diskussion in einer CDU-Mitgliederversammlung in Lichtenberg am 18.5.1965, 18 May 1965, DP 2/1509, Bl. 99, BArch Berlin; Fragen auf einem FGB-Forum in Schleiz am 20. Mai 1965, DP 2/1509, Bl. 100, BArch Berlin; Fragen zum FGB auf der Aussprache im Intelligenz-Klub Freital am 14.5.1965, DP 2/1509, Bl. 104, BArch Berlin. Fragen auf dem FGB-Forum in Erfurt am 13. Mai 1965, DP 2/1509, Bl. 101, BArch Berlin.

57 "Intakte Ehe – Interessant?" *Für Dich*, May 1965, 16–17.
58 "Das Gleichgewicht," *Für Dich*, June 1965, 11.
59 "Ehe Arbeit Notstandsfolgen," *Für Dich*, July 1965, 16.
60 Sitzung des Ausschusses für Arbeit und Sozialpolitik der Volkskammer der Deutschen Demokratischen Republik, DA 1/6422, BArch Berlin.
61 Sitzung des Ausschusses für Arbeit und Sozialpolitik der Volkskammer der Deutschen Demokratischen Republik.
62 Sitzung des Ausschusses für Arbeit und Sozialpolitik der Volkskammer der Deutschen Demokratischen Republik.
63 Stenografisches Protokoll: Beratung des Verfassungs- und Rechtsausschusses der Volkskammer, 10 December 1965, DA 1/4614, BArch Berlin.
64 Stenografisches Protokoll: Beratung des Verfassungs- und Rechtsausschusses der Volkskammer, 10 December 1965, DA 1/4614, BArch Berlin.
65 *Stenographische Protokolle der Volkskammer der Deutschen Demokratischen Republik* (Berlin: Volkskammer, 1965), 521.
66 *Stenographische Protokolle der Volkskammer der Deutschen Demokratischen Republik*, 529. For a biography of Roberta Gropper, see "Roberta Gropper," last accessed 23 December 2016, http://www.bundesstiftung-aufarbeitung.de /wer-war-wer-in-der-ddr-%2363%3b-1424.html?ID=4386. Gropper was born in 1897 and joined the KPD in 1919. She immigrated to the Soviet Union during the war, where she was imprisoned for "anti-Soviet" activities. She returned to Berlin in 1947, joined the SED, and became active in women's issues.
67 *Stenographische Protokolle der Volkskammer der Deutschen Demokratischen Republik*, 521.
68 *Stenographische Protokolle der Volkskammer der Deutschen Demokratischen Republik*, 534.
69 *Stenographische Protokolle der Volkskammer der Deutschen Demokratischen Republik*, 535.
70 *Stenographische Protokolle der Volkskammer der Deutschen Demokratischen Republik*, 535.
71 Childs, *The GDR*, 124.
72 Quint, *The Imperfect Union*, 23.
73 Verfassung der Deutschen Demokratischen Republik, 6 April 1968, http://www .documentarchiv.de/ddr/verfddr.html#KAPITEL 1–2.
74 Neumaier and Ludwig, "The Individualization of Everyday Life," 297.
75 Jarausch, "Care and Coercion," 60.
76 Neumaier and Ludwig, "The Individualization of Everyday Life," 301–2.
77 Meyer and Schulze, *Familie im Umbruch*, 47–8.
78 Meyer and Schulze, *Familie im Umbruch*, 49.
79 Meyer and Schulze, *Familie im Umbruch*, 49.
80 Meyer and Schulze, *Familie im Umbruch*, 53.
81 Meyer and Schulze, *Familie im Umbruch*, 54.

82 Allen-Thompson and Dodds, *The Wall in My Backyard*. American academics Pam Allen-Thompson and Dinah Dodds' 1994 study featured interviews with former East German women recounting their daily lives and the discrepancies between law and social expectations.

83 Allen-Thompson and Dodds, *The Wall in My Backyard*, 62.

84 Allen-Thompson and Dodds, *The Wall in My Backyard*, 62.

85 Allen-Thompson and Dodds, *The Wall in My Backyard*, 44. See also Ansorg and Hürtgen. "The Myth of Female Emancipation," 165; and Langenhan and Roß, "The Socialist Glass Ceiling," 177–8.

86 Allen-Thompson and Dodds, *The Wall in My Backyard*, 47.

87 Allen-Thompson and Dodds, *The Wall in My Backyard*, 94.

88 Allen-Thompson and Dodds, *The Wall in My Backyard*, 127.

89 Allen-Thompson and Dodds, *The Wall in My Backyard*, 131.

90 Allen-Thompson and Dodds, *The Wall in My Backyard*, 131.

91 Allen-Thompson and Dodds, *The Wall in My Backyard*, 127.

92 For biography of Erich Honecker, see Regina Haunhorst and Irmgard Zündorf, "Biografie Erich Honecker," in *LeMO-Biografien*, Lebendiges Museum Online, Stiftung Haus der Geschichte der Bundesrepublik Deutschland, http://www.hdg. de/lemo/biografie/erich-honecker.html. Honecker was born in 1912 and joined a communist youth organization at the age of ten. He was imprisoned by the Nazis in 1937 before being liberated by the Red Army in April 1945. He led the communist youth organization the Free German Youth (Freie Deutsche Jugend, FDJ), between 1946 and 1955 before rising to become Ulbricht's successor. See also Harsch, *Revenge of the Domestic*, 308, 312–13, for her discussion of the effects of Honecker's maternalist policies.

93 For a longer discussion of the term, see Jarausch, "Care and Coercion," 62–5.

94 Frieda Nadig, "Neuregelung des Familienrechts," *Gleichheit* 7, July 1957, 242.

95 Manfred Mielke, "Der neue Güterstand in der Ehe," *Frankfurter Allgemeine Zeitung*, BuZ6.

96 "Die Zukunft der Notare," *Der Spiegel* 28, 9 July 1958, 22.

97 "Die Zukunft der Notare," 25.

98 Moeller, *Protecting Motherhood*, 185.

99 Buske, *Fräulein Mutter und Ihr Bastard*, 234.

100 "Familienrechtsänderungsgesetz," *Bundesgesetzblatt*, 18 August 1961, 1222.

101 §6, "Familienrechtsänderungsgesetz," 1226.

102 §8, "Familienrechtsänderungsgesetz," 1226.

103 Kontrollratsgesetz Nr. 16 (*Ehegesetz*), 20 February 1946; "Familienrechtsänderungsgesetz," 1226.

104 §10, "Familienrechtsänderungsgesetz," 1226–7.

105 Heineman, *What Difference Does a Husband Make*, 150–1; see also Buske, *Fräulein*, 343.

106 Heineman, *What Difference Does a Husband Make?*, 154–5; VDBT, [7.] Deutscher Bundestag, 147. Sitzung, 31 January 1975, 10188–10208;

"Familienrechtsänderungsgesetz," 1227. However, the 1961 legislation allowed one party to sue the instigating spouse and challenge the divorce proceedings.

107 Bericht der Bundesregierung über die Situation der Frauen in Beruf, Familie und Gesellschaft, Deutscher Bundestag, Drucksache V/909, XVII, 1. The Committee for Women's and Youth Matters discussed the proposal in eight meetings, determining a set of requirements for the Enquete.

108 Bericht der Bundesregierung über die Situation der Frauen in Beruf, Familie und Gesellschaft, Drucksache V/909, XVII.

109 Bark and Gress, *A History of West Germany*, 472.

110 Ruth Führer, "Vorkämpferin für die Gleichberechtigung. Die erste Bundesministerin Elisabeth Schwarzhaupt," *Deutschlandfunk Kultur*, November 14, 2011. https://www.deutschlandfunkkultur.de/vorkaempferin-fuer-die -gleichberechtigung.932.de.html?dram:article_id=131355

111 Bark and Gress, *A History of West Germany*, 499–509.

112 Bericht der Bundesregierung über die Lage der Familien in der Bundesrepublik Deutschland, Deutscher Bundestag, Drucksache V/2532, 25 January 1968, 7, https://dserver.bundestag.de/btd/05/025/0502532.pdf.

113 Süß, "Social Security," 203–4.

114 Bericht der Bundesregierung über die Lage der Familien in der Bundesrepublik Deutschland, 8.

115 Bericht der Bundesregierung über die Lage der Familien in der Bundesrepublik Deutschland, 239.

116 Bericht der Bundesregierung über die Lage der Familien in der Bundesrepublik Deutschland, 236.

117 Bericht der Bundesregierung über die Lage der Familien in der Bundesrepublik Deutschland, 237.

118 Müller-Freienfels, "The Marriage Law Reform of 1976," 187.

119 Ferree, *Varieties of Feminism*, 55.

120 Allen, *Women in Twentieth-Century Europe*, 96. See also Silies, *Liebe, Lust und Last*.

121 VDBT, 7. Wahlperiode, 40. Sitzung, 8 June 1973, 2229, https://dserver.bundestag .de/btp/07/07040.pdf.

122 Nelson, "Berlin's 'Palace of Tears.'"

123 Gesetzentwurf der Bundesregierung Erstes Gesetz zur Reform des Ehe- und Familienrechts (1. EheRG), Deutscher Bundestag 7. Wahlperiode Drucksache 7/650, 1 June 1973, 6–7.

124 Gesetzentwurf der Bundesregierung Erstes Gesetz zur Reform des Ehe- und Familienrechts (1. EheRG), 7–11.

125 Bericht der Bundesregierung über die Lage der Familien in der Bundesrepublik Deutschland, Drucksache V/2532, 25 January 1968, 2226, https://dserver .bundestag.de/btp/07/07040.pdf.

126 Bericht der Bundesregierung über die Lage der Familien in der Bundesrepublik Deutschland, 2227.

127 Bericht der Bundesregierung über die Lage der Familien in der Bundesrepublik Deutschland, 2226.
128 Bericht der Bundesregierung über die Lage der Familien in der Bundesrepublik Deutschland, 2227.
129 Bericht der Bundesregierung über die Lage der Familien in der Bundesrepublik Deutschland, 2230.
130 Bericht der Bundesregierung über die Lage der Familien in der Bundesrepublik Deutschland, 2235.
131 Bericht der Bundesregierung über die Lage der Familien in der Bundesrepublik Deutschland, 2228.
132 Bericht der Bundesregierung über die Lage der Familien in der Bundesrepublik Deutschland, 2235.
133 Bericht der Bundesregierung über die Lage der Familien in der Bundesrepublik Deutschland, 2235.
134 Bericht der Bundesregierung über die Lage der Familien in der Bundesrepublik Deutschland, 2235.
135 Zweiter Bericht und Antrag des Rechtsausschusses (6. Ausschuß) zu dem von der Bundesregierung eingebrachten Entwurf eines Ersten Gesetzes zur Reform des Ehe- und Familienrechts (1. EheRG), Drucksache 7/4361, 28 November 1975, https://dserver.bundestag.de/btd/07/043/0704361.pdf
136 For more on Willy Brandt's *Ostpolitik*, see Miard-Delacroix, *Willy Brandt*, 113–42.
137 Allen, *Women in Twentieth-Century Europe*, 82.
138 Allen, *Women in Twentieth-Century Europe*, 82.
139 Allen, *Women in Twentieth-Century Europe*, 105.
140 Sheffer, *Burned Bridge*, 134.

Conclusion

1 Gorondi, "Hungary Touts Family Policies"; Sussmann, "The Poland Model."
2 "Programm für Deutschland. Wahlprogramm der Alternative für Deutschland für die Wahl zum Deutschen Bundestag am 24. September 2017," Alternative für Deutschland, last modified 22–3 April 2017, https://www.afd.de/wp-content/uploads/2017/06/2017-06-01_AfD-Bundestagswahlprogramm_Onlinefassung.pdf.
3 "'Mehr Kinder? Aber nur deutsche!' Die Familienpolitik der AfD," Heinrich Böll Stiftung, https://www.gwi-boell.de/de/2018/02/19/mehr-kinder-aber-nur-deutsche-die-voelkische-familienpolitik-der-afd.
4 "Programm für Deutschland."
5 "'Mehr Kinder? Aber nur deutsche!'"
6 Penn and Massino, *Gender Politics*; Betts and Crowley, "Introduction: Domestic Dreamworlds"; Regulska and Smith, eds., *Women and Gender in Postwar Europe*.
7 Bonnie G. Smith, "Introduction," in Regulska and Smith, eds., *Women and Gender in Postwar Europe*, 2.

8 Francisca de Haan, "Women as the 'Motor of Modern Life': Women's Work in Europe West and East since 1945," in Regulska and Smith, eds., *Women and Gender in Postwar Europe*, 93.
9 de Haan, "Women as the 'Motor of Modern Life,'" 94.
10 Smith, "Introduction," 3.
11 Allen, *Women in Twentieth-Century Europe*, 97.
12 Herzog, *Sexuality in Europe*, 100.
13 de Haan, "Women as the 'Motor of Modern Life,'" 90.
14 de Haan, "Women as the 'Motor of Modern Life,'" 92.
15 Allen, *Women in Twentieth-Century Europe*, 104–5.
16 Harsch, "Society, the State, and Abortion"; https://doi.org/10.1086/ahr/102.1.53; Herzog, *Sex after Fascism*, 193.
17 Allen, *Women in Twentieth-Century Europe*, 81, 82, 84.
18 Allen, *Feminism and Motherhood*, 211.
19 Harsch, "Vanguard of the Working Mother," 171.
20 Allen, *Women in Twentieth-Century Europe*, 107.
21 Organisation for Economic Co-operation and Development, "The Pursuit of Gender Equality: An Uphill Battle," 4 October 2017, chrome-extension:// efaidnbmnnnibpcajpcglclefindmkaj/https://www.oecd.org/germany/Gender2017 -DEU-en.pdf.
22 "Germany to be short of 384,000 Kita places 'by 2023,'" *The Local*, 20 October 2022, https://www.thelocal.de/20221020/germany-to-be-short-of-384000-kita-places-by-2023.

Bibliography

Archival Sources

Archiv der deutschen Frauenbewegung, Kassel
    NL-P-11 Elisabeth Selbert
    NL-K-16 DEF Nachlass
Archiv der Akademie der Künste
    Kempowski-Biografien
Archiv des Liberalismus, Gummersbach
    A5-50 Bundesfrauenausschuss und Bundesfrauenreferat
    N1-3000 Nachlass Thomas Dehler
    N2-6 Nachlass Herta Ilk
    L4-126 LDPD Zentralvorstand
    L2-120 LDPD Politischer Ausschuss
    A45-50 FDP Ostbüro
Bundesarchiv, Berlin-Lichterfelde
    DA 1 Volkskammer der DDR
    DP 1 Ministerium der Justiz
    DY30/IV Sozialistische Einheitspartei Deutschlands
    DO 4 Staatssekretär für Kirchenfragen
    DO 1 Ministerium des Innern
    DC 20 Ministerrat der DDR
    DY34 Bundesvorstand des Freien Deutschen Gewerkschaftsbundes
    DC-20-I/4 Beschluss- und Sitzungsreihe des Präsidiums des Ministerrates
    DA5 Staatsrat der DDR
    DP 2/ Oberstes Gericht der DDR
    DC 9 Presseamt beim Vorsitzenden des Ministerrates
    DY 31 Demokratischer Frauenbund Deutschlands
Bundesarchiv, *Koblenz*
    B141 Bundesinnenminister der Justiz

B411 Deutscher Juristentag
B106 Bundesministerium des Innern
B136 Bundeskanzleramt
NL 1151 Marie-Elisabeth Lüders
B211 Deutscher Frauenrat
Bundesbeauftragte für die Unterlagen des Staatssicherheitsdienstes (Stasi) der
    ehemaligen Deutschen Demokratischen Republik Archiv, Berlin
    MfS JHS 001 Z 9/56, BStU 0003
    MfS HA XX 5244, BstU 000002
    MfS HA XX 465, BstU 000160
    BStU 000154, MfS HA XX 465
    MfS ZAIG N2. 1074, BstU 000006
Evangelischen Zentralarchiv, Berlin
    EZA 99 Kirchenkanzlei der EKD, Aussenstelle Berlin
Friedrich-Ebert-Stiftung, Bonn
    DGB-Archiv
    DGB-Archiv/Frauen
    PV-Bestand/Ref. Organisation
    SPD Ostbüro 0247
    SPD-Parteivorstand/Frauen Referat
Konrad-Adenauer-Stiftung, Sankt Augustin
    01-237-026/2 NL Eduard Wahl
    VII-013-924 Ost-CDU
Katholischer Deutscher Frauenbund Archiv, Köln
    2-32-3, Nachlass Weber
Parlamentsarchiv des Deutschen Bundestags, Berlin
    Z5 Parlamentarischer Rat
    II 409 Gesetzesdokumentation
    Protokolle der Ausschüsse des Bundestages
Staatsbibliothek, Berlin

Newspapers and Magazines

Gleichheit
Genossin
DIE ZEIT
Der Spiegel
Frankfurter Allgemeine Zeitung
Frankfurter Rundschau
Neue Zeitung
Union in Deutschland

Neues Deutschland
Berliner Zeitung
Constanze
Für Dich
Die Frau von heute

Internet Sources

Blume, Dorlis, and Irmgard Zündorf. "Otto Grotewohl." https://www.hdg.de/lemo
/biografie/otto-grotewohl.html.

"Die historischen Wurzeln des Deutschen Frauenrates." Accessed 7 October 2016.
https://www.frauenrat.de/deutsch/verband/geschichte.html.

"Die Verfassung des Deutschen Reichs of 11 August 1919." Accessed 2 February 2015.
http://www.gesetze-im-internet.de/wrv/BJNR013830919.html.

Düwell, Kurt. "Robert Lehr." Accessed 31 December 2016. http://www.kas.de/wf/de
/37.8217

"Eduard Wahl." Accessed 13 January 2017. http://www.leo-bw.de/web/guest/detail/-
/Detail/details/PERSON/wlbblb_personen/118770799/person.

"Elisabeth Schwarzhaupt." Accessed 26 December 2016. http://www.kas.de/wf/de/37.8331.

Gesetz der Arbeit zur Förderung und Pflege der Arbeitskräfte, zur Steigerung der
Arbeitsproduktivität und zur weiteren Verbesserung der materiellen und kulturellen
Lage der Arbeiter und Angestellten, 1950. http://www.verfassungen.de/de/ddr
/gesetzderarbeit50.htm.

Hospes, Ulrike. "Luise Rehling." Accessed 10 December 2016. http://www.kas.de/wf
/de/37.8289.

Husemann, Mirjam. "Walter Ulbricht 1893–1973." Modified 17 September 2014.
https://www.dhm.de/lemo/biografie/walter-ulbricht.

"Käthe Kern." Modified October 2009. http://bundesstiftung-aufarbeitung.de/wer
-war-wer-in-der-ddr-%2363%3B-1424.html?ID=1671.

"Ludwig Metzger." Modified 16 December 2016. http://www.lagis-hessen.de/pnd
/118581570.

Marx, Stefan. "Franz-Josef Wuermeling." Accessed 26 December 2016. http://www.kas
.de/wf/de/71.9969.

"Max Reimann." Accessed 13 January 2017. http://www.bundesarchiv.de/cocoon
/barch/0000/z/z1961z/kap1_5/para2_29.html;jsessionid=AA5E6B25C23
DC06935908E89BA435723?highlight=true&search=%22Reimann,%20
Max%22&stemming=false&field=all#highlightedTerm.

Reichsbürgergesetz. 15 September 1935. http://www.verfassungen.de/de/de33-45
/reichsbuerger35.htm.

Schmalz, Grete. "Gesetzlicher Mutterschutz Gestern und heute." *Friedrich Ebert
Stiftung.* http://library.fes.de/gmh/main/pdf-files/gmh/1950/1950-06-a-282.pdf.

Socialist Unity Party Program. April 1946. http://www.cvce.eu/de/obj/politisches_
    programm_der_sed_berlin_21_und_22_april_1946-de-d9c5faf7-5c39-43fa-aa3f-
    88d5431e3746.html.
"Weber, Karl." Accessed 14 January 2017. http://www.munzinger.de/document
    /00000010949.
Zündorf, Irmgard. "Biografie Hilde Benjamin." Modified 22 February 2016.
    http://www.hdg.de/lemo/biografie/hilde-benjamin.html.
– "Josef Frings." Modified 2 August 2016. https://www.hdg.de/lemo
    /biografie/joseph-frings.html.

Printed Primary Sources

Benjamin, Hilde. *Vorschläge zum neuen deutschen Familienrecht*. Berlin: Deutscher
    Frauen Verlag, 1949.
Das Bürgerliche Gesetzbuch für das Deutsche Reich (BGB) (1896).
Die Verfassung des Deutschen Reichs, 11 August 1919. http://www.documentarchiv
    .de/wr/wrv.html#ERSTER_ABSCHNITT02.
Gesetz zur Vereinheitlichung des Rechts der Eheschließung und der Ehescheidung im
    Lande Österreich und im übrigen Reichsgebiet (Ehegesetz). 6 July 1938.
Grundgesetz für die Bundesrepublik Deutschland. 23 May 1949. http://www
    .documentarchiv.de/brd/1949/grundgesetz.html.
Hagemeyer, Maria. *Der Entwurf des Familiengesetzbuches der "Deutschen Demokratischen
    Republik."* Bonn: Bundesministerium für gesamtdeutsche Fragen, 1955.
Hedemann, Justus Wilhelm. *Das Volksgesetzbuch der Deutschen*. Munich: C.H.
    Beck'sche Verlagsbuchhandlung, 1941.
Hedemann, Justus Wilhelm, Heinrich Lehmann, and Wolfgang Siebert.
    Volksgesetzbuch. Arbeitsberichte der Akademie für Deutsches Recht, vol. 22.
    Munich: Beck, 1942.
Kommission zur Ausarbeitung des Entwurfs eines Bürgerlichen Gesetzbuches.
    Entwurf eines bürgerlichen Gesetzbuches für das Deutsche Reich: Erste Lesung. Berlin:
    J. Guttentag, 1888.
Verfassung der Deutschen Demokratischen Republik. 6 April 1968. http://www
    .documentarchiv.de/ddr/verfddr.html#KAPITEL%201-2.
Verfassung der Deutschen Demokratischen Republik. 7 October 1949. http://www
    .documentarchiv.de/ddr/verfddr1949.html.
Verhandlungen des Deutschen Bundestags, 1949–1975.
Verhandlungen des Deutschen Reichstags, 1871–1933.
Wernicke, Kurt, Georg Hans Booms, and Walter Vogel. *Der Parlamentarische Rat,
    1948–1949: Akten u. Protokolle.* Boppard am Rhein: Boldt, 1975.
Wolle-Egenolf, Waldemar and Hildegard. *Der Gleichheitsgrundsatz von Mann und Frau
    (Art. 3 Abs. 2 d. Bonner Grundgesetzes) im neuen deutschen Familienrecht.* Bonn:
    Gesellschaft z. Gestaltung öffentl. Lebens, 1952.

Secondary Literature

Allen, Ann Taylor. *Feminism and Motherhood in Western Europe, 1890–1970: The Maternal Dilemma*. New York: Palgrave Macmillan, 2005.

- *Women in Twentieth-Century Europe*. New York: Palgrave Macmillan, 2008.

Allen-Thompson, Pam, and Dinah Dodds. *The Wall in My Backyard: East German Women in Transition*. Amherst: University of Massachusetts Press, 1994.

Amos, Heike. *Die Entstehung der Verfassung in der Sowjetischen Besatzungszone/DDR 1946–1949*. Münster: LIT, 2006.

Anderson, Stewart. *A Dramatic Reinvention: German Television and Moral Renewal after National Socialism, 1956–1970*. New York: Berghahn, 2020.

Ansorg, Leonore, and Renate Hürtgen. "The Myth of Female Emancipation: Contradictions in Women's Lives." In *Dictatorship as Experience: Towards a Socio-Cultural History of the GDR*, edited by Konrad Hugo Jarausch, 163–76. New York: Berghahn Books, 1999.

Ashwin, Sarah. *Gender, State, and Society in Soviet and Post-Soviet Russia*. London: Routledge, 2000.

Balbier, Uta. *Kalter Krieg auf der Aschenbahn: Der Deutsch-deutsche Sport 1950–1972: Eine politische Geschichte*. Paderborn: Schoeningh Ferdinand GmbH, 2006.

Barck, Simone, Martina Langermann, and Siegfried Lokatis. *Zwischen "Mosaik" und "Einheit" – Zeitschriften in der DDR*. Berlin: Christoph Links Verlag, 1999.

Baring, Arnulf. *Uprising in East Germany: June 1953*. Ithaca: Cornell University Press, 1972.

Bark, Dennis L., and David Gress. *A History of West Germany*, 2nd ed. Oxford, UK, and Cambridge, MA: Blackwell, 1993.

Baumert, Gerhard. *Deutsche Familien nach dem Kriege*. Darmstadt: Roether, 1954.

Berend, Ivan. *Case Studies on Modern European Economy: Entrepreneurship, Inventions, and Institutions*. London: Routledge, 2013.

Berghahn, Volker. *Modern Germany: Society, Economy, and Politics in the Twentieth Century*. Cambridge: Cambridge University Press, 1987.

Bessel, Richard. *Germany 1945: From War to Peace*. New York: HarperCollins, 2010.

Betts, Paul. *Within Walls: Private Life in the German Democratic Republic*. Oxford: Oxford University Press, 2012.

Betts, Paul, and David Crowley. "Introduction: Domestic Dreamworlds: Notions of Home in Post-1945 Europe." *Journal of Contemporary History* 40, no. 2 (2005): 213–36.

Biedermann, Thomas. *Deutschland in der Nachkriegszeit 1945–1949: Restauration oder Neubeginn?* Hamburg: Verlag Thomas Biedermann, 2011.

Biegler, Dagmar. *Frauenverbände in Deutschland*. Opladen: Leske and Buske, 2001.

Biess, Frank. *Homecomings: Returning POWs and the Legacies of Defeat in Postwar Germany*. Princeton: Princeton University Press, 2006.

- "Men of Reconstruction – The Reconstruction of Men: Returning POWs in East and West Germany, 1945–1955." In *Home/Front: The Military, War, and Gender in Twentieth-Century Germany*, edited by Karen Hagemann and Stefanie Schüler-Springorum, 335–58. Oxford: Berg, 2002.

Blackbourn, David. *The Long Nineteenth Century: A History of Germany, 1780–1918*. Oxford: Oxford University Press, 1998.

Blasius, Dirk. *Ehescheidung in Deutschland 1794–1945*. Göttingen: Vandenhoeck & Ruprecht, 1987.

Boak, Helen. *Women in the Weimar Republic*. Oxford: Oxford University Press, 2015.

Bock, Gisela. *Zwangssterilisation im Nationalsozialismus: Studien zur Rassenpolitik und Frauenpolitik*. Opladen: Westdeutscher Verlag, 1986.

Boehling, Rebecca. "Gender Roles in Ruins: German Women and Local Politics under American Occupation, 1945–1947." In *Gender and the Long Postwar: The United States and the Two Germanys, 1945–1989*, edited by Karen Hagemann and Sonya Michel, 51–72. Washington, DC: Woodrow Wilson Center Press, 2014.

Bolz, Alexander. *Jugendweihen in Deutschland: Idee, Geschichte und Aktualität eines Übergangsrituals*. Leipzig: Rosa-Luxemburg-Stiftung Sachsen, 1998.

Bösch, Frank. *Geteilte Geschichte: Ost- und Westdeutschland 1970–2000*. Göttingen: Vandenhoeck & Ruprecht, 2015.

Bostdorff, Denise M. *Proclaiming the Truman Doctrine: The Cold War Call to Arms*. College Station: Texas A&M University Press, 2008.

Böttger, Barbara. *Das Recht auf Gleichheit und Differenz: Elisabeth Selbert und der Kampf der Frauen um Art. 3 II Grundgesetz*. Münster: Verlag Westfälisches Dampfboot, 1990.

Braas, Gerhard. *Die Entstehung der Länderverfassungen in der Sowjetischen Besatzungszone Deutschlands 1946/47*. Köln: Verlag Wissenschaft und Politik, B. von Nottbeck, 1987.

Breithaupt, Dirk. "Nathan, Hans." In *Neue Deutsche Biographie* 18 (1997), 745.

Brentzel, Marianne. "Unruhe und Aufstieg: Der 17. Juni 1953." In *Die Machtfrau Hilde Benjamin*, edited by Marianne Brentzel, 213–38. Berlin: Links Verlag, 1997.

Bruce, Gary. *Resistance with the People: Repression and Resistance in Eastern Germany (1945–1955)*. Lanham: Rowman and Littlefield, 2003.

Bruehoefener, Friederike. "Defining the West German Soldier: Military, Masculinity, and Society in West Germany, 1945–1989." PhD diss., University of North Carolina at Chapel Hill, 2014.

Brühöfener, Friederike, Karen Hagemann, and Donna Harsch. *Gendering Post-1945 German History: Entanglements*. Oxford and New York: Berghahn, 2019.

Budde, Gunilla-Friederike. *Frauen Arbeiten: Weibliche Erwerbstätigkeit in Ost- und Westdeutschland nach 1945*. Göttingen: Vandenhoeck & Ruprecht, 1997.

Buggeln, Marc, and Michael Wildt. *Arbeit im Nationalsozialismus*. Berlin: Walter de Gruyter, 2014.

Buske, Sybille. *Fräulein Mutter und Ihr Bastard: Eine Geschichte der Unehelichkeit in Deutschland, 1900–1970*. Göttingen: Wallstein Verlag, 2004.

Castillo, Greg. *Cold War on the Home Front: The Soft Power of Midcentury Design*. Minneapolis: University of Minnesota Press, 2009.

Chaperon, Sylvie. "'Feminism Is Dead. Long Live Feminism!': The Women's Movement in France at Liberation, 1944–1946." In *When the War Was Over: Women, War, and Peace in Europe, 1940–1956*, edited by Claire Duchen and Irene Bandhauer-Schöffmann. London: Leicester University Press, 2000.

Chappel, James G. "Nuclear Families in a Nuclear Age: Theorising the Family in 1950s West Germany." *Contemporary European History* 26, no. 1 (2017): 85–109.

Chartier, Roger. *On the Edge of the Cliff: History, Language, and Practices*. Baltimore: Johns Hopkins University Press, 1997.

Childs, David. *The GDR (RLE: German Politics): Moscow's German Ally*. Abingdon-on-Thames: Routledge, 1988.

Clay, David Large. *Germans to the Front: West German Rearmament in the Adenauer Era*. Chapel Hill: University of North Carolina Press, 1996.

Coser, Lewis A. "Some Aspects of Soviet Family Policy." *American Journal of Sociology* 56, no. 5 (1951): 424–37.

Creuzberger, Stefan, and Dierk Hoffmann. *"Geistige Gefahr" und "Immunisierung Der Gesellschaft": Antikommunismus und Politische Kultur in der frühen Bundesrepublik*. Munich: Oldenbourg Verlag, 2014.

Crosby, Margaret Barber. "The Civil Code and the Transformation of German Society: The Politics of Gender Inequality 1814–1919." PhD diss., Brown University, Providence, 2001.

– *The Making of a German Constitution: A Slow Revolution*. Oxford: Berg, 2008.

Davis, Belinda. "The Personal Is Political: Gender, Politics, and Political Activism in Modern German History." In *Gendering Modern German History: Rewriting Historiography*, edited by Karen Hagemann and Jean H. Quataert, 107–27. New York: Berghahn, 2007.

Demokratischer Frauenbund Deutschlands. *Geschichte des DFD*. Leipzig: Verlag für die Frau, 1989.

Dollard, Catherine L. *The Surplus Woman: Unmarried in Imperial Germany, 1871–1918*. New York: Berghahn, 2009.

Drummer, Heike. *Ein Glücksfall für die Demokratie: Elisabeth Selbert (1896–1986): Die große Anwältin der Gleichberechtigung*. Frankfurt am Main: Eichborn, 1999.

Evans, Ellen Lovell. *The German Center Party, 1870–1933: A Study in Political Catholicism*. Carbondale: Southern Illinois University Press, 1981.

Fehrenbach, Heide. "Rehabilitating Fatherland: Race and German Remasculinization." *Signs* 24, no. 1 (1998): 107–27.

Ferree, Myra Marx. *Varieties of Feminism: German Gender Politics in a Global Perspective*. Stanford: Stanford University Press, 2012.

Fidelis, Malgorzata. *Women, Communism, and Industrialization in Postwar Poland*. Cambridge: Cambridge University Press, 2010.

Fiedler, Anke, and Michael Meyen. *Fiktionen für das Volk: DDR-Zeitungen als PR-Instrument: Fallstudien zu den Zentralorganen Neues Deutschland, Junge Welt, Neue Zeit, und Der Morgen*. Münster: LIT, 2011.

Fishman, Sarah. *From Vichy to the Sexual Revolution: Gender and Family Life in Postwar France*. Oxford: Oxford University Press, 2017.

Forbes, Neil. *Doing Business with the Nazis: Britain's Economic and Financial Relations with Germany, 1931–1939*. New York: Psychology Press, 2000.

Fraenkel, Ernst. *The Dual State: A Contribution to the Theory of Dictatorship*. New York and London: Oxford University Press, 1941.

Frank, Mario. *Walter Ulbricht: Eine Deutsche Biografie*. Berlin: Siedler, 2001.

Franzius, Christine. *Bonner Grundgesetz und Familienrecht: Die Diskussion um die Gleichberechtigung von Mann und Frau in der westdeutschen Zivilrechtslehre der Nachkriegszeit (1945–1957)*. Frankfurt am Main: Vittorio Klostermann, 2005.

Freeland, Jane. "Behind Closed Doors: Domestic Violence, Citizenship, and State-Making in Divided Berlin, 1969–1990." PhD diss., Carleton University, Ottawa, 2015.

Frevert, Ute. "Frauen auf dem Weg zur Gleichberechtigung – Hindernisse, Umleitungen, Einbahnstraßen." In *Zäsuren nach 1945: Essays zur Periodisierung der deutschen Nachkriegsgeschichte*, edited by Martin Broszat, 113–30. Munich: Walter de Gruyter, 1990.

Fühner, Ruth. "Vorkämpferin für die Gleichberechtigung. Die erste Bundesministerin Elisabeth Schwarzhaupt," Deutschlandfunk Kultur, 14 November 2011. https://www.deutschlandfunkkultur.de/vorkaempferin-fuer-die-gleichberechtigung.932.de.html?dram:article_id=131355.

Führer, Karl Christian, et al. "Öffentlichkeit – Medien – Geschichte." *Archiv für Sozialgeschichte* 41 (2001): 1–38.

Fulbrook, Mary. *Anatomy of a Dictatorship: Inside the GDR, 1949–1989*. Oxford and New York: Oxford University Press, 1995.

– *A History of Germany, 1918–2014: A Divided Nation*. Chichester, UK, and Malden, MA: Wiley Blackwell, 2014.

Garner, Curt. "Public Service Personnel in West Germany in the 1950s: Controversial Policy Decisions and Their Effects on Social Composition, Gender Structure, and the Role of Former Nazis." In *West Germany under Construction: Politics, Society, and Culture in the Adenauer Era*, edited by Robert G. Moeller, 135–95. Ann Arbor: University of Michigan Press, 1997.

Genth, Renate. *Frauenpolitik und Politisches Wirken von Frauen im Berlin der Nachkriegszeit 1945–1949*. Berlin: Trafo Verlag Dr Wolfgang Weist, 1996.

Gerhard, Ute. "Family Law and Gender Equality: Comparing Family Policies in Postwar Western Europe." In *Children, Families, and States: Time Policies of Childcare, Preschool, and Primary Education in Europe*, edited by Karen Hagemann, Konrad H. Jarausch, and Cristina Allemann-Ghionda, 75–93. New York: Berghahn, 2011.

- *Frauen in der Geschichte des Rechts: Von der frühen Neuzeit bis zur Gegenwart.* Munich: C.H. Beck, 1997.

Gille-Linne, Karin. *Verdeckte Strategien: Herta Gotthelf, Elisabeth Selbert, und die Frauenarbeit der SPD 1945–1949.* Bonn: Dietz, 2011.

Gimbel, John. *The American Occupation of Germany: Politics and the Military, 1945–1949.* Stanford: Stanford University Press, 1968.

Goldman, Wendy Z. *Women, the State, and Revolution: Soviet Family Policy and Social Life, 1917–1936.* Cambridge: Cambridge University Press, 1993.

Gorondi, Pablo. "Hungary Touts Family Policies as Alternative to Immigration," AP News, 5 September 2019. https://apnews.com/article/279dfc17b13340e0bc 272717cf75b768.

Granieri, Ronald J. *The Ambivalent Alliance: Konrad Adenauer, the CDU/CSU, and the West, 1949–1966.* New York: Berghahn, 2003.

Gray, William Glenn. *Germany's Cold War: The Global Campaign to Isolate East Germany, 1949–1969.* Chapel Hill: University of North Carolina Press, 2003.

De Grazia, Victoria. *How Fascism Ruled Women: Italy, 1922–1945.* Berkeley: University of California Press, 1992.

Gross, Michael B. *The War against Catholicism: Liberalism and the Anti-Catholic Imagination.* Ann Arbor: University of Michigan Press, 2004.

Großekathöfer, David. *"Es ist ja jetzt Gleichberechtigung": Die Stellung der Frau im nachehelichen Unterhaltsrecht der DDR.* Köln: Böhlau, 2003.

Grünbaum, Robert. *Deutsche Einheit: Ein Überblick 1945 bis heute.* Berlin: Metropol, 2010.

Hachtmann, Rüdiger. *Industriearbeit im "Dritten Reich": Untersuchungen zu den Lohn- und Arbeitsbedingungen in Deutschland 1933–1945.* Göttingen: Vandenhoeck and Ruprecht, 1989.

Hagemann, Karen. "Between Ideology and Economy: The 'Time Politics' of Child Care and Public Education in the Two Germanys." *Social Politics: International Studies in Gender, State, and Society* 13 (2006): 239–41.

- "Civil Society Gendered." In *Civil Society and Gender Justice: Historical and Comparative Perspectives*, edited by Gunilla-Friederike Budde, Karen Hagemann, and Sonya Michel, 17–42. New York: Berghahn, 2008.

- "Geschichtswissenschaft, Medien und kollektives Gedächtnis: Zum 'Mythos Trümmerfrauen.'" *Neue Politische Literatur* 4 (2015): 203–12.

- "Halbtags oder Ganztags? Zeitpolitiken von Kinderbetreuung und Schule in Europe im historischen Vergleich." In *Halbtags oder Ganztags? Familie, Frauenarbeit, und Zeitpolitik von Kinderbetreuung und Schule in Europa im historischen Vergleich*, edited by Karen Hagemann and Konrad Jarausch, 20–83. Weinheim: Beltz-Juventa, 2014.

- "Mobilizing Women for War: The History, Historiography, and Memory of German Women's War Service in the Two World Wars." *Journal of Military History* 75, no. 4 (2011): 1055–93.

- "'Rationalization of Family Work': Municipal Family Welfare and Urban Working-Class Mothers in Interwar Germany." *Social Politics* 4, no. 1 (1997): 19–48.
- "A West-German *"Sonderweg"*? Family, Work, and the Half-Day Time Policy of Childcare and Schooling." In *Children, Families, and States: Time Policies of Childcare, Preschool, and Primary Education in Europe*, edited by Cristina Allemann-Ghionda, Karen Hagemann, and Konrad H. Jarausch, 275–300. New York: Berghahn, 2011.

Hagemann, Karen, Donna Harsch, and Friederike Bruehoefener. *Gendering Post-1945 German History: Entanglements*. New York: Berghahn, 2019.

Hagemann, Karen, and Sonya Michel. "Gender and the Long Postwar: Reconsiderations of the United States and the Two Germanys, 1945–1989." In *Gender and the Long Postwar: Reconsiderations of the United States and the Two Germanys, 1945–1989*, edited by Karen Hagemann and Sonya Michel, 1–27. Baltimore: Johns Hopkins University Press, 2014.

Hagemeyer, Maria. *Zum Familienrecht der Sowjetzone*. Bonn: Bundesministerium für Gesamtdeutsche Fragen, 1958.

Harsch, Donna. *German Social Democracy and the Rise of Nazism*. Chapel Hill: University of North Carolina Press, 1993.
- "Public Continuity and Private Change? Women's Consciousness and Activity in Frankfurt." *Journal of Social History* 27 (1993): 29–58.
- *Revenge of the Domestic: Women, the Family, and Communism in the German Democratic Republic*. Princeton: Princeton University Press, 2007.
- "Society, the State, and Abortion in East Germany, 1950–1972." *American Historical Review* 102, no. 1 (1997): 53–84. https://doi.org/10.1086/ahr/102.1.53.
- "Vanguard of the Working Mother: The East German Family between Change and Continuity." In *The Family in Modern Germany*, edited by Lisa Pine, 171–200. London: Bloomsbury Academic, 2020.

Haupt, Heinz-Gerhard, and Jürgen Kocka. *Comparative and Transnational History: Central European Approaches and New Perspectives*. New York: Berghahn, 2009.
- "Comparative History: Methods, Aims, Problems." In *Comparison and History: Europe in Cross-National Perspective*, edited by Deborah Cohen and Maura O'Connor, 23–40. Abingdon: Routledge, 2004.

Hauser, Andrea. "Alle Frauen unter einem Hut? – Zur Geschichte des Stuttgarter Frauenausschusses." In *Frauen in der deutschen Nachkriegszeit*, edited by Annette Kuhn, 102–9. Düsseldorf: Schwann Düsseldorf, 1984.

Heineman, Elizabeth D. "Single Motherhood and Maternal Employment in Divided Germany: Ideology, Policy, and Social Pressures in the 1950s." *Journal of Women's History* 12 (2000): 146–72.
- *What Difference Does a Husband Make? Women and Marital Status in Nazi and Postwar Germany*. Berkeley: University of California Press, 2003.

Heinemann, Sylvia. *"Frauenfragen sind Menschheitsfragen": Die Frauenpolitik der Freien Demokratinnen von 1945 bis 1963*. Sulzbach: Helmer, 2012.

Henicz, Barbara, and Margrit Hirschfeld. "Der Club Deutscher Frauen in Hannover." In *Frauen in der deutschen Nachkriegszeit*, edited by Annette Kuhn, 127–34. Düsseldorf: Schwann Düsseldorf, 1984.

- "Die erste Frauenzusammenschlüsse." In *Frauen in der deutschen Nachkriegszeit*, edited by Annette Kuhn, 94–101. Düsseldorf: Schwann Düsseldorf, 1984.

- "'Wenn die Frauen wüßten, was sie könnten, wenn sie wollten': Zur Gründungsgeschichte des Deutschen Frauenrings." In *Frauen in der deutschen Nachkriegszeit*, edited by Annette Kuhn, 135–56. Düsseldorf: Schwann Düsseldorf, 1984.

Henke, Klaus-Dietmar. *Widerstand und Opposition in der DDR*. Köln: Böhlau, 1999.

Herf, Jeffrey. *Divided Memory: The Nazi Past in the Two Germanys*. Cambridge, MA: Harvard University Press, 1997.

Herzog, Dagmar. "East Germany's Sexual Evolution." In *Socialist Modern: East German Everyday Culture and Politics*, edited by Katherine Pence and Paul Betts, 71–95. Ann Arbor: University of Michigan Press, 2008.

- *Sex after Fascism: Memory and Morality in Twentieth-Century Germany*. Princeton: Princeton University Press, 2007.

- *Sexuality in Europe: A Twentieth-Century History*. Cambridge: Cambridge University Press, 2011.

Hoffmann, Dierk. *Otto Grotewohl (1894–1964): Eine Politische Biographie*. Munich: Oldenbourg, 2009.

Holz, Petra. *Zwischen Tradition und Emanzipation: Politikerinnen in der CDU in der Zeit von 1945 bis 1957*. Königstein im Taunus: Ulrike Helmer Verlag, 2004.

Hong, Young-Sun. "'The Benefits of Health Must Spread among All': International Solidarity, Health, and Race in the East German Encounter with the Third World." In *Socialist Modern: East German Everyday Culture and Politics*, edited by Katherine Pence and Paul Betts, 183–210. Ann Arbor: University of Michigan Press, 2008.

- *Welfare, Modernity, and the Weimar State, 1919–1933*. Princeton: Princeton University Press, 1998.

Hunt, Lynn. *The New Cultural History*. Berkeley: University of California Press, 1989.

Icken, Angela. *Der Deutsche Frauenrat: etablierte Frauenverbandsarbeit im gesellschaftlichen Wandel*. Opladen: Leske & Budrich, 2002.

Ironside, Kristy. *A Full-Value Ruble: The Promise of Prosperity in the Postwar Soviet Union*. Cambridge, MA: Harvard University Press, 2021.

Jahn, Hans Edgar. *Die deutsche Frage von 1945 bis heute: Der Weg der Parteien und Regierungen*. Zarrentin am Schaalsee: v. Hase und Koehler, 1985.

Jarausch, Konrad H. *After Hitler: Recivilizing Germans, 1945–1995*. Oxford and New York: Oxford University Press, 2006.

- "Care and Coercion: The GDR as Welfare Dictatorship." In *Dictatorship as Experience: Towards a Socio-Cultural History of the GDR*, edited by Konrad H. Jarausch, 47–72. New York: Berghahn Books, 1999.

– "'Die Teile als Ganze erkennen': Zur Integration der beiden deutschen Nachkriegsgeschichten." *Zeitgeschichte Forschungen/Studies in Contemporary History* 1 (2004): 10–30.

Jeffords, Susan. "The 'Remasculinization' of Germany in the 1950s: Discussion." *Signs* 24 (1998): 163–9.

Joesten, Joachim. *The German Press in 1947.* New York: New Germany Reports, 1947.

John, Michael. *Politics and the Law in Late Nineteenth-Century Germany: The Origins of the Civil Code.* Oxford: Clarendon, 1989.

Kaelble, Hartmut. *Der Historische Vergleich: Eine Einführung zum 19. und 20. Jahrhundert.* Frankfurt am Main: Campus Verlag, 1999.

Kaiser, Monika. "Change and Continuity in the Development of the Socialist Unity Party of Germany." *Journal of Contemporary History* 30 (1995): 687–703.

Kannappel, Petra. *Die Behandlung von Frauen im nationalsozialistischen Familienrecht.* Darmstadt and Marburg: Hessischen Historischen Kommission Darmstadt und der Historischen Kommission für Hessen, 1999.

Kirchner, Emil, and James Sperling. *The Federal Republic of Germany and NATO: 40 Years After.* New York: Springer, 2016.

Klein, Michael. *Westdeutscher Protestantismus und politische Parteien: Anti-Parteien-Mentalität und parteipolitisches Engagement von 1945 bis 1963.* Tübingen: Mohr Siebeck, 2005.

Klessmann, Christoph. "Abgrenzung und Verflechtung: Aspekte der geteilten und zusammengehörigen deutschen Nachkriegsgeschichte." *Aus Politik und Zeitgeschichte (APuZ)* 29–30 (1993): 30–41.

– *Deutsche Vergangenheiten – Eine gemeinsame Herausforderung: Der schwierige Umgang mit der doppelten Nachkriegsgeschichte*, edited by Christoph Klessmann. Berlin, 1999.

– *The Divided Past: Rewriting Post-War German History*, edited by Christoph Klessmann. Oxford: Berg, 2001.

– *Die doppelte Staatsgründung.* Göttingen: Vandenhoeck & Ruprecht, 1982.

– *Zwei Staaten, Eine Nation: Deutsche Geschichte 1955–1970.* Göttingen: Vandenhoeck & Ruprecht, 1988.

Kocka, Jürgen. *Civil Society and Dictatorship in Modern German History.* Hanover: University Press of New England, 2010.

Koonz, Claudia. *Mothers in the Fatherland: Women, the Family, and Nazi Politics.* New York: St. Martin's Press, 1987.

Kos, Franz-Josef. "Politische Justiz in der DDR. Der Dessauer Schauprozeß vom April 1950." *Vierteljahrshefte für Zeitgeschichte* 44 (1996): 395–429.

Langenhan, Dagmar, and Sabine Roß. "The Socialist Glass Ceiling: Limits to Female Careers." In *Dictatorship as Experience: Towards a Socio-Cultural History of the GDR,* edited by Konrad Hugo Jarausch, 177–94. New York: Berghahn Books, 1999.

Lauterer, Heide-Marie. *Parlamentarierinnen in Deutschland 1918/19–1949.* Sulzbach: Helmer, 2002.

Lepp, Claudia. *Tabu der Einheit? Die Ost-West-Gemeinschaft der evangelischen Christen und die deutsche Teilung (1945–1969)*. Göttingen: Vandenhoeck & Ruprecht, 2005.

Lister, Ruth. *Citizenship: Feminist Perspectives*, 2nd ed. New York: NYU Press, 2003.

Mai, Günther. "The United States in the Allied Control Council: From Dualism to Temporary Division." In *The United States and Germany in the Era of the Cold War, 1945–1990*: vol. 1: *1945–1968: A Handbook*, edited by Detlef Junker, Philipp Gassert, and Wilfried Mausbach, 50–6. Cambridge: Cambridge University Press, 2004.

Maier, Charles S. *Dissolution: The Crisis of Communism and the End of East Germany*. Princeton: Princeton University Press, 1999.

Maier, Friederike. "Zwischen Arbeitsmarkt und Familie – Frauenarbeit in den alten Bundesländern." In *Frauen in Deutschland, 1945–1992*, edited by Gisela Helwig and H.M. Nickel, 257–79. Bonn: Bundeszentrale für Politische Bildung, 1993.

Major, Patrick. *The Death of the KPD: Communism and Anti-Communism in West Gemany, 1945–1956*. Oxford: Clarendon, 1997.

Markovits, Inga. "Civil Law in East Germany – Its Development and Relation to Soviet Legal History and Ideology." *Yale Law Journal* 78, no. 1 (1968): 1–51.

– "Constitution Making after National Catastrophes: Germany in 1949 and 1990." *William & Mary Law Review* 49 (2008): 1307–46. http://scholarship.law.wm.edu/wmlr/vol49/iss4/9.

– *Justice in Lüritz: Experiencing Socialist Law in East Germany*. Princeton: Princeton University Press, 2010.

Mattes, Monika. "Economy and Politics: The Time Policy of the East German Childcare and Primary School System." In *Children, Families, and States: Time Policies of Childcare, Preschool, and Primary Education in Europe*, edited by Cristina Allemann-Ghionda, Karen Hagemann, and Konrad H. Jarausch, 344–63. New York: Berghahn, 2011.

May, Elaine Tyler. *Homeward Bound: American Families in the Cold War Era*. New York: Basic Books, 1988.

Mazower, Mark. *Dark Continent: Europe's Twentieth Century*. New York: Vintage, 2000.

Merkel, Ina. "Sex and Gender in the Divided Germany: Approaches to History from a Cultural Point of View." In *The Divided Past: Rewriting Postwar German History*, edited by Christoph Klessmann. Oxford: Berg, 2001.

Merkel, Ina, and Felix Mühlberg. "Eingaben und Öffentlichkeit." In *"Wir sind doch nicht die Mecker-Ecke der Nation": Briefe an das DDR-Fernsehen*, edited by Ina Merkel, 11–46. Köln: Bohlau, 1998.

Meyer, Sibylle, and Eva Schulze. *Familie im Umbruch: Zur Lage der Familien in der ehemaligen DDR*. Stuttgart: Kohlhammer, 1992.

Miard-Delacroix, Helene. *Willy Brandt: The Life of a Statesman*. London: I.B. Tauris, 2016.

Millington, Richard. *State, Society, and Memories of the Uprising of 17 June 1953 in the GDR*. London: Palgrave Macmillan, 2014.

Möller, Monika. "Der Frauenausschuss in Hamburg-Harburg." In *Frauen in der deutschen Nachkriegszeit*, edited by Annette Kuhn, 110–21. Düsseldorf: Schwann Düsseldorf, 1984.

Moeller, Robert G. "Heimkehr ins Vaterland: Die Remaskulinisierung Westdeutschlands in den Fünfziger Jahren." *Militärgeschichtliche Zeitschrift* 60 (2001): 403–36.

– *Protecting Motherhood: Women and the Family in the Politics of Postwar West Germany*. Berkeley: University of California Press, 1993.

– "The 'Remasculinization' of Germany in the 1950s: Introduction." *Signs* 24 (1998): 101–6.

– *West Germany under Construction: Politics, Society, and Culture in the Adenauer Era*. Ann Arbor: University of Michigan Press, 1997.

Mouton, Michelle. *From Nurturing the Nation to Purifying the Volk: Weimar and Nazi Family Policy, 1918–1945*. Cambridge and New York: Cambridge University Press, 2007.

Mühlberg, Felix. *Bürger, Bitten, und Behörden: Geschichte der Eingabe in der DDR*. Berlin: Karl Dietz Verlag, 2004.

Müller-Freienfels, W. "The Marriage Law Reform of 1976 in the Federal Republic of Germany." *International and Comparative Law Quarterly* 28 (1979): 184–210.

Naimark, Norman M. *The Russians in Germany: A History of the Soviet Zone of Occupation, 1945–1949*. Cambridge, MA: Belknap Press of Harvard University Press, 1995.

Nelson, Soraya Sarhaddi. "Berlin's 'Palace of Tears,' a Reminder of Divided Families, Despair." National Public Radio, 10 November 2014. https://www.npr.org/sections/parallels/2014/11/10/362294465/near-old-border-of-east-germany-a-reminder-of-despair.

Neumaier, Christoph, and Andreas Ludwig. "The Individualization of Everyday Life: Consumption, Domestic Culture, and Family Structures." In *A History Shared and Divided: East and West Germany Since the 1970s*, edited by Frank Bösch, 293–347. New York: Berghahn, 2018.

Niehuss, Merith. *Familie, Frau, und Gesellschaft: Studien zur Strukturgeschichte der Familie in Westdeutschland 1945–1960*. Göttingen: Vandenhoeck & Ruprecht, 2001.

Nödinger, Ingeborg. "'Mitwissen, mitverantworten und mitbestimmen': Zu den Anfängen des Demokratischen Frauenbundes Deutschland." In *Frauen in der deutschen Nachkriegszeit*, edited by Annette Kuhn, 122–6. Düsseldorf: Schwann Düsseldorf, 1984.

Noelle-Neumann, Elisabeth, and Erich Peter Neumann. *The Germans: Public Opinion Polls, 1957–1966*. Westport: Greenwood Press, 1981.

Notz, Gisela. *Frauen in der Mannschaft: Sozialdemokratinnen im Parlamentarischen Rat im Deutschen Bundestag 1948/49–1957*. Bonn: J.H.W. Dietz, 2003.

– *Mehr als bunte Tupfen im Bonner Männerclub: Sozialdemokratinnen im deutschen Bundestag 1957–1969: Mit 12 Biographien*. Bonn: J.H.W. Dietz, 2007.

Obertreis, Gesine. *Familienpolitik in der DDR 1945–1980*. Opladen: Leske & Budrich, 1986.

Oertzen, Christine von. *Pleasure of a Surplus Income: Part-time Work, Gender Politics, and Social Change in West Germany, 1955–1969.* New York: Berghahn, 2007.

- *Teilzeitarbeit und die Lust am Zuverdienen: Geschlechterpolitik und Gesellschaftlicher Wandel in Westdeutschland 1948–1969.* Göttingen: Vandenhoeck & Ruprecht, 1999.

Oertzen, Christine von, and Almut Rietzschel. "Das 'Kuckucksei' Teilzeitarbeit: Die Politik der Gewerkschaften im deutsch-deutschen Vergleich." In *Frauen arbeiten: Weibliche Erwerbstätigkeit im deutsch-deutschen Vergleich,* edited by Gunilla-Friederike Budde, 212–51. Göttingen: Vandenhoeck & Ruprecht, 1997.

Offen, Karen. *European Feminisms, 1700–1950: A Political History.* Stanford: Stanford University Press, 2000.

Olivo, Christiane. *Creating a Democratic Civil Society in Eastern Germany: The Case of the Citizen Movements and Alliance 90.* Houndmills and New York: Palgrave, 2001.

Opelt, Karin. *DDR-Erwachsenenbildung.* Münster: Waxmann Verlag, 2005.

Oppelland, Torsten. "Domestic Political Developments I: 1949–1969." In *The Federal Republic of Germany Since 1949: Politics, Society, and Economy before and after Unification,* edited by Klaus Larres and Panikos Panayi, 74–99. Abingdon-on-Thames: Routledge, 1996.

- *Gerhard Schroeder (1910–1989): Politik zwischen Staat, Partei und Konfession.* Düsseldorf: Droste, 2002.

Ostermann, Christian. *Uprising in East Germany 1953: The Cold War, the German Question, and the First Major Upheaval behind the Iron Curtain.* Budapest: Central European University Press, 2011.

Overmans, Rüdiger. *Deutsche Militärische Verluste im zweiten Weltkrieg.* Munich: R. Oldenbourg, 1999.

Pedersen, Susan. "Comparative History and Women's History." In *Comparison and History: Europe in Cross-National Perspective,* edited by Deborah Cohen and Maura O'Connor, 85–102. London: Routledge, 2004.

Pence, Katherine. "'You as a Woman Will Understand': Consumption, Gender, and the Relationship between State and Citizenry in the GDR's Crisis of 17 June 1953." *German History* 19 (2001): 218–52.

Penn, Shana, and Jill Massino. *Gender Politics and Everyday Life in State Socialist Eastern and Central Europe.* New York: Palgrave, 2009.

Pierson, Paul. "Increasing Returns, Path Dependence, and the Study of Politics." *American Political Science Review* 94 (2000): 251–67.

Pine, Lisa. *Nazi Family Policy, 1933–1945.* Oxford: Berg, 1997.

Poiger, Uta G. *Jazz, Rock, and Rebels: Cold War Politics and American Culture in a Divided Germany.* Berkeley: University of California Press, 2000.

- "A New, 'Western' Hero? Reconstructing German Masculinity in the 1950s." *Signs* 24 (1998): 147–62.

Quataert, Jean. *Reluctant Feminists in German Social Democracy, 1885–1917.* Princeton: Princeton University Press, 1979.

Quint, Peter E. *The Imperfect Union: Constitutional Structures of German Unification*. Princeton: Princeton University Press, 1997.

Radbruch, Gustav, and Günter Spendel. *Biographische Schriften*. Heidelberg: C.F. Müller, 1988.

Rahden, Till von. "Fatherhood, Rechristianization, and the Quest for Democracy in Postwar West Germany." In *Raising Citizens in the Century of the Child*, edited by Dirk Schumann, 141–65. New York: Berghahn, 2012.

Ramet, Sabrina Petra. "Protestantism in East Germany, 1949–1989: A Summing Up." In *Protestantism and Politics in Eastern Europe and Russia: The Communist and Post-Communist Eras*, edited by Sabrina P. Ramet, 160–96. Durham: Duke University Press, 1992.

Regulska, Joanna, and Bonnie G. Smith, eds. *Women and Gender in Postwar Europe: From Cold War to European Union*. Abingdon and New York: Routledge, 2012.

Reich-Hilweg, Ines. *Männer und Frauen sind gleichberechtigt: Das Gleichberechtigungsgrundsatz (Art. 3 Abs. 2 GG) in der parlamentarischen Auseinandersetzung 1948-1957 und in der Rechtsprechung des Bundesverfassungsgerichts*. Frankfurt am Main: Europäische Verlagsanstalt, 1979.

Reimann, Mathias, and Joachim Zekoll. *Introduction to German Law*, 2nd ed. The Hague: Kluwer Law International, 2005.

Richter, Michael. *Die Ost-CDU: Beiträge zu ihrer Entstehung und Entwicklung*. Weimar: Böhlau, 1995.

Rodnick, David. *Postwar Germans: An Anthropologist's Account*. New Haven: Yale University Press, 1948.

Rogers, Daniel E. *Politics after Hitler: The Western Allies and the German Party System*. New York: NYU Press, 1995.

Rölli-Alkemper, Lukas. *Familie im Wiederaufbau: Katholizismus und Bürgerliches Familienideal in der Bundesrepublik Deutschland, 1945–1965*. Paderborn: Schöningh, 2000.

Rossi-Duria, Anna. "Italian Women Enter Politics." In *When the War Was Over: Women, War, and Peace in Europe, 1940–1956*, edited by Claire Duchen and Irene Bandhauer-Schöffmann. London: Leicester University Press, 2000.

Rouette, Susanne. *Sozialpolitik als Geschlechterpolitik: Die Regulierung der Frauenarbeit nach dem ersten Weltkrieg*. Frankfurt am Main and New York: Campus, 1993.

Ruhl, Klaus-Jörg, ed. *Frauen in der Nachkriegszeit 1945–1963*. Munich: Deutscher Taschenbuch Verlag, 1988.

Sabrow, Martin. "Historisierung der Zweistaatlichkeit." *Aus und Zeitgeschichte* 3 (2007), 19–24.

Sachse, Carola. *Der Hausarbeitstag. Gerechtigkeit und Gleichberechtigung in Ost und West 1939-1994*. Göttingen: Wallstein-Verlag, 2002.

Sandstrom, Glenn, and Olof Gardarsdottir, "Long-Term Perspectives on Divorce in the Nordic Countries – Introduction." *Scandinavian Journal of History* 43, no. 1 (2018): 1–17.

Schäfer, Bernd. *The East German State and the Catholic Church, 1945–1989*. New York: Berghahn, 2010.

- "Weskamm, Wilhelm * 13.5.1891, † 21.8.1956 Katholischer Bischof." In *Wer war wer in der DDR?* Berlin: Ch. Links Verlag, 1992.

Schaser, Angelika. *Frauenbewegung in Deutschland 1848–1933*. Darmstadt: Wissenschaftliche Buchgesellschaft, 2006.

Schelsky, Helmut. *Wandlungen der Deutschen Familie*. Stuttgart: Ferdinand Enke Verlag, 1954.

Schissler, Hanna. "German and American Women between Domesticity and the Workplace." In *The United States and Germany in the Era of the Cold War, 1945–1990*, vol. 1: *1945–1968*, edited by Detlef Junker, Philip Gassert, and Wilfried Mausbach, 559–65. Cambridge: Cambridge University Press, 2004.

Schrank, Ralf. *Heraeus – ein Familienunternehmen schreibt Industriegeschichte: Von der Einhorn-Apotheke zum Weltkonzern*. Munich: Piper, 2001.

Schreiter, Katrin. *Designing One Nation: The Politics of Economic Culture and Trade in Divided Germany*. Oxford: Oxford University Press, 2020.

Schroeder, Klaus. *Der SED-Staat: Geschichte und Strukturen der DDR 1949–1990*. Köln: Böhlau, 2013.

Schubert, Werner. "Die Stellung der Frau im Familienrecht und in den familienrechtlichen Reformprojekten der NS-Zeit." In *Frauen in der Geschichte des Rechts*, edited by Ute Gerhard, 828–50. Munich: C.H. Beck, 1997.

Schwab, Dieter. "Gleichberechtigung und Familienrecht im 20. Jahrhundert." In *Frauen in der Geschichte des Rechts*, edited by Ute Gerhard, 790–827. Munich: C.H. Beck, 1997.

Schwarz, Hans-Peter. *Konrad Adenauer: From the German Empire to the Federal Republic, 1876–1952*. New York: Berghahn, 1995.

Scott, Joan W. "Gender: A Useful Category of Historical Analysis." *American Historical Review* 91 (1986): 1053–75.

- "Gender: Still a Useful Category of Analysis?," *Diogenes* 57 (2010): 7–14.

- *Gender and the Politics of History*. New York: Columbia University Press, 1999.

Sheffer, Edith. *Burned Bridge: How East and West Germans Made the Iron Curtain*. Oxford: Oxford, 2014.

Silies, Eva-Maria. *Liebe, Lust und Last: Die Pille als weibliche Generationserfahrung in der Bundesrepublik 1960–1980*. Göttingen: Wallstein Verlag, 2010.

Sneeringer, Julia. *Winning Women's Votes: Propaganda and Politics in Weimar Germany*. Chapel Hill: University of North Carolina Press, 2002.

Sperlich, Peter W. *Oppression and Scarcity: The History and Institutional Structure of the Marxist-Leninist Government of East Germany and Some Perspectives on Life in a Socialist System*. Westport: Praeger, 2006.

Spicka, Mark E. *Selling the Economic Miracle: Reconstruction and Politics in West Germany, 1949–1957*. New York: Berghahn Books, 2007.

Stark, John. "The Overlooked Majority: German Women in the Four Zones of Occupied Germany, 1945–1949: A Comparative Study." PhD diss., Ohio State University, Columbus, 2003.

Steininger, Christian. "Die freie Presse: Zeitung und Zeitschrift." In *Die Kultur der 50er Jahre*, edited by Werner Faulstich, 231–48. Munich: Wilhelm Fink, 2002.

Steinweis, Alan E., and Robert D. Rachlin. *The Law in Nazi Germany: Ideology, Opportunism, and the Perversion of Justice*. New York: Berghahn, 2013.

Stitziel, Judd. "Shopping, Sewing, Networking, Complaining: Consumer Culture and the Relationship between State and Society in the GDR." In *Socialist Modern: East German Everyday Cultures and Politics*, edited by Katherine Pence and Paul Betts, 253–86. Ann Arbor: University of Michigan Press, 2008.

Stoehr, Irene. "Cold War Communities: Women's Peace Politics in Postwar West Germany, 1945–1952." In *Home/Front: The Military, War, and Gender in Twentieth-Century Germany*, edited by Karen Hagemann and Stefanie Schüler-Springorum, 311–33. Oxford: Berg, 2002.

– *Emanzipation zum Staat? Der Allgemeine Deutsche Frauenverein-Deutscher Staatsbürgerinnenverband (1893–1933)*. Pfaffenweiler: Centaurus-Verlagsgesellschaft, 1990.

Stolleis, Michael. *History of Social Law in Germany*. Heidelberg: Springer, 2013.

– *The Law under the Swastika: Studies on Legal History in Nazi Germany*. Chicago: University of Chicago Press, 1998.

Stone, O.M. "The New Fundamental Principles of Soviet Family Law and Their Social Background." *International and Comparative Law Quarterly* 18 (1969): 392–423.

Summerfield, Penny. "'It Did Me Good in Lots of Ways': British Women in Transition from War to Peace." In *When the War Was Over: Women, War, and Peace in Europe, 1940–1956*, edited by Claire Duchen and Irene Bandhauer-Schöffmann. London: Leicester University Press, 2000.

Süß, Winfried. "Social Security, Social Inequality, and the Welfare State in East and West Germany." In *A History Shared and Divided: East and West Germany since the 1970s*, edited by Frank Bösch, 191–238. New York: Berghahn, 2018.

Sussmann, Anna Louie. "The Poland Model – Promoting 'Family Values' with Cash Handouts." *The Atlantic*, 14 October 2019. https://www.theatlantic.com /international/archive/2019/10/poland-family-values-cash-handouts/599968.

Taborsky, Edward. "The 'New Course' in the Soviet Economy." *Southern Economic Journal* 23 (1956): 160–79.

Thurnwald, Hilde. *Gegenwarts-Probleme Berliner. Familien: Eine soziologische Untersuchung an 498 Familien*. Berlin: Weidmann, 1948.

Timm, Annette F. *The Politics of Fertility in Twentieth-Century Berlin*. Cambridge: Cambridge University Press, 2010.

Timmer, Karsten. *Vom Aufbruch zum Umbruch: Die Bürgerbewegung in der DDR 1989*. Göttingen: Vandenhoeck & Ruprecht, 2000.

Treber, Leonie. *Mythos Trümmerfrauen: Von der Trümmerbeseitigung in der Kriegs-
und Nachkriegszeit und der Entstehung eines deutschen Erinnerungsortes*. Essen:
Klartext, 2014.

Tscharntke, Denise. *Re-Educating German Women: The Work of the Women's Affairs
Section of British Military Government, 1946-1951*. Frankfurt am Main and New
York: P. Lang, 2003.

Usborne, Cornelie. *The Politics of the Body in Weimar Germany: Women's Reproductive
Rights and Duties*. Ann Arbor: University of Michigan Press, 1992.

Utrata, Jennifer. *Women without Men: Single Mothers and Family Change in the New
Russia*. Ithaca: Cornell University Press, 2015.

Vierhaus, Rudolf, and Ludolf Herbst. *Biographisches Handbuch der Mitglieder des
Deutschen Bundestages 1949-2002*. Munich: Saur, 2002.

Walpole, Norman C. *Area Handbook for Germany*. Department of the Army,
1964.

Weber, Hermann. "Pieck, Wilhelm." In *Neue Deutsche Biographie 20* (2001):
421-2.

Wehler, Hans-Ulrich. *The German Empire 1871-1918*, translated by Kim Traynor.
Leamington: Berg, 1985.

Weinberg, Gerhard. *A World at Arms: A Global History of World War II*, 2nd ed.
Cambridge and New York: Cambridge University Press, 2005.

Weitz, Eric D. *Creating German Communism, 1890-1990: From Popular Protests to
Socialist State*. Princeton: Princeton University Press, 1997.

– "The Ever-Present Other: Communism in the Making of West Germany." In *The
Miracle Years: A Cultural History of West Germany, 1949-1968*, edited by Hanna
Schissler, 219-32. Princeton: Princeton University Press, 2001.

Wengst, Udo. *Beamtentum zwischen Reform und Tradition: Beamtengesetzgebung in
der Gründungsphase der Bundesrepublik Deutschland 1948-1953*. Düsseldorf: Droste
Verlag, 1988.

– *Thomas Dehler: 1897-1967. Eine politische Biographie*. Munich: R. Oldenbourg
Verlag, 1997.

Wentker, Hermann. *Justiz in der SBZ/DDR 1945-1953: Transformation und Rolle ihrer
zentralen Institutionen: Veröffentlichungen zur SBZ-/DDR-Forschung im Institut für
Zeitgeschichte*. Munich: Oldenbourg Verlag, 2001.

Werner, Michael, and Bénédicte Zimmermann. "Beyond Comparison: Histoire Croisée
and the Challenge of Reflexivity." *History and Theory* 45 (2006): 30-50.

– "Vergleich, Transfer, Verflechtung: Der Ansatz der Histoire Croisée und
die Herausforderung des Transnationalen." *Geschichte und Gesellschaft*
28 (2002): 607-36.

Wurzbacher, Gerhard. *Leitbilder gegenwaertigen deutschen Familienlebens Methoden,
Ergebnisse und sozialpaedagogische Forderungen einer soziologischen Analyse*.
Stuttgart: Enke, 1969.

Zachmann, Karin. *Mobilisierung der Frauen: Technik, Geschlecht und Kalter Krieg in der DDR*. Frankfurt am Main and New York: Campus, 2004.

Zatlin, Jonathan R. "Ausgaben und Eingaben: Das Petitionsrecht und der Untergang der DDR." *Zeitschrift für Geschichtswissenschaft* 45 (1997): 902–17.

Zepp, Marianne. *Redefining Germany: Reeducation, Staatsbürgerschaft, und Frauenpolitik im US-Amerikanisch Besetzten Nachkriegsdeutschland*. Göttingen: V&R Unipress, 2007.

Index

GERMAN AND EUROPEAN STUDIES

General Editor: James Retallack